CHARMING SMALL HOTEL GUIDES
ITALY

INCLUDING
SICILY & SARDINIA

CHARMING SMALL HOTEL GUIDES

ITALY

INCLUDING
SICILY & SARDINIA

Edited by Chris Gill

300 Raritan Center Parkway,
CN 94, Edison, N.J. 08818

Published by Hunter Publishing Inc, 300 Raritan
Center Parkway, CN 94, Edison, N.J. 08818. Tel 201 225 1900.

First published 1988 by
Papermac, a division of Macmillan Publishers Limited
and subsequently (1990 edition)
by Duncan Petersen Publishing Ltd,
5 Botts Mews, London W2 5AG

Conceived, designed and produced by
Duncan Petersen
Edited by Fox and Partners, The Old Forge,
Norton St Philip, Bath, U.K.

Typeset by Lineage Ltd, Watford, Herts
Originated by Regent Publishing Services, Hong Kong
Printed by G. Canale & C. SpA, Turin

ISBN 1-55650-260-5

Contents

Introduction

Here is a new accommodation guide series with a singular focus on places which are both charming and small: in Italy for example, the recommendations have usually fewer than 30 rooms, rarely more than 40.

The *Charming Small Hotel Guides* look different from others on the market; their descriptive style is different; and they are compiled differently. They are, in fact, designed to satisfy what we believe to be the real needs of today's traveller; needs which, at best, have been served at best haphazardly by existing guides.

Our entries employ, above all, words: they contain not one symbol. They are written by people with something to say, not a bureaucracy which has long since lost the ability to distinguish the praiseworthy from the mediocre. The editorial team is small and highly experienced at assessing and writing about hotels; at noticing all-important details. Every entry, however brief, aims to give a coherent and definite feel of that place. And we have placed great emphasis on consistency.

These are features which will reveal their worth only as you use your *Charming Small Hotel Guide*. Its other advantages are more obvious: the use of colour photographs to depict 80 or so of the entries, which are particularly appealing; and the ease of reference, with clear geographical designations for all entries.

Small Italian hotels

Small hotels have always had the special appeal that they can offer the traveller a personal welcome and personal attention, whereas larger places are necessarily more institutional. But the distinction has become particularly clear in Italy during recent years with the energetic restoration of historic buildings to create singular hotels. Of course, Italy's cities and towns have always had their share of *pensioni* which, at their best, are the stuff of a guide such as this; but you need a guide like this to distinguish the seedy from the delightful.

The establishments described in this guide are simply the 275 small hotels, *pensioni*, *alberghi* and bed-and-breakfast places that we believe most discriminating travellers would prefer to stay in, given the choice. Some undeniably pricey places are included ... Italy is no longer a particularly cheap destination; but there are a number of places in this guide costing less than L40,000.

Italy is peculiar in having some significant areas notably lacking in hotels of our type. These areas are discussed in special **Area introductions.**

Our ideal hotel has a peaceful, pretty setting; the building itself is either handsome, appealing, historic, or has a distinct character. The rooms are spacious, but on a human scale – not grand or intimidating. The decorations and furnishings are harmonious, comfortable and impeccably maintained, and include antique pieces meant to be used, not revered. The proprietors and staff are dedicated, thoughtful and sensitive in their pursuit of their guests' happiness – friendly and welcoming without being intrusive. Last but not least, the food, whether simple or ambitious, is fresh, interesting and carefully prepared.

Of course, not every hotel scores top marks on each of these counts. But it is surprising how many do respectably well on most fronts.

Going to Italy

We are pleased to acknowledge the assistance of two UK tour operators in preparing this second edition. Our inspectors travelled to Italy courtesy of Magic of Italy, who operate a large and varied programme featuring many of the hotels in the guide. Telephone 01/081-743 9555. We had helpful reports on many hotels from Art in Europe, who make use of the book in planning their guided cultural tours. Telephone (0993) 868864.

How to find an entry

In this guide, the entries are arranged in a sequence starting in the north and working southwards, in sweeps from west to east. Sicily and Sardinia come last.

To find a hotel, simply browse through headings at the top of the pages until you find the area you want to visit. Or, use the two indexes at the back of the book. One lists the hotels by name; the other lists their locations by the nearest town or village.

On pages 10 to 13 there are, in addition, maps showing the location of all the entries.

Reporting to the guide

The guide is greatly strengthened by reports from people who have stayed in the hotels recommended here, or who have found other places which seem to deserve an entry. On page 195 is further information on reporting to the guide.

How to read an entry

At the top of each entry is a coloured bar highlighting the name of the town or village where the establishment is located, along with a categorization which gives some clue to its character. These categories are as far as possible self-explanatory. The term villa needs, perhaps, some qualification: it is reserved for places with gardens which have something of the air of a country house, whether in a town or at the seaside.

Introduction

Fact boxes

The factbox given for each hotel follows a standard pattern which requires little explanation; but:

Under **Tel** we give the telephone number starting with the area code used within the country; when dialling from another country, omit the initial nought of this code.

Under **Location** we give information on the setting of the hotel and on its parking arrangements.

Under **Food & drink** we list the meals available.

The **Prices** are per person, including tax and service for 1990 wherever possible. Normally, a range is given, representing the smallest and largest amounts you might pay in different circumstances – typically, the minimum is half the cost of the cheapest double room in low season, while the maximum is the cost of the dearest single in high season. Thus, with an appropriate allowance for inflation, you can usefully estimate the cost of rooms in years following publication. If no bed and breakfast price is given, this is because we understand that dinner is inescapable. After the B & B price, we give either the price for dinner, bed and breakfast, or for full board – or, instead, an indication of the cost of individual meals. After all this basic information comes, where space allows, a summary of reductions available for long stays or for children.

Our lists of facilities in bedrooms cover only mechanical gadgets and not ornaments such as flowers or consumables such as toiletries or free drinks.

Under **Facilities** we list public rooms and then outdoor and sporting facilities which are either part of the hotel or immediately on hand; facilities in the vicinity are not listed, though they sometimes feature at the end of the main description in the **Nearby** section, which is necessarily selective.

We use the following abbreviations for **Credit cards:**
AE American Express
DC Diners Club
MC MasterCard (Access/Eurocard)
V Visa (Barclaycard/Bank Americard/Carte Bleue)

The final entry in a factbox is normally the name of the proprietor(s); but where the hotel is run by a manager we give his or her name instead.

Unfamiliar terms
Some overseas visitors to Italy, particularly from North America, may be mystified by the terms **'self-catering'** and **'bargain breaks'**. The first means that cooking facilities such as a kitchenette or small kitchen are provided for making one's own meals, as in a rental apartment. The second means off-season price reductions are available.

Master location map

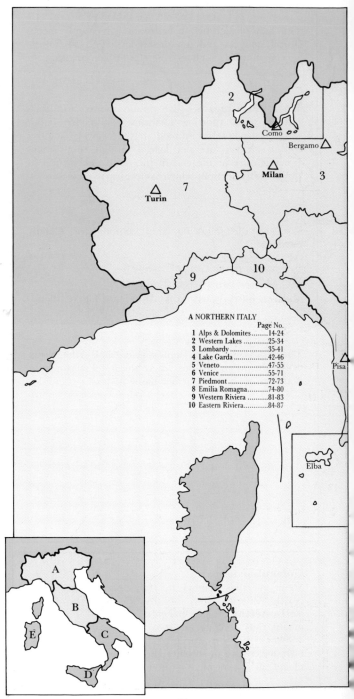

Como

Bergamo △

△ Milan

3

△ Turin

7

9

10

A NORTHERN ITALY

△ Pisa

Elba

A

B

E

C

D

(Continued on following two pages)

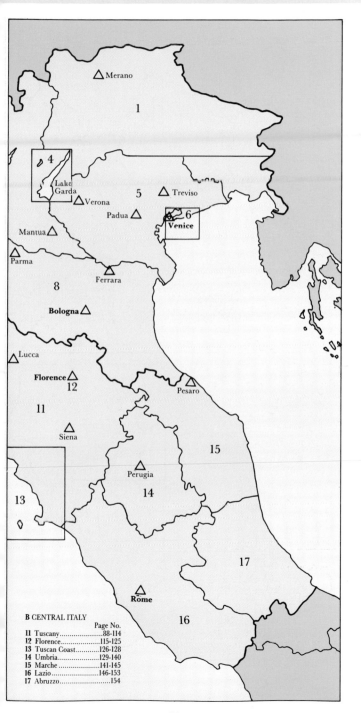

Merano

1

4

Lake Garda

Verona

5

Treviso

Padua

6

Venice

Mantua

Parma

Ferrara

8

Bologna

Lucca

Florence

12

Pesaro

11

Siena

15

Perugia

14

13

17

Rome

16

B CENTRAL ITALY

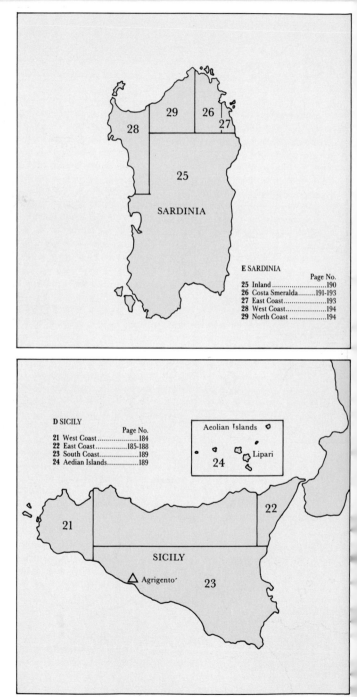

E SARDINIA

29 26 27 28 25 SARDINIA

D SICILY

Aeolian Islands

24 Lipari

21 22 SICILY

△ Agrigento 23

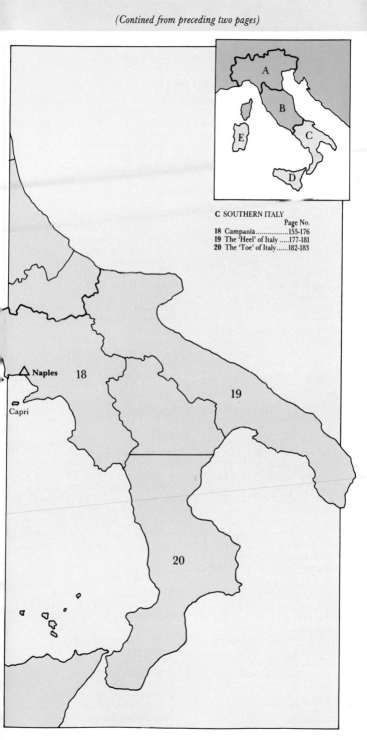

C SOUTHERN ITALY

Naples

Capri

18

19

20

Alps & Dolomites

Cappella

This is a good (and unusually small) example of the classical Sud Tirol hotel – modern (less than 20 year old), but built in Alpine chalet style; thoroughly comfortable and welcoming, with richly traditional furnishings and decoration; well equipped with sports facilities; and set in spectacular mountain scenery, with skiing or walking from the door, depending on the season, and beautiful views from the bedroom balconies and the grassy garden.

Nearby Sella group and other Dolomites.

Colfosco, Val Badia 39030 Bolzano
Tel (0471) 836183
Location 2 km NW of Corvara; car parking
Food & drink breakfast, lunch, dinner
Prices FB L86,000-L135,000; reduction for children
Rooms 31 double, 13 with bath, 18 with shower; 6 single, 2 with bath, 4 with shower; 3 family rooms with bath; all rooms have central heating, phone, radio, TV
Facilities dining-room, bar, TV, playroom; beauty parlour, sauna; covered swimming-pool, table tennis, tennis, bowls
Credit cards AE, DC, V
Children welcome over 3
Disabled no special facilities
Pets small ones only accepted
Closed mid-Apr to mid-June, end Sep to mid-Dec
Proprietors Josef and Renata Pizzinini

Menardi

This old farmhouse has long served the needs of travellers on the road north from Cortina, which over the years has been extended up the valley until it now almost embraces the hotel. The Menardi family has seen the place evolve over the years from country inn to restaurant to *pensione* to hotel, without losing its rustic warmth and essentially Tirolean style – despite the introduction of elegant antiques and modern comforts. Despite its size (slightly over our usual limit), there is no question that the Menardi also retains the atmosphere of a small family-run establishment.

Nearby Dolomite mountains.

Via Majon 110, Cortina d'Ampezzo 32043 Belluno
Tel (0436) 2400
Location 1.5 km from middle of resort, on road to Dobbiaco; ample car parking and covered garage
Food & drink breakfast, lunch, dinner
Prices rooms L55,000-L160,000
Rooms 40 double, 8 single; all with bath; all rooms have central heating, phone
Facilities dining-room, bar, reading-room, card-playing-room, TV room, taverna
Credit cards V
Children accepted
Disabled access difficult
Pets dogs not accepted
Closed Oct to mid-Dec and mid-Apr to mid-June
Proprietors Menardi family

Alps & Dolomites

Town hotel, Bressanone

Elefante

Bressanone is a pretty little town at the foot of the Brenner Pass, more Austrian than Italian. The same is true of the charming old Elefante, which owes its name to a beast which was led over the Alps for the amusement of Emperor Ferdinand of Austria. The only stable which could house the exhausted creature was that next to the inn, and the innkeeper, quick to see the possibilities, painted an elephant on the side of his inn and changed its name.

There is an air of solid, old-fashioned comfort throughout. Green-aproned staff lead you through corridors packed with heavily carved and beautifully inlaid pieces of antique furniture. The colours here are rich and sumptuous – scarlets, greens, copper, gold and suddenly an enormous display of purple iris and tulips in a simple iron pot. The bedrooms are generous and handsomely furnished with antique and solid old pieces.

The breakfast room is panelled entirely in intricately carved wood – very Tyrolean – and the main restaurant is wood-floored, with a moulded ceiling and windows looking out on to a little garden area. Much of the produce here comes from a large walled garden across the street, and the adjacent farm belonging to the hotel. The formal sitting-room has been decorated in 18thC style, with mirrors, chandeliers and plush armchairs.

Nearby cathedral; Novacella monastery (3 km); the Dolomites.

Via Rio Bianco 4,
Bressanone 39042 Bolzano
Tel (0472) 32750
Location at N end of town, in gardens with car parking and garages
Food & drink breakfast, lunch, dinner
Prices rooms L85,000; DB&B L130,000
Rooms 28 double, all with bath and shower; 16 single, 15 with bath, one with shower; all rooms have central heating, colour TV, phone
Facilities 2 dining-rooms, sitting-room, bar; outdoor swimming-pool
Credit cards not accepted
Children welcome **Disabled** not suitable **Pets** accepted by arrangement
Closed mid-Nov to late Feb
Proprietor Wolfgang Heiss

Alps & Dolomites

Locanda al Castello

Cividale is a small town in the hills east of Udine, not far from the Yugoslav border. This crenellated red-brick building, though properly described as a restaurant with rooms, is a quiet, welcoming and restful place to stay, with a large terrace with easy chairs and sunshades. Much of the food is grilled over open fires. Both dining-rooms are rather large and lack character, but the bedrooms more than compensate. They are simply decorated but spacious, with honest rustic wooden furniture which gives a somewhat Alpine feel, and fabrics chosen to add to the rusticity. The tiled bathrooms are spotlessly clean.

Nearby cathedral, archaeological museum and Tempietto of Cividale del Friuli; Venice (17 km).

Via del Castello 18, Cividale del Friuli 33043 Udine
Tel (0432) 733242
Location 1.5 km NW of middle of Cividale del Fruili; with private car parking
Food & drink breakfast, lunch, dinner
Prices rooms L44,800-L84,000
Rooms 10 rooms, all with bath or shower; all rooms have phone
Facilities 2 dining-rooms, large terrace
Credit cards V
Children accepted
Disabled no special facilities
Pets dogs not accepted
Closed few days in Feb
Proprietor Roberto Cidarmas

Castel Pergine

A tiny winding mountain road leads you to the hilltop on which is perched Castel Pergine – a medieval castle, surrounded by woods, with marvellous views in all directions. Inside, two enormous, vaulted rooms with rustic chairs and tables and mullioned windows serve as a restaurant. The bedrooms are simple, some with whitewashed stone walls, some panelled in a soft tan wood. Window boxes with bright geraniums add a splash of colour, and the old carved wooden beds are lightened by gay duvets. There is a tranquil walled garden for the use of guests only – the main tower of the hotel and its capacious restaurant and bar are open to the public.

Nearby Lago di Caldonazzo (2.5 km), Trento (10 km).

Pergine 38057 Trento
Tel (0461) 531158
Location 1.5 km S of Pergine on road to Levico Terme, with private walled garden and car parking at gates
Food & drink breakfast, lunch, dinner
Prices rooms L34,000-L68,000; 40% reduction for children under 6
Rooms 18 double, 8 with shower; 5 single, 4 with shower; all rooms have phone
Facilities dining-room, bar, sitting-room
Credit cards not accepted
Children welcome **Disabled** not suitable **Pets** accepted
Closed mid-Oct to Apr; restaurant only, Mon
Proprietor Luigi Fontanara

Alps & Dolomites

Converted castle, San Paolo

Schloss Korb

Rising up above the fertile vineyards and orchards that surround the outskirts of Bolzano is the 11thC medieval tower which forms the centrepiece of Schloss Korb.

The entrance to the hotel is a riot of colour – flowering shrubs and plants set against the golden stone walls. Inside, furnishings and decorations are in traditional style, and antiques and fresh flowers abound. Reception is a cool, dark, tiled hall, set about with brass ornaments and armoury – the oldest part of the hotel. Surrounding the main restaurant areas is a terrace hanging out over the valley and awash with plants.

The bedrooms in the castle are generous in size, with separate sitting-areas and lovely views out over the vineyards. Duvet covers give a warm, friendly feel. The detached annexe behind the main building has its own dining-room, heated indoor pool and lift/elevator – the last being the attraction for some of the older guests.

The daughter of the family (shadowed everywhere by her enormous Great Dane) speaks fluent English.

Nearby sights of Bolzano; Merano within reach; the Dolomites.

Missiano, San Paolo 39050 Bolzano
Tel (0471) 633222
Location 8 km W of Bolzano, in gardens on estate with vineyards and large car park
Food & drink breakfast, lunch, dinner
Prices rooms L70,000-L140,000; reductions for children in family room
Rooms 54 double, 2 single, all with bath or shower; all rooms have central heating, phone

Facilities dining-room, conference rooms, bar, sitting-rooms (one with TV); sauna, beauty salon, outdoor and heated indoor swimming-pools, tennis
Credit cards not accepted
Children welcome **Disabled** lift to annexe bedrooms, but access awkward for wheelchairs **Pets** accepted
Closed Nov to Mar
Proprietors Dellago family

Alps & Dolomites

Converted castle, Merano

Castel Labers

On the hillside to the east of Merano, Castel (or Schloss) Labers is surrounded by its own vineyards, orchards and mountain walks through alpine pastures. The hotel has been in the Neubert family since 1885, but the building itself dates back to the 11thC.

An impressive stone staircase with wrought-iron balustrades leads from the white-walled entrance hall and up to the bedrooms. These all have charming wooden double doors, with sealed wooden floors, simple old furniture, and goose feather duvets in crisp white cotton covers.

The castle gardens are packed with trees and flowering shrubs, which can be admired from the conservatory restaurant, whose windows are draped in country cottons. Leading off this is another restaurant area, with a church-like vaulted wooden ceiling and old panelling round the walls. Fresh local produce is well presented and deliciously cooked.

Nearby promenades along the Passirio river in Merano; Tirolo Castle (5 km); Passirio valley, the Dolomites.

Via Labers 25, Merano
39012 Bolzano
Tel (0473) 34484
Location 2.5 km E of Merano, with private grounds, gardens and vineyard; garage and courtyard car parking (locked at night)
Food & drink breakfast, lunch, dinner
Prices rooms L80,000-L120,00; DB&B L75,000-L95,000; reductions for children sharing parents' room
Rooms 22 double, 20 with bath, 2 with shower; 9 single, 2 with bath, 7 with shower;
10 family rooms, all with bath; all rooms have central heating, phone
Facilities dining-room, dining/conservatory, bar, music/reading room, conference room; outdoor heated swimming-pool, tennis
Credit cards AE, DC, MC, V
Children welcome **Disabled** not suitable **Pets** dogs accepted, but not in the dining-room in evening.
Closed Nov to mid-Mar
Proprietors Stapf-Neubert family

Alps & Dolomites

Converted castle, Merano

Castel Freiberg

The Freiberg is every inch the grand medieval castle. It commands an exposed hilltop position high above Merano, but its ramparts enclose a beautiful sheltered garden with sweet-scented shrubs, and its walls conceal a hotel which is at once luxurious, welcoming and full of character. The entrance is very grand, with suits of armour and ancient weapons along the whitewashed walls, and vaulted ceilings. Throughout the castle there are small sitting areas, usually by a window with superb eagle's-eye views down over the valley. The small, intimate bar with an old painted wooden bench adjoins a tiny chapel, but by far the most stunning rooms are the dining-rooms, completely panelled in honey-coloured wood with enormous wood-burning stoves.

The house-boys, in black-and green-striped jackets, lead you to the bedrooms – rather anonymous, but with fitted carpets and all the trimmings.

Nearby promenades along Passirio River in Merano; Passirio valley, the Dolomites.

Via Fragsburg, Merano
39012 Bolzano
Tel (0473) 44196
Location 8 km NE of Merano, with walled garden and park; car parking close to hotel, and garaging available
Food & drink breakfast, lunch, dinner
Prices rooms L140,000-L250,000
Rooms 28 double, all with bath and shower; 7 single, all with bath and shower; all rooms have phone, radio, sitting area; TV on request
Facilities 3 dining-rooms, basement taverna, TV room, 2 sitting-rooms, bar, chapel, veranda; indoor and outdoor heated swimming-pools, fitness room
Credit cards AE, DC, MC, V
Children welcome, although few guests bring them
Disabled not suitable
Pets not accepted
Closed Nov to mid-Apr
Proprietors Bortolotti family

Alps & Dolomites

Converted castle, Merano

Fragsburg

A lovely drive along a narrow country lane, through mixed woodland and past Alpine pastures where goats and cattle graze, brings you to the wooded outcrop, high up to the east of Merano, where sits the hotel Fragsburg (or Castel Verruca).

The original building is 300 years old, in traditional chalet style with carved wooden shutters and balconies decked with flowering plants. Recent extensions to provide more bedrooms are sympathetic in style.It enjoys splendid views (notably of the Texel Massif), shared by many of the bedrooms; these are decorated in sparkling white, with abundant wood panelling, some old and some new. Downstairs, the low-ceilinged dining areas are panelled, with gay checked table-cloths and rustic benches and chairs. You can eat out on the balcony which runs the length of the hotel – not recommended if you suffer from vertigo, as it juts right out over the precipitous mountainside, and the tops of tall pines sway about alarmingly only a few feet away from you. In the extensive wooded garden there are areas for lazing in the sun – including one reserved for naturists.

Nearby promenades along the Passirio river in Merano; Passirio valley, the Dolomites.

Via Fragsburg 3/a, PO Box 210, Freiberg, Merano 39012 Bolzano
Tel (0473) 44071
Location 6 km NE of Merano, with gardens; ample car parking space, and garages available
Food & drink breakfast, lunch, dinner
Prices rooms L70,000-L120,000
Rooms 14 double, 10 with bath, 4 with shower; 3 single, all with shower; 2 family rooms; all rooms have central heating, phone, balcony, TV
Facilities dining-rooms, sitting-room, terrace; table-tennis, heated outdoor swimming-pool
Credit cards not accepted
Children welcome
Disabled not suitable
Pets dogs accepted by arrangement
Closed Nov to Easter
Proprietors Ortner family

Alps & Dolomites

Medieval manor, Merano

Castel Rundegg

Despite its smart facilities, this ancient white-painted house retains a lot of charm. The pretty sitting-room, with plush seats and antiques, overlooking the garden through delicate wrought iron gates. The restaurant has a cellar-like atmosphere, with its stone-vaulted ceiling and alcove rooms. The bedrooms are luxurious, and many of them have special features – the turret room, reached up spiral steps, commands a 360-degree view.

Nearby promenades along Passirio river; Passirio valley, the Dolomites.

Via Scena 2, Merano 39012 Bolzano
Tel (0473) 34364
Location on E side of town; in gardens, with car parking and garages
Food & drink breakfast, lunch, dinner
Prices DB&B L121,000-L149,000; reductions for children under 12
Rooms 22 double, 20 with bath, 2 with shower; 5 single, all with shower; 2 family rooms, both with bath; all rooms have central heating, colour TV, radio, minibar, phone
Facilities 3 dining-rooms, bar, sitting-room; heated indoor swimming-pool, health and beauty farm
Credit cards AE, DC, MC, V
Children welcome
Disabled lift/elevator available
Pets small dogs accepted on request
Closed last 3 weeks Jan
Proprietors Sinn family

Alps & Dolomites

Town villa, Merano

Villa Mozart

Here is a truly extraordinary hotel. Set in a peaceful residential area of Merano, it has been entirely decorated in the Jugend style of art nouveau, with not a single detail overlooked.

The villa was built in 1907 and was renovated to the existing design in the late 1970s. Black and white are dominant throughout, with splashes of colour sparingly applied. In the airy conservatory, where breakfast is served, gauze curtains throw a soft light on posies of vivid fresh flowers; in the dining-room, a single yellow tulip next to a black candle picks up the soft yellow of the walls. The bedrooms are done out in black, gold and soft yellows, with the honey-coloured parquet floors giving warmth and contrast to the beautiful black-and-white patterned rugs.

Every last knife, teacup and finger plate in the Villa Mozart is part of a 'homogeneous whole', the design principle laid down by Josef Hoffmann in 1901. But this is no museum piece – the seats are for relaxing on, the rugs for walking over and the elegant staff (uniformed in black and white, of course) make a good job of cosseting their guests. And the kitchen too is dedicated to perfection.

Nearby promenades along Passirio river in Merano.

Via San Marco 26, Merano
39012 Bolzano
Tel (0473) 30630
Location in peaceful
residential area; with garden
and covered car parking
Food & drink breakfast,
dinner
Prices rooms L142,000-
L284,000; DB&B L178,000
Rooms 8 double, all with
bath; 2 single, both with
shower; all rooms have
colour TV, phone, radio,
minibar, health-beds
Facilities bar, restaurant,
breakfast conservatory;
heated indoor swimming-
pool, sauna, solarium
Credit cards AE, MC, V
Children accepted
Disabled lift/elevator
Pets not accepted
Closed Nov to Easter
Proprietors Andreas and
Emmy Hellrigl

Stefaner (see opposite)

Alps & Dolomites

Country hotel, Merano

Der Punthof

The original building of the Punthof, which now houses reception, breakfast rooms and a few bedrooms, dates back to the Middle Ages, when it was a farmhouse. To this have been added little detached chalets with kitchen facilities and a separate restaurant. Despite these alterations however, much of the charm of the old building has been retained. The breakfast rooms have simple, rustic furniture and traces of the original decorative paintings on the panelled walls. Antiques are dotted around, with plenty of fresh flowers.

Nearby promenades along Passirio River in Merano.

Via Steinach 25, Merano
39022 Bolzano
Tel (0473) 48553
Location about 3 km NW of Merano, in village; in small park with parking for 40 cars
Food & drink breakfast, dinner
Prices rooms L42,400-L164,000
Rooms 16 double, 3 with bath, 13 with shower; 2 single, both with shower; all rooms have central heating, colour TV, radio, minibar, phone, safe
Facilities breakfast room, sitting-room, dining-room, bar; outdoor swimming-pool, tennis, sauna, solarium
Credit cards DC, V
Children welcome **Disabled** no special facilities **Pets** accepted in certain rooms
Closed mid-Nov to Feb
Proprietors Wolf family

Mountain chalet, Tires

Stefaner

This relatively modern chalet, standing high up in a beautiful Dolomite valley, is more a home than a hotel: furnishings are simple and cosy, with plenty of plants, comfy armchairs and pretty crockery ornaments. Downstairs on one side is a large sitting-room, and on the other is the restaurant, with gaily striped padded chairs and a ceramic wood-burning stove. The bedrooms are bright and airy, and most have pretty little balconies, decorated with geraniums and carved wood. The views are spectacular. The proprietors have the charm, and the enthusiasm, to make their visitors welcome.

Nearby Bolzano; Dolomite mountains.

San Cipriano, Tires 39050 Bolzano
Tel (0471) 642175
Location about 20 km NW of Bolzano at northern end of San Cipriano; in garden with ample car parking
Food & drink breakfast, dinner
Prices DB&B L36,000-L45,000
Rooms 13 double, 2 with bath, 11 with shower; 2 single, both with shower
Facilities dining-room, sitting-room, bar, terrace
Credit cards not accepted
Children welcome
Disabled access possible – lift/elevator to bedrooms
Pets accepted
Closed mid-Nov to mid-Dec
Proprietor Mathilde Goller-Villgrattner

Alps & Dolomites

Villa Anna Maria

Champoluc is the main community of a steep-sided valley running up to the Swiss border, between the famous peaks of the Matterhorn and Monte Rosa – a small-time ski resort in winter, a base for mountaineering (and less strenuous walking) in summer. The Anna Maria is a 1920s villa in a quiet wooded setting on the fringe of the village, with flowery terraces outside and wood panelling and country decorations within. Bedrooms are simply furnished but cosy, and most have private bathrooms. Cooking revolves around specialities of the Val d'Aosta.
Nearby skiing, skating in winter; walking, fishing in summer.

Via Croues 5, Champoluc
11020 Aosta
Tel (0125) 307128
Location on outskirts of village
27 km N of Verrès on S506; ample car parking
Food & drink breakfast, lunch, dinner
Prices rooms L60,000-L105,000; meals L30,000-L40,000
Rooms 15 double (12 twin), 6 with bath, 4 with shower; 5 single, 2 with shower; all rooms have central heating
Facilities dining-room, sitting-room, small bar, games room, ski locker; sun terrace
Credit cards V
Children accepted if well behaved
Disabled no special facilities
Pets not accepted **Closed** mid-Sep to Dec, late Apr to late Jun, depending on weather **Proprietor** Domenico Origone

Il Capricorno

Sauze d'Oulx is not renowned for attracting discerning travellers – it is a resolutely downmarket ski resort in winter, and not a pretty sight in summer.

But the wooded slopes above the resort are pretty all-year-round and the Capricorno, isolated among the trees, breaks all the local rules by being small, traditional in style and cosily charming. Although modern in style from the outside, the chalet is all rough beams, hand-made furniture and blazing log fires within.

Mariarosa is the cook, and well able to meet the demands of the gourmets who stray across the nearby border from France.
Nearby walking in summer, skiing in winter.

Case Sparse 21, Le Clotès,
Sauze d'Oulx 10050 Torino
Tel (0122) 85273
Location on slopes above Sauze d'Oulx; car parking space, but no access in winter
Food & drink breakfast, lunch, dinner
Prices rooms L146,000; meals L45,000-L60,000
Rooms 8 double, all with shower; central heating
Facilities dining-room, sitting-room, bar; sun terrace
Credit cards none
Children accepted only by special arrangement
Disabled no special facilities
Pets accepted only in bedrooms
Closed May to mid-Jun, mid-Sep to Nov **Proprietors** Carlo and Mariarosa Sacchi

Western Lakes

Country villa, Alzate Brianza

Villa Odescalchi

This rather grand 17thC building is a popular spot used by local companies for small business conferences, but it is also worth considering for holiday purposes too. The main salon, furnished with antiques and plush sofas and chairs, leads out to the gardens and park behind. An open gallery runs all around the top of the room, and many of the bedrooms lead off this narrow rectangle – tall, quite spacious rooms, decorated in autumn colours with modern furnishings. The dining-room is pleasantly situated in a modern conservatory extension.

Nearby Como (10 km), Milan (42 km), Bergamo (46 km).

Via Anzani 12, Alzate Brianza 22040 Como
Tel (031) 630822
Location close to middle of town off road for Como, with large private park and car parking opposite entrance
Food & drink breakfast, lunch, dinner
Prices rooms L94,000-L133,000; FB L130,000
Rooms 14 double, 8 single, 3 family rooms, all with bath or shower; all rooms have

phone, minibar, colour TV
Facilities sitting-room, dining-room, 2 conference rooms, bar; outdoor heated swimming-pool, tennis
Credit cards AE
Children welcome
Disabled not suitable
Pets dogs allowed
Closed never
Manager Federico Bruschini

Lakeside villa, Argegno

Belvedere

It is odd to walk into this small old villa on the shore of Lake Como and find an English-style bar upholstered in tartan. But when you meet the jolly owner and discover that his wife is a Scot, the friendly British guest-house atmosphere is explained.

In front of the house is a sunny, gravelled terrace where you can enjoy a drink, or eat out if the weather permits. In the dining-room, with views out over the lake, the old painted ceiling remains, and antiques are scattered around. The bedrooms are simply, even basically furnished, and some are a little cramped; those at the back are possibly rather noisy, but those at the front have splendid views of the lake.

Nearby Valle di Intelvi; boat trips on lake.

Via Milano 8, Argegno 22010 Como
Tel (031) 821116
Location on shores of Lake Como; private car parking
Food & drink breakfast, lunch, dinner
Prices rooms L37,000-L74,000; meals L25,000-L30,000
Rooms 17 double (7 twin), 11

with bath or shower; one single
Facilities dining-room, bar, sitting-room; boats for hire in summer
Credit cards DC, MC, V
Children welcome **Disabled** not suitable **Pets** accepted, but not in dining-room
Closed Nov to Mar
Proprietors Giorgio and Jane Cappelletti

Western Lakes

Lakeside hotel, Cannero Riviera

Cannero

Cannero is one of the quietest resorts on Lake Maggiore and its most desirable hotels lie right on the shore. Only the ferry landing-stage and a quiet dead-end road separate the Cannero from the waters of Maggiore.

The building was once a monastery, though only an old stone column, a couple of vaulted passageways and a quiet courtyard suggest it is anything other than a modern hotel. The emphasis is on comfort and relaxation and the atmosphere is very friendly, thanks largely to the smiling Signora Gallinotto. Downstairs, big windows and terraces make the most of the setting. The restaurant focuses on the lake, with an outdoor terrace running alongside.

The bedrooms are light and well cared for, and have adequate bathrooms. There are gorgeous views of lake and mountains from the front rooms, though many guests are just as happy overlooking the pool at the back – which, if anything, is quieter. By day this provides a delightfully peaceful spot to take a dip or lounge under yellow and white parasols.

Nearby Borromean Islands – daily connections by boat; Ascona (21 km), Locarno (25 km) and other resorts of Lake Maggiore.

Lungo Lago 3-2, Cannero Riviera, Lago Maggiore 28051 Novara
Tel (0323) 788046
Location in resort, overlooking lake, with garden and 2 car parks
Food & drink breakfast, lunch, dinner
Prices rooms L45,000; DB&B L64,000; FB L70,000; 10% reduction for children under 10
Rooms 30 double, 15 with bath, 15 with shower; 6 single, 3 with bath, 3 with shower; all rooms have central heating, phone
Facilities sitting-room, piano bar, dining-room, lakeside terrace; tennis, pool, solarium, boat, windsurfing, 2 bicycles
Credit cards AE, DC, MC, V
Children welcome; separate dining-room for children, baby-sitter on request
Disabled 8 rooms accessible; lift/elevator **Pets** accepted if well behaved, but not in main sitting-room
Closed Nov to mid-Mar
Proprietors Sga Gallinotto and sons

Western Lakes

Lakeside hotel, Arona

Giardino

There is little point in staying in Arona without views of Lake Maggiore, and the Giardino's great attraction is a large terrace shaded by a magnificent awning of well-trained wisteria, looking across the road to the waterfront. Rooms (with lake views for a modest premium) have been decorated with a modest attempt at individuality – for example tartan carpets, marble tops, brass and china lamp fittings. The dining-room is strictly average in ambience and decoration, but in season there will be the Piedmontese speciality of *porcine* (*cèpe* mushrooms) in several guises It is a family business with friendly, willing staff.

Nearby Colosso di San Carlone (1.5 km); Stresa (16 km); Borromean islands (regular boats); Baveno, Pallanza.

Via Repubblica 1, Arona 28041 Novara **Tel** (0322) 45994 **Location** five minutes from station; car parking nearby on and off road **Food & drink** breakfast, lunch, dinner **Prices** rooms L81,000-L114,000; meals L30,000-L50,000 **Rooms** 56 double, all with	bath and shower; all rooms have central heating, TV, minibar, phone **Facilities** dining-room, sitting-room, TV room, bar, disco in basement; tennis **Credit cards** AE, DC, V **Children** welcome **Disabled** no special facilities **Pets** welcome **Closed** never **Proprietor** Ezio Bertalli

Restaurant with rooms, Soriso

Al Sorriso

The village of Soriso lies some way from the lake of Orta and has no special charm (despite its name which with the addition of an 'r' – as in the name of the hotel – comes to mean a 'smile'). The real reason for coming here is the food. In the whole of Italy there are less than a dozen restaurants which are awarded two or more Michelin stars and this is one of them. Among the specialities are pumpkin flowers with truffle sauce, celery soup with prawns in thyme and slices of lamb with marjoram. The dining-room is the picture of elegance and the service is highly professional. The bedrooms are quite plush, but unremarkable.

Nearby Orta San Giulio (8 km), Milan (78 km).

Soriso 28018 Novara **Tel** (0322) 983228 **Location** in village of Soriso, S of Lake Orta; car parking on road **Food & drink** breakfast, lunch, dinner **Prices** rooms L70,000-L100,000; meals about L70,000-L80,000 **Rooms** 5 double, 3 single; all with bath or shower; all	rooms have phone, TV, minibar **Facilities** bar, dining-room **Credit cards** MC, V **Children** not suitable **Disabled** no special facilities **Pets** dogs not accepted **Closed** 2 weeks Jan, 3 weeks Aug; restaurant only, Mon and Tue lunch **Proprietors** Angelo and Luisa Valazza

Western Lakes

Lakeside hotel, Bellagio

Florence

Bellagio is the pearl of Lake Como. It stands on a promontory at the point where the lake divides into two branches, and the views from its houses, villas and gardens are superb. The Florence is a handsome 18thC building occupying a prime position on the main piazza overlooking the lake. A terrace under arcades, where drinks and snacks are served, provides a welcoming entry to the hotel and the interior is no less appealing. Whitewashed walls, high vaulted ceilings and beams create a cool, attractive foyer; to one side, elegant and slightly faded seats cluster round an old stone fireplace. The atmosphere of rustic old-world charm is carried through to the vaulted dining-room.

The hotel has been in the same family for 150 years, and is now in the hands of the amiable Ketzlar family, who speak good English.

Bedrooms have the same old-fashioned charm as the public rooms, furnished with antiques and attractive fabrics; the most sought after, naturally, are those with balconies and views over the lake. Breakfast can be taken on a delightful lakeside terrace under shady trees across the street from the hotel, watching the various craft ply across the lake.

Recent reports contain conflicting views: one speaks of 'five idyllic days' here, another of 'dilapidated furnishings', uncomfortable beds and 'third-rate' food and service. Who's right?

Nearby Villa Serbelloni (in Bellagio); tour of the Madonna del Ghisallo (37 km); ferry and motor boat trips around Como.

Piazza Mazzini, Bellagio
22021 Como
Tel (031) 950342
Location on main piazza overlooking lake, with waterside terrace and garage
Food & drink breakfast, lunch, dinner
Prices rooms L48,000-L97,000; meals L25,000
Rooms 32 double, 23 with bath, 8 with shower; 6 single; all rooms have central heating
Facilities dining-room, bar, reading and TV room, terrace
Credit cards AE, DC, MC, V
Children accepted
Disabled no special facilities
Pets well behaved ones accepted, but not in restaurant
Closed 3rd week Oct to mid-Apr
Proprietor Ronald Ketzlar

Western Lakes

Du Lac

A congenial family atmosphere, light sunny rooms and, above all, a delightful setting on the central piazza combining to make the Hotel du Lac one of the most popular hotels in Bellagio. One of the most inviting features is the arcaded terrace where drinks are served to guests and passers-by. Clients seeking more privacy have sole use of a room garden for sunbathing and admiring the views. The decoration is essentially modern and not altogether inspiring, but the dining-room is particularly spacious and light, overlooking the lake, and several of the bedrooms have their own terrace.

Nearby Villa Serbelloni (in Bellagio).

Pza Mazzini 32, Bellagio 22021 Como
Tel (031) 950320
Location overlooking lake, in middle of resort
Food & drink breakfast, lunch, dinner
Prices rooms L65,000-L106,000; reductions for children
Rooms 33 double, 30 with bath, 3 with shower; 10 single, 6 with bath, 4 with shower; 5 family rooms, all with bath; all rooms have central heating, phone, hairdrier
Facilities dining-room, sitting-room, bar, TV room, terrace, roof garden
Credit cards AE, MC, V
Children welcome **Disabled** no special facilities **Pets** not accepted in dining-room
Closed mid-Oct to mid-Apr
Proprietors Leoni family

La Pergola

While most hotels in Bellagio are concentrated around the main piazza and waterfront, La Pergola is tucked away in the tiny, quiet village of Pescallo just to the south. It faces the eastern shores of Como, its lakeside terrace commanding beautiful views. Parts of the house are 500 years old. There are handsome flagstone floors, antiques, vaulted ceilings and an air of rustic simplicity. It is a small, modest family-run place where mother does the cooking (mainly fish from the lake) and the rest of the family look after the hotel. The bedrooms are all simple and old-fashioned but not without charm. And, being some of the cheapest rooms in one of the most popular resorts of the lakes, they are booked up well ahead in season.

Nearby Villa Serbelloni at Bellagio; lake tours.

Pescallo, Bellagio 22021 Como
Tel (031) 950263
Location one km S of Bellagio, overlooking lake; ample car parking
Food & drink breakfast, lunch, dinner
Prices DB&B L66,000
Rooms 12 rooms, 2 with bath; 2 single
Facilities dining-room, bar, terrace
Credit cards AE, DC, MC, V
Children accepted
Disabled no special facilities
Pets accepted
Closed Nov to Mar; restaurant only, Tue
Proprietor Sga M Mazzoni

Western Lakes

Lakeside guest-house, Isola dei Pescatori

Verbano

The Isola dei Pescatori, a tiny dot in Lake Maggiore, may not have the *palazzo* or gardens of neighbouring Isola Bella (unlike the other islands it has never belonged to the wealthy Borromean family), but it is just as charming in its own way. The cafés and slightly shabby, painted fishermens' houses along the front are, perhaps, reminiscent of a Greek island – though not an undiscovered one.

The Verbano is a large russet-coloured villa occupying one end of the island, its garden and terraces looking across the lake to Isola Bella. It does not pretend to be a hotel of great luxury, but it can offer lots of character and local colour, and the Zacchera family are friendly hosts. There are beautiful views from the bedrooms, and 11 of the 12 have balconies. Each room is named after a flower – some are prettily and appropriately furnished with painted furniture, others are slightly faded and old-fashioned.

But the emphasis in this small hotel is really on the restaurant. The cook has been here for about 30 years and home-made pastas are her speciality. If weather prevents eating on the terrace you can still enjoy views of the lake through the big windows of the dining-room.

Nearby Isola Bella (5 minutes by boat); Stresa, Pallanza, Baveno all linked to the island by regular ferry service.

Via Ugo Ara 2, Isola dei Pescatori, Stresa 28049 Novara
Tel (0323) 30408
Location on tiny island with waterside terraces; regular boats from Stresa, where there is ample car parking space
Food & drink breakfast, lunch, dinner
Prices rooms L100,000; meals L30,000
Rooms 12 double, 8 with bath, 4 with shower; all rooms have central heating
Facilities dining-room, sitting-room, bar, terrace
Credit cards AE, DC, MC, V
Children accepted
Disabled no special facilities
Pets accepted
Closed never
Proprietors Zacchera family

Western Lakes

Lakeside hotel, Orta San Giulio

Leon d'Oro

In itself, the Leon d'Or is unremarkable. The bedrooms, although comfortable, are small, their furnishings are modern and anonymous, and as a room the restaurant is nothing more than pleasant. But the hotel enjoys a position which is unbeatable for beautiful lake views. From its shady vine-clad terraces on the water's edge, there are superb and commanding views of the enchanting little island of San Giulio and the wooded shore rising up behind – and the big windows provide views that are almost as wide as from within the restaurant. Another bonus of the location is the adjoining Piazza Motta, an animated square of extraordinary beauty.

Nearby island of San Giulio (quick trip by boat).

Orta San Giulio, Lago d'Orta 28016 Novara
Tel (0322) 90254
Location just off main piazza, with terrace right on lake; some car parking 100 m away
Food & drink breakfast, lunch, dinner
Prices rooms L49,000-L77,000; meals L24,000
Rooms 26 double, 4 with bath, 22 with shower; 5 single, all with shower; one family room with shower; all rooms have central heating; phone in 12 rooms
Facilities restaurant, lake terrace, bar, TV, solarium
Credit cards AE, MC, V
Children accepted **Disabled** access difficult **Pets** accepted
Closed Jan
Proprietors Maddalena and Giuseppina Ronchetti

Lakeside hotel, Orta San Giulio

Orta

Lying on the main square of Orta San Giulio, the Orta enjoys beautiful views across the lake. Its endearingly shabby classical facade flanks the southern side of the piazza and the tables of its flowery terrace spill out on to the square. On the lakeside, the tables along the restaurant terrace have a bird's-eye view of the cluster of houses forming the lovely little island of San Giulio. Sitting areas are light and surprisingly spacious for a hotel of its size, though furnishings are rather old-fashioned and the atmosphere a trifle staid.

Nearby island of San Giulio (quick trip by motor or rowing-boat).

Orta San Giulio 28016 Novara
Tel (0322) 90253
Location on central square of Orta San Giulio, overlooking lake; garage
Food & drink breakfast, lunch, dinner
Prices rooms L48,000-L96,000; meals L27,000
Rooms 24 double, 9 with bath, 15 with shower; 5 single with shower; 6 family rooms, 2 with bath, 4 with shower; all rooms have central heating, phone, view of lake; TV on request
Facilities dining-room with lakeside terrace, bar, TV room, sitting-room
Credit cards AE, DC, MC, V
Children accepted **Disabled** some rooms suitable **Pets** accepted **Closed** Nov to Feb
Proprietors Marina Bianchi and Adriano Oglina

Western Lakes

Country hotel, Orta San Giulio

La Bussola

The Bussola is a modern hotel in a splendid position, amid lawns, flowering shrubs and shady trees on a hill looking down on the lake and the little island of San Giulio.

Few of the bedrooms match up to the expectations aroused by the reception area, where antique features like beams and stone walls merge successfully with modern furnishings. The restaurant is simple, light and spacious and there is understandable competition for space on the narrow lakeside terrace. Specialities are smoked salmon and fillet of salmon trout with cream of courgettes.

Nearby old town of Orta; San Giulio island.

Orta San Giulio 28016
Novara
Tel (0322) 90198
Location on hillside, above
Orta; garage and plenty of
open car parking
Food & drink breakfast,
lunch, dinner
Prices rooms L53,000-
L100,000 (half board only,
Jun-Sep)
Rooms 14 double, 2 single;
11 with bath, 5 with shower;
all rooms have phone; 7
rooms have minibar
Facilities dining-room with
terrace, bar, TV room;
outdoor swimming-pool
Credit cards AE, MC, V
Children welcome; baby
listening **Disabled** not
suitable **Pets** dogs not
accepted in dining-room
Closed 10 days in Nov
Proprietor Mario Tassera
family

Restaurant with rooms, Ranco

Sole

Gastronomy, it seems, has always been the strength of the Sole at Ranco. It started off as a coaching inn and 'casa del vino' in 1872; now it is an elegant restaurant, and the fish specialities for which Carlo Brovelli is renowned include such delicacies as salmon stuffed with pike mousse in ginger sauce and prawns in pastry with wild asparagus. Meals are taken on the terrace or in the refined setting of the restaurant, smartly combining modern and antique furnishing. Bedrooms are swish suites.

Nearby castle at Angera (3 km), Arona (19 km).

Piazza Venezia 5, Ranco,
Lago Maggiore 21020
Varese
Tel (0331) 976507
Location 10 km NW of Sesto
Calende, in village, with
garden and ample private
car parking
Food & drink breakfast,
lunch, dinner
Prices rooms L180,000;
meals approx L85,000
Rooms 8 twin-bedded suites,
all with bath; all rooms have
central heating, minibar,
lake-view terrace, air-
conditioning, safe, TV
Facilities dining-room,
reading-room, conference
room, bar, lakeside terrace
Credit cards AE, DC, V
Children accepted if well
behaved **Disabled** no special
facilities **Pets** accepted, but
not in dining-room or some
bedrooms
Closed Jan
Proprietor Carlo Brovelli

Western Lakes

Lakeside hotel, Lenno

San Giorgio

This large white 1920s villa on the shores of Lake Como stands out against a backdrop of wooded hills and immaculate gardens running right down to the shore.

The San Giorgio's gardens are a delight. A path lined with potted plants leads down through neatly tended lawns to the lakeside terrace and the low-lying stone wall which is all that divides the gardens from the pebble beach and the lake. There are palm trees, arbours and stone urns where geraniums flourish. For a trip on the lake you need not go far – the ferry landing-stage lies close by.

The interior is no disappointment. The public rooms are large and spacious, leading off handsome halls. There are antiques wherever you go and attractive touches such as pretty ceramic pots and copper pots brimming with flowers. The restaurant is a lovely light room with breathtaking views and the salon is equally inviting, with its ornate mirrors, fireplace and slightly faded antiques. Even the ping-pong room has a number of interesting antique pieces.

Bedrooms are large and pleasantly old-fashioned. Antiques and beautiful views are the main features, but there is nothing grand or luxurious about them – hence the reasonable prices. Half-board terms are available for stays of several days.

Nearby Tremezzo, Cadenabbia, Villa Carlotta (2-4 km); Bellagio (10 min boat crossing from Cadenabbia).

Via Regina 81, Lenno, Tremezzo 22019 Como
Tel (0344) 40415
Location on lakefront in private park, with parking for 30 cars, garage for 6
Food & drink breakfast, lunch, dinner
Prices rooms L48,000-L106,000; meals L28,000
Rooms 26 double, 20 with bath, 6 with shower; 3 single, one with bath; all rooms have central heating
Facilities dining-room, hall, reading-room, ping-pong room, terrace; tennis,
Credit cards MC, V
Children accepted
Disabled access difficult
Pets not accepted
Closed Oct to Apr
Proprietor Margherita Cappelletti

Western Lakes

Villa Flora

This is a modest, home-like *pensione* with no pretensions occupying a large pinkish-orange villa of indeterminate age. Its greatest asset is the lakeside situation, well below the road which runs through the little medieval village of Torno. Your bedroom could be spacious, with a parquet floor and 1960s furniture, or cramped with smarter laminated units; but it will be simple. The restaurant, too, is functional but spotlessly clean, and has a terrace overlooking the lake. The sitting-room is rather quaint: with its brocade and ornate ceiling it seems unchanged since the turn of the century.

Nearby cathedral and town of Como; Bellagio (23 km).

Via Torrazza 10, Lago di Como, Torno 22020 Como
Tel (031) 419222
Location 7 km NE of Como; car parking nearby
Food & drink breakfast, lunch, dinner
Prices rooms L70,000-L90,000; meals L22,000-L45,000; reductions for children
Rooms 20 double, all with shower; 3 family rooms, all with shower; all rooms have phone
Facilities restaurant with terrace, breakfast area, sitting-room, bar; jetty, private beach
Credit cards MC, V
Children accepted
Disabled not suitable
Pets accepted
Closed Nov to Feb; restaurant only, Tue
Proprietor Sg Cavadini

Stella d'Italia

Mario Ortelli represents the third generation of his family to run this popular little hotel on the shores of Lake Lugano. Bedrooms are large but simple, with a 1950s feel; the little sitting-room has a pleasantly lived-in atmosphere, with pictures, comfy furniture and books – many in English. But the most appealing feature is the slightly unkempt garden and gravelled terrace, shaded by pergolas, which juts right into the lake.

Nearby Lugano (10 km), Menaggio (Lake Como) (20 km), Como (50 km).

Piazza Roma 1, San Mamete, 22010 Como Valsolda; postal address PO Box 46, 6976 Castagnola, Switzerland
Tel (0344) 68139
Location 8 km E of Lugano, 3 km from Swiss border; garage parking for 14 cars
Food & drink breakfast, lunch, dinner
Prices rooms L53,000-L82,000
Rooms 31 double, 4 single; 23 with bath, 12 with shower; all rooms have central heating, balcony, phone
Facilities 2 sitting-rooms, bar, dining-room, terrace; private beach
Credit cards AE, DC, MC, V
Children accepted
Disabled not very suitable
Pets small dogs only accepted
Closed mid-Oct to Apr; restaurant only, Wed
Proprietors Ortelli family

Lombardy

Lombardy hotels

Lombardy is an enormous region, stretching from the high Alps bordering Switzerland almost as far as the Adriatic and Ligurian seas. It contains Lake Como, and Lakes Maggiore and Garda form its boundary in the west and east respectively; the many charming hotels in these popular tourist areas are covered in the separate sections immediately before and after this one, which covers the hotels in and around Bergamo, Mantua and Milan.

Of all big, glossy Italian cities, none is glossier than Milan and only Rome is bigger. Despite its considerable heritage – notably a marvellous cathedral, important art collections and the world's most famous opera house – its role as Italy's economic capital dominates the visitor's view, and most steer clear. The result is that Milan's hotels are business-oriented – and as big and glossy as the city itself.

Conveniently located in the same central area as the recommended Gran Duca di York – that is, within walking distance of all or most of the major sights and the smart shops – the Manzoni (Tel 705700) falls only just outside our usual size limits and is calm, comfortable, and reasonably priced. Very handy for the Stazione Centrale (which is not in fact entirely central) is the slightly cheaper and more modern Florida (Tel 670 5921). If the budget will stand extravagance, the Duomo (Tel 8833) has the merits of a historic building and an unrivalled position – close, of course, to the duomo itself and to the famous central shopping arcades.

Gran Duca di York

On paper there is nothing remarkable about this traditional little city hotel – behind its grand entrance it is relatively plain, and some of the bedrooms (though spacious) verge on the basic. But it has rather more warmth and character than most of its ilk, with paintings and ornaments dotted around, and its position is a good one – the Biblioteca Ambrosiana next door contains some remarkable paintings, and the neighbourhood (being business-dominated) is notably quiet at night. But this position has its price: be prepared for a walk of 300 m or 400 m to find a choice of worthwhile restaurants.

Nearby *duomo*, Poldi-Pezzoli museum, La Scala, Brera Palace and Gallery, all within walking distance.

Via Moneta 1/a, (Piazza Cordusio), Milan 20123
Tel (02) 874863
Location about 300 m W of the *duomo*; public (paying) garage nearby
Food & drink breakfast
Prices rooms L90,000-L120,000
Rooms 21 double, 6 single, 6 suites, all with bath or shower; all rooms have central heating, air-conditioning, phone, TV
Facilities breakfast room, sitting-room/bar
Credit cards AE
Children accepted
Disabled no special facilities
Pets not accepted
Closed Aug
Proprietor Dr Visentini

Lombardy

Antica Locanda Solferino

The last thing you might expect to find close to the centre of glossy Milan: a simple and modestly priced hotel of great character and charm, with a rather countrified atmosphere. Bedrooms are on the small side, but are prettily decorated and furnished with rustic antiques, and are not without modern conveniences; unusually for Italy, the bathrooms have not been given the chrome-and-glass treatment. As if the position and prices were not sufficient attractions, the restaurant which forms part of the inn is highly popular in its own right; it is cosily traditional in style, with more than a hint of Parisian bistros. Not surprisingly, you need to book in advance.

Nearby Brera gallery within walking distance.

Via Castelfidardo 2,
Milan 20121
Tel (02) 6570129
Location on tiny street
between Arena and Piazza
della Repubblica; no car
parking space
Food & drink breakfast,
lunch, dinner
Prices rooms L64,300-
L91,600; meals from L30,000

Rooms 10 double, one single,
all with bath; all rooms
have central heating, phone
Facilities dining-room
Credit cards V
Children accepted **Disabled**
no special facilities **Pets** accepted
Closed 10 days in Aug;
restaurant only, Sat lunch
and Sun mid-July to mid-Sep
Manager Curzio Castelli

Castello di San Gaudenzio

Voghera is a small town south of Milan, where the plain of the Po starts to give way to hills; the Castello lies half-way between the town and the river, convenient for travellers on both the A7 and the A21. It is a brick-built 14thC castle in lush grounds, immaculately restored and sensitively furnished in mainly modern styles, which caters for big banqueting parties but also takes small numbers of guests. The public areas and bedrooms are superbly spacious, and for what you get the prices are modest.

Nearby Pavia (Carthusian monastery) (25 km).

Cervesina, Voghera 27050
Pavia
Tel (0383) 75025
Location 6 km N. Voghera,
in hamlet; in large ground,
with ample car parking
Food & drink breakfast,
lunch, dinner
Prices rooms L95,000-
L160,000, suites L220,000;
meals L30,000
Rooms 9 double with bath,
one single with shower, two
suites; all rooms have central
heating, TV, minibar,

phone, radio
Facilities dining-room,
sitting-room/bar, meeting
rooms, banqueting hall
Credit cards AE, DC, MC, V
Children welcome
Disabled access difficult
Pets not accepted
Closed never
Proprietors Stefano Natali

Lombardy

Agnello d'Oro

The Agnello d'Oro lies in the heart of the old city – a picturesque, tall and incredibly narrow building facing a tiny square with a fountain. The interior exudes charm and character. An antique desk and walls cluttered with ceramics, copper masks (made by the *padrone*) and various trophies for gastronomic excellence make up the tiny reception area, and the dining-room is a cosy trattoria with red checked table-cloths and a collection of bottles and copper pots covering every inch of wall and ceiling. The menu mainly features local dishes including the Bergamo speciality of small birds with *polenta*. Bedrooms verge on the basic; but they are reasonably priced.

Nearby Colleoni chapel, Piazza Vecchia, church of Santa Maria Maggiore (all in upper town); Carrara gallery (lower town).

Via Gombito 22, Bergamo 24100
Tel (035) 249883
Location in the heart of the old upper town, on a small piazza; no private car parking
Food & drink breakfast, lunch, dinner
Prices rooms L40,200-L69,400; meals about L35,000
Rooms 16 double, 4 with bath, 12 with shower; 4 single, all with shower; all rooms have central heating, phone, colour TV
Facilities dining-room, bar
Credit cards AE, DC, MC, V
Children accepted
Disabled no special facilities
Pets accepted
Closed never
Proprietor Pino Capozzi

Gourmet

Bergamo's reputation for gastronomy is well deserved, and the food at the Gourmet is about as good as you will find anywhere in the upper city. 'Tagliatelle' with artichokes and prawns, turbot with butter and capers, truffle and caviar soufflé – these are just a few of the dishes you might find on the menu. But the Gourmet is also a comfortable place to stay the night – the 12 bedrooms are spacious, light and civilized, with smart furnishings of high quality in modern Italian style, and luxury bathrooms. In summer meals are taken on a delightful flowery veranda, overlooking the lower city.

Nearby Piazza Vecchia, Colleoni Chapel, Church of Santa Maria Maggior in upper town; Carrara Academy in lower town.

Via San Vigilio 1, Bergamo Alta 24100
Tel (035) 256110
Location in upper town; private car parking
Food & drink breakfast, lunch, dinner
Prices rooms L69,000-L104,000; meals about L40,000
Rooms 10 rooms, all with bath or shower; all rooms have phone, TV, minibar
Facilities dining-room with terrace, sitting-room, bar
Credit cards AE, DC, MC, V
Children accepted **Disabled** not suitable **Pets** not accepted
Closed restaurant only, Tue
Managers Aldo Beretta and Franco Tassi

NORTHERN ITALY

Lombardy

Town hotel, Sabbioneta

Al Duca

Sabbioneta was built in the 16thC by the great Gonzaga family
as an ideal fortified city; now it is a sad backwater, but still
retains some of its finest monuments. The Al Duca is a family-
run, no-frills hotel close to the central square. The façade is
classical Renaissance, the hallway retains the original columns
and pink marble stairway, but the rest is almost entirely renovated. Bedrooms are bright and airy with modern light-wood
furniture, some of them large. But the main emphasis is on the
restaurant – a relaxed, modest trattoria with pink table-cloths,
ladder-back chairs and flowers on every table. The dishes are
regional and the set meals moderately priced.
Nearby Palazzo del Giardino (gallery of antiquities); Parma,
Mantua, Modena all within reach.

Via della Stamperia 18,
Sabbioneta 46018 Mantova
Tel (0375) 52474
Location very close to main
piazza, on fairly quiet street
with car parking available
Food & drink breakfast,
lunch, dinner
Prices rooms L43,000-
L68,000; lunch and dinner
L15,000-L25,000
Rooms 9 double, one single,
all with bath or shower; all
rooms have central heating,
intercom
Facilities breakfast room,
dining-room, bar
Credit cards AE, MC, V
Children accepted
Disabled no special facilities
Pets accepted
Closed Jan
Proprietor Giovanni Savi

Restaurant with rooms, Bergamo

Il Sole

On the corner of the lovely Piazza Vecchia, the Sole catches a lot
of Bergamo's tourist trade. Primarily this is a place to eat. The
restaurant doesn't have quite the same cosy charm as the Agnello
d'Oro (page 37) but there is a cheerful atmosphere and you are
unlikely to be disappointed either by food or service – and when
weather permits you can eat in an attractive courtyard. In comparison to the restaurant standards, the bedrooms are fairly basic
and uninspired. But the cost of a night's accommodation is low,
and for location – right in the heart of the old city – it is hard to
beat.
Nearby Colleoni chapel, church of Santa Maria Maggiore (both
at far end of square); Carrara Accademy in lower town.

Via Bartolomeo Colleoni 1,
Piazza Vecchia, Citta Alta,
Bergamo 24100
Tel (035) 218238
Location in corner of piazza,
in upper town; car parking
awkward
Food & drink breakfast,
lunch, dinner
Prices rooms L52,000
Rooms 11 double, all with
shower or bath
Facilities dining-room, bar,
courtyard
Credit cards AE, DC, MC, V
Children accepted
Disabled no special facilities
Pets small ones only accepted
Closed restaurant only, Thu
Proprietor Mauro Dipilato

Lombardy

Restaurant with rooms, Capriate San Gervasio

Vigneto

Capriate San Gervasio is a few minutes' drive from the main autostrada from Milan to Venice, convenient for an overnight stop. The Vigneto is a comfortable villa, perched on a river bank, surrounded by a beautifully kept small garden and terrace. The bedrooms are reasonably sized, with modern furniture, decorated in rather sombre beige and tans; those at the front look out over the tree-lined banks of the river. The dining-room is formal, with many pictures on the walls, and looks out over the covered terrace where you can eat in the summer months. The restaurant is popular with the locals.
Nearby Bergamo (17 km), Milan (35 km).

Capriate San Gervasio 24042
Bergamo
Tel (02) 909 39351
Location 12 km SW of
Bergamo, 2 km N of A4, on
banks of River Adda; with
private car parking
Food & drink breakfast,
lunch, dinner
Prices rooms L80,000-
L110,000; meals L35,000-
L50,000

Rooms 12 rooms, all with
shower; all rooms have
phone, TV
Facilities 2 sitting-rooms,
dining-room, conference
facilities
Credit cards AF., V
Children accepted
Disabled no special facilities
Pets not accepted
Closed Aug; restaurant only,
Tue **Proprietor** Casina Rosella

Lombardy

Town hotel, Mantua

Broletto

The huge cobbled Piazza Sordello and the arcaded Piazza delle Erbe boast the finest buildings of Mantua, and the little Broletto lies conveniently between the two. It is a new building in an old shell and apart from the façade and stone-arched entrance the only real evidence of age is the old timber beams in a couple of the bedrooms. Elsewhere it is light, modern and essentially functional. Bedrooms are small, bright and spotlessly clean, and there is a modest little breakfast-room on the first floor. As a modestly priced and welcoming base, with friendly staff, the Broletto serves its purpose well.

Nearby apartments of the Palazzo Ducale (Piazza Sordello); Parma, Modena and Verona all within reach.

Via Accademia 1,
Mantua 46100
Tel (0376) 326784
Location in heart of city, close to Teatro Bibiena; car parking available
Food & drink breakfast
Prices L68,000-L107,000
Rooms 8 double, 2 with bath, 6 with shower; 9 single, all with shower; all rooms have

central heating, air-conditioning, minibar, phone, radio
Facilities breakfast room
Credit cards AE, MC, V
Children accepted
Disabled no special facilities
Pets small ones only
Closed 24 Dec-3 Jan
Proprietor Augusto Bodoardo

Town hotel, Mantua

San Lorenzo

The San Lorenzo stands close to the famous Piazza delle Erbe, and from its roof-top terrace there are fine views of historic Mantua. Although it is comparatively new, the hotel feels old. A simple façade with arcades conceals a rather grand lobby: ornate gilt mirrors, gleaming antiques and chandeliers. The first-floor salon is comfortable, quiet and civilized, with smart furnishings, huge bowls of carnations and coloured urns. The bedrooms are less impressive – a trifle gloomy – though a few have original antiques and all are in good taste.

Nearby Piazza Sordello, Palazzo Ducale; Parma, Modena, Verona all within reach.

Piazza Concordia 14,
Mantua 46100 Mantova
Tel (0376) 220500
Location in historic heart of city, with private paying garage 60 m away
Food & drink breakfast
Prices rooms L127,000-L190,000
Rooms 28 double, 18 with bath, 10 with shower; 10 single, 6 with bath, 4 with shower; 3 suites, all with

bath; all rooms have central heating, phone
Facilities sitting areas, bar, TV room, breakfast room, roof-top terrace
Credit cards AE, DC, MC, V
Children accepted
Disabled no special facilities
Pets small ones only
Closed never
Managers Giuseppe and Ottorino Tosi

Lombardy

Restaurant with rooms, Pomponesco

Il Leone

Pomponesco was once a flourishing town under the Gonzaga family. Now it is a shadow of its former self, surrounded by unsightly modern suburbs. But the old part still has a certain faded charm, and just off the main piazza lies the Leone – an old peeling building which once belonged to a 16thC nobleman.

As the name suggests, this is primarily a place to eat. There are only eight bedrooms and by far the most attractive features are the dining areas. The *pièce de rèsistance* is the coffered 16thC ceiling and frieze in the main restaurant. Elsewhere the decoration is suitably elegant: 'old master' paintings, gilt wall lamps, a terrazzo floor and tables immaculately laid. Food here is among the best in the region, and local specialities include the traditional dish of braised beef with 'polenta' which was one of the popular dishes of the Gonzagas.

Beyond the restaurant a flower-filled inner courtyard leads to the bedrooms. These are built around an inviting pool and garden area where a country house atmosphere prevails.

In contrast with the Renaissance elegance of the restaurants, the bedrooms have a stark modernity. But they are peaceful, bright, comfortable and well maintained.

Nearby Mantua, Modena, Parma all within reach.

Piazza IV Martiri 2,
Pomponesco 46030 Mantova
Tel (0375) 86077
Location on small piazza, next to river Po, with garden and car parking
Food & drink breakfast, lunch, dinner
Prices rooms L41,000-L67,000; DB&B L63,000
Rooms 6 double, 3 single; all with shower; all rooms have central heating, phone, minibar
Facilities dining-room, bar, TV room; swimming-pool
Credit cards AE, DC, MC, V
Children accepted
Disabled access difficult
Pets accepted
Closed Jan; restaurant only, Sun pm and Mon
Proprietor Fernando Mori

Lake Garda

Lakeside villa, Gardone Riviera

Villa Fiordaliso

A pink villa on the banks of Lake Garda in shady gardens of pines, palms and cypresses, the Fiordaliso is one of the most exclusive hotels of northern Italy. This *fin de siècle* villa's main claim to fame is the fact that Claretta Petacci, life-long friend of Mussolini (who set up headquarters nearby), stayed here for a few months. No expense has been spared in its conversion to a restaurant and hotel. Throughout, there is a wealth of marble and alabaster, inlaid woodwork and silk tapestries: the atmosphere is one of formal opulence. But the place is pleasantly small and the restaurant is divided into four rooms, each with an individual feature such as mosaic glass windows or antique fireplace. In summer you can eat by the lakeside or take drinks on the terrace.

The Fiordaliso is first and foremost a restaurant and its dishes, many of them French-influenced, have earned it a high reputation in the region. The food is beautifully presented, and served from fine crystal and china.

Of the show-piece bedrooms, Claretta's is the *pièce de résistance*. The sumptuous decoration even extends to the bathroom, which is built of Carrara marble. The other rooms are smaller but exceptionally comfortable – and the best have some truly beautiful views.

Nearby Vittoriale estate (1 km); Sirmione, Desenzano within reach; hydrofoil and ferry tours up and down the western side of Lake Garda.

Via Zanardelli 132, Gardone Riviera 25083 Brescia
Tel (0365) 20158
Location on main road through resort, in private park overlooking lake; private car parking available
Food & drink breakfast, lunch, dinner
Prices rooms L128,000; DB&B L127,000
Rooms 6 double, 4 with bath, 2 with shower; all rooms have central heating, minibar, TV, radio, phone
Facilities dining-room, piano bar; private beach
Credit cards AE, DC, MC, V
Children not very suitable
Disabled not suitable
Pets not accepted
Closed Jan and Feb
Proprietors Pierantonio Ambrosi, Monica Giudici

Lake Garda

Lakeside hotel, Gardone Riviera

Montefiori

The Montefiori is up the hill-side from lake Garda, secluded in extensive gardens and park-land. It actually consists of three villas; by 1989 there will be a fourth, adding another 80 beds (along with another Olympic-size pool and other facilities). At present this is quite an exclusive place and not in the least impersonal. Bedrooms are tastefully furnished in Venetian or Florentine style and nearly all have balconies facing the lake; the dining-room is a suave combination of modern and traditional styles. In the garden, cypresses, palms and exotic plants flourish.
Nearby walks in the hills; boat trips to Desenzano, Sirmione, Torri del Benaco, Malcesine.

Gardone Riviera, Lago di Garda 25083 Brescia
Tel (0365) 21118
Location 200 m from Gardone Riviera, with 2 private car parks
Food & drink breakfast, lunch, dinner
Prices rooms L70,000-L120,000; DB&B L90,000-L100,000
Rooms 35 rooms, 7 with bath, 28 with shower; all rooms have central heating, TV, phone, radio
Facilities 3 sitting-rooms, 3 bars, dining-room; outdoor swimming-pool, bowls, tennis
Credit cards AE, MC, V
Children accepted **Disabled** no special facilities **Pets** accepted **Closed** never
Proprietor Giacomini Franca

Lakeside villa, Gardone Riviera

Villa del Sogno

The Villa del Sogno ('Dream Villa') deserves its name, thanks to a remarkable position, overlooking Lake Garda and secluded in its own luxuriant park (with a pleasant swimming-pool). Inside, the villa is comfortable and traditional, with some handsome turn-of-the-century features and furnishings but also a smart modern 'American' bar. All the bedrooms have a lake view and there is also a vast terrace. Sadly though, the cooking is nothing to write home about.
Nearby Gardone Riviera (2 km); boat trips on Lake Garda.

Via Zanardelli 107, Fasano di Gardone Riviera, Lago di Garda 25083 Brescia
Tel (0365) 20228
Location 2 km NE of Fasano di Gardone Riviera; in grounds with garage and ample car parking
Food & drink breakfast, lunch, dinner
Prices rooms L90,000-L200,000
Rooms 33 double, 2 single, all with bath or shower; all rooms have central heating, phone, TV
Facilities dining-room, American bar, sitting-rooms (one with TV), terrace; heated outdoor swimming-pool, tennis
Credit cards AE, DC, MC, V
Children not encouraged
Disabled no special facilities
Pets small dogs accepted in rooms only
Closed mid-Oct to Mar
Proprietors Calderan family

Lake Garda

Lakeside hotel, Gargnano

Baia d'Oro

Gargnano is a picturesque resort on the west shores of Lake Garda. The Baia d'Oro is a distinctive old yellow-and-green building, lying right on the shore, its little pier jutting out into the dark blue waters of Garda and its terrace commanding superb views of the mountains beyond. This outside terrace provides the focal point of the hotel: in the summer months you breakfast, lunch and dine outside. If you are lucky enough to arrive by boat you can moor at the pier for the night and step straight into the hotel.

It is a small, friendly establishment run by the Terzi family. Gianbattista is however first and foremost an artist – you can see some of his water-colours of the lakes in the rooms of the hotel. It is his wife, a naturally warm hostess, who devotes all her time to maintaining high standards in the hotel. In 25 years she has transformed the building, first from a private home to a *pensione* and now to a delightful hotel which retains its former intimacy.

The main public room is the restaurant – a light and inviting area with baskets brimming with fruit, bowls of freshly cut flowers, pretty arches and glass doors opening on to the terrace. The great majority of the main dishes here are fish – either from the sea or straight from the lake. Bedrooms are bright and lovingly cared for, six of them with lakeside balconies.

Nearby Gardone Riviera, Desenzano, Sirmione, Garda, Malcesine – all reached by hydrofoil or ferry.

Via Gamberera 13, Gargnano 25084 Brescia
Tel (0365) 71171
Location in resort, with private car parking
Food & drink breakfast, lunch, dinner
Prices rooms L62,000-L104,000; meals L35,000
Rooms 11 double, 2 with bath, 11 with shower; 2 single with shower; all rooms have central heating, phone, minibar
Facilities dining-room, bar, TV room, sitting-room
Credit cards AE, MC, V
Children small children not accepted **Disabled** access difficult **Pets** dogs accepted
Closed Oct to Easter
Proprietors Terzi family

Lake Garda

Giulia

From a *pensione* with no private bathrooms, the Giulia has gradually been upgraded over the years to a three-star hotel. But happily it retains the atmosphere of a family-run guesthouse – albeit a large one. It is a beautiful, big spacious villa, built over a hundred years ago in Victorian style with Gothic touches. Signora Bombardelli, the proud owner, has been here for 40 years, and thanks to all her hard work (for which she has received various awards) the Giulia is one of the most delightful places to stay on the entire lake.

For a start, it has a wonderful location, with gardens and terraces running practically on the water's edge. Inside, light and airy rooms lead off handsome corridors – a beautiful dining-room with Murano chandeliers, gold walls and elegant seats; a civilized sitting-room with Victorian armchairs; and bedrooms which range from light and modern to large rooms with timbered ceilings, antiques and balconies overlooking garden and lake.

At garden level a second, simpler dining-room opens out on to a terrace with ample space and gorgeous views. At any time of day, it is a lovely spot to linger among the palm trees and watch the boats plying the blue waters of Garda.

Nearby hydrofoil and ferry services to villages and towns around Lake Garda.

Gargnano, Lago di Garda
25084 Brescia
Tel (0365) 71022
Location 150 m from middle of resort, with garden and terrace down to lake; private car park
Food & drink breakfast, lunch, dinner
Prices DB&B L80,000-L85,000; FB L85,000-90,000
Rooms 14 double, 3 single; all with bath or shower; all rooms have central heating, intercom, phone
Facilities dining-room, veranda taverna, sitting-room, TV room, terrace; beach, swimming-pool, sauna
Credit cards V
Children accepted
Disabled access difficult
Pets accepted
Closed mid-Oct to mid-Mar
Proprietor Rina Bombardelli

Lake Garda

Lakeside guest-house, Sirmione

Grifone

No tour of Lake Garda is complete without a visit to the lovely lakeside village of Sirmione. The massive Castle of the Scaligers, the gardens, beaches and Roman remains bring hoards of day-trippers, which makes it sensible to stay the night and see the quieter side of Sirmione. There is nothing very special about the bedrooms of the Grifone – in fact they are rather spartan and lack the charm evoked by the old stone façade, but the advantages are low prices, a family atmosphere and an excellent location with a small garden and terrace overlooking the castle and Lake Garda. There is a good restaurant in the same building, but a reader recommends cheaper alternatives nearby.

Nearby Castle of the Scaligers, grottoes of Catullus, both at Sirmione; boat tours of Lake Garda.

Via delle Bisse, Sirmione
25019 Brescia
Tel (030) 916014
Location on waterfront, overlooking lake and castle; with small garden; car parking some distance away
Food & drink no meals served
Prices rooms L40,000-

L60,000
Rooms 17 rooms, all with bath or shower
Facilities TV room
Credit cards not accepted
Children accepted
Disabled not suitable
Pets not accepted
Closed Nov to mid-Apr
Proprietor Sga Bertaldi

Lakeside hotel, Torri del Benaco

Gardesana

The Gardesena has a plum position on the main piazza facing the busy little harbour of Torri del Benaco. The building has a long history going back to the Republic of Venice, but the entire interior was smartly modernized in the late 1970s. Bedrooms are almost all identical – rustic wood furnishings, soft green fabrics, and plenty of little extras – and most have beautiful views of the lake. The Hall of the Ancient Council makes a suitably elegant dining-room, and there are a few tables on the balcony which overlooks the lake. Breakfast is sumptuous.

Nearby Bardolino (11 km), Malcesine (21 km).

Piazza Calderini 20, Torri del Benaco, Lago di Garda
37010 Verona
Tel (045) 7225411
Location in middle of resort, on waterfront; private parking 150 m away
Food & drink breakfast, dinner
Prices rooms L50,000-L140,000; DB&B L65,000-L170,000; reduction for children sharing parents' room

Rooms 30 double, 4 with bath, 26 with shower; 3 single, all with shower; all rooms have central heating, air-conditioning, phone
Facilities dining-room, bar, TV room, lakeside terrace
Credit cards AE, DC
Children welcome
Disabled no special facilities
Pets not accepted
Closed mid-Nov to Dec
Proprietor Giuseppe Lorenzini

Veneto

Country villa, Asolo

Villa Cipriani

Asolo is a beautiful medieval hilltop village commanding panoramic views of the plains below. The Villa Cipriani is a mellow ochre-washed house on the fringes of the village, the entrance leading directly from the street into a tiled hall with Oriental-style rugs and a grandfather clock, brass wall lights and an efficient but warm welcome from reception. The hotel is part of the Cigahotels chain, but the staff are friendly and attentive.

A tall covered terrace furnished in rustic style, and with an unusual pierced minstrel gallery, leads out through glass doors into the prettiest of gardens, well stocked with flowers and partly laid to grass – a mass of roses, azaleas and mature trees. The restaurant areas dog-leg round the outside of the villa, overhanging the valley below, with views out through plate-glass windows. For cooler evenings, there is a cosy bar.

The bedrooms all have lovely views, and are decorated in comfortably old-fashioned style, with prints, fresh flowers and antiques adding interest and colour. Pretty tiles have been used for the 'en suite' bathrooms. The views, the comfort and the peaceful garden all combine to make this a most relaxing country hotel.

Nearby Treviso (35 km); Padua, Vicenza, Venice within reach.

Via Canova 298, Asolo
31011 Treviso
Tel (0423) 55444
Location on NW side of village; with small garden and private car parking
Food & drink breakfast, lunch, dinner
Prices rooms L280,000-L350,000; meals about L85,000

Rooms 31 double; all rooms have colour TV, phone, air-conditioning
Facilities dining-room, bar, conference room
Credit cards AE, DC, MC, V
Children accepted
Disabled lift/elevator
Pets accepted
Closed never
Manager Giuseppe Kamenar

Veneto

Country villa, Cavasagra

Villa Corner della Regina

Driving through the flat agricultural land west of Treviso, it is something of a surprise to come upon this stately Palladian mansion, set in its vast estate and formal grounds at the end of a gravel drive. Lemon trees in huge terracotta pots and an ancient wisteria decorate your path to the entrance on the ground floor, to the side of a vast, sweeping set of stone steps. Once inside, you are greeted with a magnificent floral display, and it is clear that much of the original grandeur of the villa has been preserved, despite the provision of modern comforts.

The grandiose central reception room runs the full width of the villa; intricately carved French windows survey the drive, with floor-to-ceiling drapes trimmed in pink contrasting with the dark panelling and matching the deeply cushioned chairs and sofas. The bedrooms are huge, light and airy. They are all decorated differently and each room has its own name: 'the Butterfly Room' or 'the Rose Room', for example. They offer a combination of both character and luxury, with period antiques, decorative painted plaster walls, abundant flowers and prints, and thick pile carpets.

The lush grounds are beautifully kept and the pool beside the villa has plenty of space for relaxation.

Nearby Palladian villas; Venice (40 km).

Cavasagra, Treviso 31050
Treviso
Tel (0423) 481481
Location 15 km W of
Treviso, 3 km S of road to
Vicenza; in formal gardens
and parkland, with ample
car parking
Food & drink breakfast,
lunch, dinner
Prices B & B L100,000-
L230,000
Rooms 4 double, 7 suites and
12 apartments, all with bath;
all rooms have TV,
telephone, minibar
Facilities dining-rooms,
breakfast room (in old
orangery), sitting-room;
heated outdoor swimming-
pool, sauna, tennis
Credit cards AE, DC, MC, V
Children accepted
Disabled not suitable
Pets dogs not accepted
Closed never
Proprietor Conte Nicolo and
Contessa Dona Dalle Rose

Veneto

Villa Condulmer

For about the price of a two-star hotel in central Venice you can stay in this lovely 18thC villa only a 20-minute drive away, and enjoy the perfect antidote to the hurly-burly of the city. The villa belonged to the last admiral of the Venetian Republic. The splendour of the era is preserved in the delightful rococo frescoes, the extravagant Murano-glass chandeliers, the period furniture and the formal gardens. Bedrooms in the main villa are quite grand, but those that have been converted from the old stables have the advantage of air-conditioning – you may well need it here in the height of summer.

Nearby Venice (18 km), Treviso (12 km).

Via Zermanese, Zerman
Mogliano 30121 Treviso
Tel (041) 457100
Location 4 km NE of
Mogliano Veneto; in large
park, with ample car parking
Food & drink breakfast,
lunch, dinner
Prices rooms L90,000-
L175,000, suites L230,000;
meals L40,000-L60,000
Rooms 45 rooms; all rooms
have phone, minibar; some
rooms have air-conditioning
Facilities dining-room,
sitting-rooms, bar,
conference facilities;
swimming-pool, tennis,
27-hole golf, riding
Credit cards AE, DC, MC, V
Children accepted **Disabled**
ground-floor bedrooms
suitable **Pets** not accepted
Closed restaurant only, Mon
and mid-Nov to mid-Mar
Proprietor Paolo Magrino

El Toulà

An old farmhouse lovingly converted by Alfredo Beltrame some 15 years ago, now a member of the Relais & Chateaux group and living up to the five C's of character, courtesy, calm, comfort and cuisine. People come from far and wide to experience the restaurant where classic dishes are re-interpreted according to new ideas. It is also a popular place for wedding parties. It would not be a bad choice for a honeymoon either; the house is secluded and extremely civilized, with large bedrooms which vary from very comfortable to extremely luxurious, and stylish bathrooms. An expensive treat.

Nearby Treviso; Padua (35 km), Venice (45 km).

Via Postumia 63, Paderno di
Ponzano, 31050 Treviso
Tel (0422) 969023
Location 10 km NW of
Treviso; in delightful park
and vineyards with private
car parking
Food & drink breakfast,
lunch, dinner
Prices rooms L200,000-
L500,000; meals L75,000-
L90,000
Rooms 10 rooms, all with
bath; all rooms have central
heating, phone, TV, minibar
Facilities dining-room,
2 sitting-rooms, conference
room; swimming-pool
Credit cards AE, DC, V
Children accepted **Disabled**
not suitable **Pets** accepted
Closed never
Manager Giorgio Zamuner

Veneto

Country villa, Dolo

Villa Ducale

Driving along the N11 highway from Padua to Venice, you follow an old canal whose banks are scattered with beautiful 18thC villas, where wealthy Venetians used to escape the heat and stench of the city in the summer months. Villa Ducale is one of them – surrounded by calm formal gardens, with statues, a fountain, trees and arbours.

The entrance to the hotel is rather grand but the welcome friendly. The marble-floored reception area leads into a tall restaurant, beautifully decorated with fresh flowers and plants and floor-to-ceiling French windows wafting in cool air from the garden. A grand staircase leads to the bedrooms. Upstairs, the floors are the original decorative wooden parquet, overlaid with patterned rugs. In the bedrooms, much of the furniture is antique and in some the original softly painted walls and ceilings remain. The larger rooms have balconies and all are of a generous size. The bathrooms have decorative tiles and gilt fittings, much in keeping with the antique style of the hotel. The smaller rooms at the rear overlook horse chestnut trees.

Villa Ducale is an ideal base for visiting both Padua and Venice, with lush countryside and the peaceful canal banks awaiting your return.

Nearby Venice (20 km), Padua (21 km), Treviso (33 km); Palladian villas.

Riviera Martiri della Liberta 75, Dolo 30031 Venezia
Tel (041) 420094
Location 2 km E of Dolo
Food & drink breakfast, dinner; lunch on request
Prices rooms L85,000-L120,000; DB&B L75,000 (minimum 3 days)
Rooms 14 double, 4 with bath, 10 with shower; one single; all rooms have phone, terrace
Facilities sitting-room, bar, TV room, dining-room, games room
Credit cards AE, DC, V
Children accepted
Disabled not suitable
Pets not accepted
Closed restaurant only, Wed
Proprietors Bressan family

Veneto

Town hotel, Padua

Donatello

So-called because it overlooks Donatello's famous equestrian statue of the Venetian soldier known as Gattamelata, this hotel is easily the best-placed in the city for tourists. Inside its slightly shabby old shell the place has been simply modernized. The bright trattoria-style restaurant has a pavement terrace with a fine view of the basilica (and is therefore called the Sant' Antonio). The food is plain, unpretentious and reasonably priced. An adequate base for exploring Padua; and Venice is only 20 minutes away by coach or (less conveniently) car.

Nearby Villas of the Brenta Canal; Vicenza (35 km), Venice (37 km); Euganean hills.

Via del Santo 102-104,
Padua 35100
Tel (049) 8750634
Location on N side of Piazza del Santo, near main entrance to basilica; with private garage
Food & drink breakfast, lunch, dinner
Prices rooms L74,000-L117,500
Rooms 38 double, 37 with bath; 4 single, one with bath, 2 with shower; all rooms have phone, minibar, TV, air-conditioning
Facilities dining-room, café, terrace, 2 bars, TV room
Credit cards AE, DC, MC, V
Children accepted
Disabled not suitable
Pets accepted
Closed mid-Dec to mid-Jan; restaurant only, Wed, and Dec to third week Jan
Proprietor Franco Moresco

Town hotel, Padua

Leon Bianco

A small lift takes you up to the public rooms of this tall terraced building in the heart of Padua. Furnishings throughout are modern, the decorations up-to-the-minute pastels; there are pink-striped sofas in the sitting-room. Modern gallery posters hang on all the walls, and fresh flowers add to the feeling of simple elegance. The bedrooms, with squeaky wooden floors, are pleasant and reasonably sized – though the concertina bathroom doors are not ideal. Breakfast can be served in the tiny roof garden when the weather permits.

Nearby Cappella degli Scrovegni (Giotto frescoes), Basilica del Santo; Venice within reach.

Piazzetta Pedrocchi 12,
Padua 35100
Tel (049) 8750814
Location in middle of town, with car parking 300 m away
Food & drink breakfast
Prices rooms L83,500-L126,000; air-conditioning L9,000 extra
Rooms 16 double, 11 with shower; 2 single, both with shower; 4 family rooms, all with bath; all rooms have colour TV, phone, minibar, air-conditioning
Facilities bar, sitting-room, breakfast room, roof terrace
Credit cards AE, DC, MC, V
Children welcome
Disabled lift/elevator to some bedrooms **Pets** welcome
Closed never
Proprietor Paulo Morosi

Veneto

Country villa, Oderzo

Villa Revedin

Amid open countryside just outside the little town of Gorgo al Monticano, the Villa Revedin is sheltered within its own mature, tree-screened park. Formal gardens at the front and an old fountain lead on to the park through cool tree-lined paths.

The villa dates from the 18thC, and the original atmosphere is well preserved in the huge main salon, which has an imposing grand piano. The restaurant (which attracts local customers, particularly for its fish specialities) is more relaxed, in the familiar Italian sophisticated-rustic style, with wooden ceiling, terracotta tiled floor and cream decorations. The hotel's sitting areas have large leather sofas and chairs, and there is a pretty open fireplace for cooler evenings.

Most of the bedrooms are of generous size, and some have balconies. All have pretty views out over the park and gardens. Although most of the furniture is modern, the tall ceilings, shuttered windows, open fireplaces and tasteful decoration lend a charm to the modern competence.

This is a luxury hotel, but its setting and helpful staff make it charming and welcoming in a way that most such hotels are not.
Nearby Treviso (32 km); Venice within reach; Venetian villas.

Via Palazzi 4, Gorgo al Monticano, Oderzo 31040 Treviso
Tel (0422) 740669
Location 4 km E of Oderzo, signposted just N of Gorgo al Monticano; in private grounds with ample car parking
Food & drink breakfast, lunch, dinner
Prices rooms L58,000-L120,000
Rooms 14 double, 14 single, 4 family rooms; all with bath and shower; all rooms have TV, radio, phone
Facilities breakfast room, dining-room, function room, bar, sitting-room, conference room (30 people)
Credit cards AE, DC, MC, V
Children very welcome
Disabled not suitable
Pets accepted by arrangement
Closed restaurant only, Jan
Proprietor Armando Salmistraro

Veneto

Locanda da Lino

The cooking at this rustic restaurant in the mountains north of Treviso is not sophisticated – a predominance of soups and pasta dishes followed by grills – but good enough to have earned a Michelin star and to have greatly impressed our inspector. The atmosphere in the beamed dining-room, its walls covered in copper and china, is delightfully friendly. The smallish but comfortable and stylish bedrooms are in an ultra-modern annexe; all are on the ground floor, and each has its own small garden to the front (for privacy rather than sitting in).

Nearby Treviso (30 km); Palladian villas.

Via Brandolini 31
Solighetto, Pieve di Soligo
31050 Treviso
Tel (0438) 82150
Location 2 km N of Pieve,
12 km W of Conegliano, at
Solighetto; in countryside,
with private car parking
Food & drink breakfast,
lunch, dinner
Prices B&B L26,000-
L31,000; meals L25,000-

L40,000
Rooms 12 double, 5 family
rooms; all rooms have central
heating, phone, TV, minibar
Facilities dining-room, bar
Credit cards AE, DC, MC
Children not accepted
Disabled access to some
rooms possible
Pets not accepted
Closed July; restaurant only,
Mon **Proprietor** Lino Toffolin

Villa Conestabile

During the 16thC, a main ambition of most of Venice's patricians was to own a country villa, not too far from the city. The Villa Conestabile was the fulfilment of one such ambition. It is not a luxury hotel, but it will cost you about half the price of a similar standard of accommodation in Venice. It still has touches of grandeur – elaborate chandeliers, grand staircases and fine period pieces of furniture, but the restaurant and bar are comparatively simple. Bedrooms are in keeping with the style of the building, and there is a spacious terrace for breakfast and evening drinks.

Nearby Treviso; Venice (20 km), Padua (30 km).

Via Roma 1, Scorze 30037
Venezia
Tel (041) 445027
Location 13 km SW of
Treviso, in village; in
extensive grounds, with
ample car parking
Food & drink breakfast,
lunch, dinner
Prices rooms L59,000-
L98,000
Rooms 18 double, 4 with
bath, 12 with shower; 6

single, 3 with shower, one
with bath; all rooms have
central heating, phone, TV
Facilities dining-room, bar,
sitting-room, TV room
Credit cards AE, MC, V
Children welcome
Disabled no special facilities
Pets small dogs only
accepted
Closed restaurant only first 3
weeks in Aug
Manager Sga Martinelli

Veneto

Town hotel, Treviso

Le Beccherie

Treviso is a charming old town, ringed by ramparts and cut through by canalized streams, and this friendly, family-run restaurant-cum-hotel lies at the heart of its intricate network of narrow one-way streets. Le Beccherie itself is a long-established, unpretentious but highly regarded restaurant on a tiny piazza, close to the splendid 13thC town hall. Above it are a few simple bedrooms, and across the piazza is a modernized annexe – known as the Albergo Campeol – containing more comfortable rooms with bathrooms.

Nearby old town of Treviso; Venice (30 km), Padua (50 km).

Piazza G Ancillotto 10, Treviso 31100
Tel (0422) 540871
Location in historic heart of city; public car parking in front of hotel
Food & drink breakfast, lunch, dinner
Prices rooms L40,000-L74,000
Rooms 18 double, 12 with shower; 9 single, 4 with shower; all rooms have central heating; 16 rooms have radio and phone
Facilities bar, dining-room, TV room
Credit cards AE, DC, MC, V
Children accepted
Disabled no special facilities
Pets not accepted
Closed restaurant only: Thu pm, Fri and 3 weeks late July
Proprietor Ado Campeol

Town hotel, Verona

Torcolo

This faded ochre building stands just a few steps away from the famous Arena, in the heart of Verona. Another attraction is the warm welcome of Signora Pomari and her daughter Marina, both of whom speak English. Public rooms are confined to the reception (where the most interesting features are the modern Italian lithographs), a tiny TV room and an equally tiny break-fast room. But breakfast can be served outside on a terrace, in the shade of white parasols. Bedrooms are decorated in a variety of styles: Italian 18thC, art nouveau and modern. Most are not as noisy as you might expect – though street-side ones can be affected by the bar next door. The neighbouring Ristorante Torcolo is, according to Signora Pomari, "good but expensive".

Nearby Piazza Bra, Castelvecchio.

Vicolo Listone 3, Verona 37121
Tel (045) 8007512
Location in middle, close to Arena; limited car parking
Food & drink breakfast
Prices rooms L51,000-L94,000
Rooms 15 double, one with bath, 14 with shower; 4 single, all with shower; all rooms have central heating, air-conditioning, phone
Facilities breakfast room, TV room, terrace
Credit cards not accepted
Children accepted
Disabled no special facilities
Pets accepted **Closed** 2 weeks Jan **Proprietor** Silvia Pomari

Veneto/Venice

Country villa, Mira Porte

Villa Margherita

Yet another country villa well placed for excursions into Venice – this one opened as a hotel only since late 1987. Villa Margherita is less imposing than some from the outside, but charmingly furnished and decorated within, particularly in the public areas. The breakfast room is gloriously light, with French windows on to the garden, while the sitting-room has *trompe l'oeil* frescos and an open fireplace. Bedrooms are plainer, but thoroughly comfortable.

Note that the highly regarded restaurant is a short walk from the main building.

Nearby Venice (10 km), Padua (30 km).

Via Nazionale 416, Mira Porte 30030 Venezia
Tel (041) 426 5800
Location on banks of Brenta river at Mira, 10 km W of Venice; ample car parking
Food & drink breakfast, lunch, dinner
Prices rooms L100,000-L200,000; meals from L33,000
Rooms 18 double, 3 with bath, 15 with shower; 1 single with shower; all rooms have central heating, phone, air-conditioning, TV, minibar
Facilities breakfast room, sitting-room, bar, restaurant (200 m walk); jogging track
Credit cards AE, DC, MC, V
Children accepted
Disabled rooms on ground floor **Pets** only small animals, by arrangement **Closed** never
Manager Valeria Sabbadin

Seaside villa, Venice Lido

Villa Mabapa

Despite the extensions to the original 1930s family house, the Villa Mabapa still manages to give the impression of a private home. What is more, it is good value, particularly in comparison with the large, better-known hotels on the beach at the Lido. The location may be slightly out of the way, but it does have the bonus of wonderfully peaceful rooms, a garden and a summer dining terrace – all of which are more than welcome after the frenzy of visiting Venice. There are two buildings – the main hotel with the public rooms and some bedrooms (the best are on the first floor) and an annexe in the garden with more up-to-date bedrooms.

Nearby Venice (10/20 minutes by ferry).

Riviera San Nicolo 16, Venice Lido 30126
Tel (041) 526 0590
Location on the lagoon side of the Lido, with fine views of city; in pretty garden
Food & drink breakfast, lunch, dinner
Prices rooms L80,000-L140,000; meals about L30,000
Rooms 47 double, 15 single, all with bath or shower; all rooms have TV, phone; 30 rooms have air-conditioning
Facilities dining-room, dining terrace, bar, sitting-room
Credit cards AE, DC, MC, V
Children accepted
Disabled some rooms suitable
Pets no dogs allowed in dining-room
Closed mid-Nov to just before Christmas
Proprietor Sg Vianello

Venice

Locanda Cipriani

This delightful little family-run restaurant and bar is only 40 minutes by regular boat from Venice (calling at Murano and Burano on the way), but in another, more peaceful world. Simple, country antique furniture and pretty plates decorate the hall, where arch-shaped wooden doors lead into the rooms. The double bedrooms (effectively small suites) overlook the garden, from which come the salads used in the excellent restaurant and the flowers which decorate the rooms and tables.

Depending on your mood and the seasons, you can eat in the restaurant itself, the covered terrace or in the open courtyard.
Nearby cathedral of Torcello.

Piazza S Fosca 29, Torcello, Venice 30012
Tel (041) 730757
Location on Torcello island; in gardens
Food & drink breakfast, lunch, dinner
Prices DB&B L220,000; FB L300,000
Rooms 2 double, 2 single, all with bath and shower; all rooms have phone; double rooms have sitting-room
Facilities 4 dining areas, bar
Credit cards DC
Children welcome
Disabled not suitable
Pets accepted at proprietor's discretion
Closed early Nov to mid-Mar
Proprietor Bonifacio Brass

Abbazia

Not much evidence remains of the Abbazia's monastic origins – spacious halls, a few antiques and a quiet atmosphere – but it is certainly a cut above the average station hotel. Guest rooms vary; some are still old-fashioned but most have been modernized, with wall-to-wall carpets, whitewashed walls, dark-wood repro antiques and excellent bathrooms. The great advantage in what is generally a noisy area is the tranquillity – many of the rooms overlook the garden now receiving the attention it deserves.
Nearby Grand Canal.

Cannaregio 66, Venice 30121
Tel (041) 717333
Location in Calle Priuli, close to railway station
Food & drink breakfast
Prices rooms L56,500-L129,000; reduction for child sharing parents' room
Rooms 35 double, 8 with bath, 13 with shower; 2 single, both with shower; all rooms have central heating, phone
Facilities breakfast room, reading-room, conference facilities
Credit cards AE, DC, MC, V
Children accepted
Disabled 3 rooms on ground floor
Pets not accepted
Closed never
Manager Franco de Rossi

Venice

Town guest-house, close to Accademia

Accademia

Book weeks in advance and you might just be lucky enough to get a room at the Accademia – a great favourite among British and French visitors to Venice (and particularly regular visitors, whose custom is cultivated). Though it is not quite the bargain it used to be, the Accademia is still a place of immense charm and character with prices that most people can afford and a very convenient but tranquil location. But what really distinguishes the *pensione* is its gardens – the spacious patio facing the canal, where tables are scattered among potted plants and classical urns, and the grassy garden at the back where wisteria, roses and fruit trees flourish.

It is thanks to the Marzollo family, who have been here since 1955, that the aristocratic charm of the villa has been preserved. It was originally built as a private mansion, and earlier this century housed the Russian consulate. There are still touches of grandeur, and the furnishings for the most part are classically Venetian. But there is no trace whatever of formality.

Reception is a spacious hallway-cum-salon, with ample seating, stretching between two gardens. The airy breakfast room has chandeliers and a beamed ceiling supported by columns; but, weather permitting, guests will inevitably opt to start their day in the garden, and end it there with evening drinks. Most of the bedrooms are rather old-fashioned, with a haphazard collection of antiques. Some are surprisingly spartan, and those on the upper floor are quite modern in style.

Nearby Accademia gallery, Grand Canal.

Fondamenta Maravegie, Dorsoduro 1058, Venice 30123
Tel (041) 5237846
Location on side canal just S of Grand Canal, with gardens front and back
Food & drink breakfast
Prices rooms L40,000-L145,000; extra bed L35,000
Rooms 20 double, 8 with bath, 8 with shower; 6 single, 5 with bath; all rooms have central heating, phone
Facilities breakfast room, bar, sitting-room
Credit cards AE, DC, MC, V
Children welcome over 12
Disabled no special facilities
Pets not accepted
Closed never
Proprietor Franco Marzollo

Venice

Town hotel, near the Accademia

American

This shuttered, terraced *palazzo*, tucked behind the Accademia on a quiet residential canal, has in recent years been restored throughout to serve its new purpose as a hotel. The bedrooms, all of a reasonable size, were refurbished in 1989, in Venetian style. Downstairs, the little breakfast room and two adjoining sitting-rooms have old-fashioned patterned wallpapers and wood panelling; comfy chairs, some rustic wooden furniture, large paintings of Venice and Oriental-style rugs on the terrazzo floors give an air of quiet comfort.

Nearby Accademia gallery; church of Santa Maria della Salute.

San Vio 628, Venice 30123
Tel (041) 5204733
Location close to the Accademia, off Campo Santo
Food & drink breakfast
Prices rooms L90,000-L180,000
Rooms 24 double, 14 with bath, 10 with shower; 5 single, 3 with bath, 2 with shower; 5 family rooms; all with bath; all rooms have colour TV, minibar, phone, air-conditioning
Facilities breakfast room, sitting-room, TV room
Credit cards AE, DC, MC, V
Children babies and toddlers not welcome
Disabled some rooms on ground floor **Pets** small dogs only welcome **Closed** never
Proprietor Umberto Graffi

Town hotel, near Fenice theatre

Ateneo

The Ateneo is partly an old *palazzo*, once the home of an aristo-cratic Venetian family. It is now a relatively simple place, but the classical Venetian style is in evidence – Murano glass chandeliers, flocked walls, fancy mirrors, carved bedheads and reproduction Venetian armchairs. Bedrooms are small but carefully and neatly furnished and reasonably quiet; and the bathrooms are spotless. The lack of a restaurant is no problem in an area liberally endowed with lively-looking trattorias. Just one draw-back: there is no garden – just a courtyard in front, strictly reserved for the plants.

Nearby Teatro la Fenice; Piazza San Marco.

San Marco 1876, Venice 30124
Tel (041) 5200588
Location very close to Fenice theatre, with some rooms facing canal
Food & drink breakfast
Prices rooms L71,000-L181,000
Rooms 16 double, 4 with bath, 10 with shower; 3 single; 4 family rooms with bath or shower; all rooms have air-conditioning, central heating, minibar, phone
Facilities breakfast room, sitting area, TV room
Credit cards AE, V
Children accepted
Disabled no special facilities
Pets welcome
Closed never
Proprietor Massimo Maschietto

Venice

Town guest-house, near the Accademia

Alboretti

Enthusiastic students of Venetian painting will find this little hotel the most convenient in Venice. It lies right alongside the gallery of the Accademia and the world's finest collection of Venetian art. It is also well placed for exploration further afield: a water-bus landing-stage on the Grand Canal lies just a few steps from the entrance to the hotel.

Like many small hotels in Venice, the Alboretti occupies a building which is several centuries old, but what distinguishes it from the others is the warm welcome and the genuine family atmosphere – something of a rarity in Venice. Reception is a cosy wood-panelled room with a model of a 17thC galleon in its window; the sitting-room small, but the upper TV room is a comfortable retreat (the TV is rarely used). The dining-room has recently been attractively extended, and dinner is now available.

The bedrooms have recently been renovated; the style is predominantly simple and modern, though a few rooms have an antique or two. Like the rest of the hotel, they are well cared for and spotlessly clean; but bathrooms are tiny. The most peaceful are those overlooking the pretty leafy courtyard at the back of the hotel.

Nearby Accademia gallery, Zattere, Gesuati church.

Accademia 882, Venice 30123
Tel (041) 5230058
Location between the Grand Canal and Giudecca Canal; nearest landing-stage: Accademia
Food & drink breakfast, dinner
Prices rooms L57,000-L130,500
Rooms 12 double, 3 with bath, 9 with shower; 6 single, all with shower; one family room with bath; all rooms have central heating, phone
Facilities sitting-room, dining-room, TV room, bar
Credit cards AE, MC, V
Children welcome – cots on request **Disabled** no special facilities **Pets** small dogs only accepted **Closed** never
Proprietor Anna Linguerri

Venice

Town hotel, west of St Mark's

Bel Sito

If you can't afford a room in the prestigious Gritti Palace, there are plenty of cheaper places close by. One of these is the Bel Sito, opposite the inelegantly Baroque church of Santa Maria del Giglio on the square of the same name. It is quiet despite being central – very close to one of the best shopping streets of the city. A small patio in front of the hotel, with potted plants and parasols, makes an excellent spot for watching the shoppers and tourists crossing the Campo. Bedrooms vary widely. The most inviting are those at the back, with prettily painted furniture; those overlooking the church are old-fashioned and dark in comparison.

Nearby Piazza San Marco, Accademia Gallery.

Campo Santa Maria del Giglio, San Marco 2517, Venice 30124
Tel (041) 522 3365
Location in square, opposite church, about 5 minutes' W of San Marco
Food & drink breakfast
Prices rooms L73,000-L163,500
Rooms 32 double, 4 single, all with bath or shower; all rooms have phone, minibar; some rooms have TV
Facilities 2 breakfast rooms, bar, sitting-room, terrace
Credit cards MC, V
Children accepted **Disabled** no special facilities **Pets** accepted by prior arrangement **Closed** never
Proprietor Sg Serafino

Town guest-house, on the Zattere

Calcina

Over a hundred years ago, the great art historian Ruskin singled out the Calcina for its low prices and stunning views; the prices remain low by Venetian standards – and the view south to the Giudecca can hardly have changed at all. The *pensione's* position on the spacious stone-flagged quay of the Zattere has other advantages too – it is out of the main tourist bustle, but not too far out. The Calcina has recently been totally renovated, happily without loss of its character. There are now many more private bathrooms, but the simple old-fashioned furnishings remain. This lack of sophistication seems only to enhance the romantic appeal of Ruskin's House, as it is known. Waterfront rooms are booked up weeks, even months ahead.

Nearby Accademia gallery, Gesuati church.

Zattere 780, Venice 30123
Tel (041) 5206466
Location on the Zattere waterfront
Food & drink breakfast
Prices rooms L41,000-L124,000
Rooms 30 double, 10 with bath, 16 with shower; 10 single; all rooms have central heating, phone
Facilities sitting area, TV room, terrace overlooking lagoon
Credit cards all accepted
Children welcome if under parents' control
Disabled no special facilities
Pets accepted if not too big
Closed Nov to Feb
Manager Alessandro Szemere

Venice

Town guest-house, island of Giudecca

Casa Frollo

You are unlikely to fall upon the Casa Frollo by chance. For many years this distinguished 17thC 'palazzo' on the island of Giudecca was a private residence and that is the way it likes to remain. There is no hotel sign, just a small plaque outside saying Casa Frollo. Ring the bell and the sturdy wooden door mysteriously opens revealing a cool courtyard and a quiet, sweet smelling garden beyond. A flight of stone stairs takes you up to the main salon – a beautiful big room of Renaissance furnishings and a fine collection of paintings from old and modern masters. But perhaps the greatest attraction is the grand panorama across the lagoon to the Doges' Palace – just a five-minute ferry ride away.

Bedrooms are simpler than the grandeur of the salon might suggest and bathrooms, where they exist, are somewhat spartan. But all is crisp and clean and the rooms are tastefully furnished, with whitewashed walls, quarry tiled floors and antique wardrobes. The Casa Frollo offers none of the luxuries of hotels just across the water – no porter, no English-speaking staff, and no one to let you in after midnight – but for character and slightly eccentric charm it is hard to beat. Traditionally a favourite among the French 'literati', it is now becoming popular with British visitors who are looking for something entirely different.

Nearby Piazza San Marco (about five minutes across the water).

Giudecca 50, Fondamenta delle Zitelle, Venice 30123
Tel (041) 522 2723
Location on island of Giudecca facing Venice; with garden; nearest landing-stage Zitelle
Food & drink breakfast
Prices rooms L42,000-L97,500

Rooms 26 rooms, 8 with bath or shower
Facilities breakfast/sitting area
Credit cards not accepted
Children not very suitable
Disabled not suitable
Pets accepted
Closed end Nov to mid-Mar
Proprietor Flora Soldan

Venice

Town guest-house, near the station

Ai Due Fanali

The station hotels of Venice (like those of most cities) are not usually noted for being the most salubrious, but there are of course exceptions – including the Due Fanali. It is a tiny family-run hotel, about five minutes from the station but across the Grand Canal and well away from the main concentration of station hotels. It is tucked in the corner of a quiet *campo* flanking the Grand Canal and in front of it there is a pretty terrace with parasols and plants. The interior is compact and simple but the best things about it are the quiet, spotlessly clean modern rooms, the friendly atmosphere and the reasonable prices.

Nearby Grand Canal.

Campo San Simeone Grande 946, Santa Croce, Venice 30135
Tel (041) 718490
Location on small square, close to station on opposite side of the Grand Canal
Food & drink breakfast
Prices rooms L39,500-L92,500
Rooms 8 double, 4 with shower; 3 single, one with shower; 6 family rooms, one with bath, 5 with shower; all rooms have central heating
Facilities bar with TV, breakfast and sitting areas, terrace
Credit cards AE, DC, MC, V
Children accepted **Disabled** no special facilities **Pets** small ones only **Closed** never
Proprietors Zanegreco family

Town villa, Venice Lido

Villa Parco

If your wish is to combine the sights of Venice with a beach holiday, the Lido is still the obvious place to stay – even if it has lost its former 'cachet'. The problem is the price of hotels – especially those right on the waterfront. This one, however, lies a few minutes' away in a quiet residential area and its prices are very reasonable.

A simple, unpretentious place, its greatest asset is the garden, where you can take breakfast and evening drinks. The building is in art nouveau style, though the furnishings are mainly modern – only one bedroom has antiques. As well as breakfast, you can get snacks from the bar.

Nearby Casino; Venice (boats every ten minutes).

Via Rodi 1, Venice Lido 30126
Tel (041) 5260015
Location about 5 minutes' walk from beach; car parking
Food & drink breakfast
Prices rooms L52,000-L145,000
Rooms 15 double, 3 with bath, 12 with shower; 2 single, all with shower; 5 family rooms, 3 with bath, 2 with shower; all rooms have central heating, phone, TV, air-conditioning, minibar
Facilities sitting-room, bar, breakfast room
Credit cards AE, DC, MC, V
Children accepted if well behaved
Disabled no special facilities
Pets small dogs and cats accepted
Closed Dec to Carnival (Feb)
Proprietors Barbaro family

Venice

Town hotel, near St Mark's

Flora

Such is the popularity of this small hotel, tucked away in a cul-de-sac close to St Mark's, that to get a room here you have to book weeks or even months in advance. You only need to glimpse the garden to understand why it is so sought after. Creepers, fountains and flowering shrubs cascading from stone urns create an enchanting setting for morning coffee and croissants, or evening drinks in summer. It is undoubtedly one of the prettiest and quietest gardens in Venice – somehow far removed from the hubbub of St Mark's.

The lobby is small and inviting, enhanced by the views of the garden through a glass arch. The atmosphere is one of friendly efficiency, reception acting as a mini tourist information bureau for the many English-speaking guests. There are some charming double bedrooms with painted carved antiques and other typically Venetian furnishings, but beware of other comparatively spartan rooms, some of which are barely big enough for one, let alone two. Prices are quite steep for a small three-star hotel but most guests agree that the setting and the intimate atmosphere make it well worth the cost.

Nearby Piazza San Marco.

Calle Larga 22 Marzo 2283/a,
San Marco, Venice 30124
Tel (041) 5205844
Location 300 m from Piazza
San Marco in cul-de-sac
Food & drink breakfast
Prices rooms L113,000-
L171,000
Rooms 32 double, 6 single, 6
family rooms; all with bath
and/or shower; all rooms
have phone; air-conditioning
at extra cost
Facilities breakfast room,
bar, sitting-room
Credit cards AE, DC, MC, V
Children accepted
Disabled no special facilities
Pets accepted
Closed mid-Nov to Jan
Proprietors Alex and Roger
Romanelli

Venice

Town hotel, west of St Mark's

Do Pozzi

In a dead-end street close to San Marco, this calm hotel enjoys one of the quietest locations of central Venice. It is also well placed for chic shopping. Bedrooms are all identical: neat, modern, in browns and beiges and fully equipped. Public rooms consist of an elegant but tiny breakfast-room and an equally tiny sitting-room with TV. Understandably more popular is the leafy courtyard at the entrance of the hotel where cats doze and guests take breakfast or evening drinks.

Ask where to lunch and dine and you will be ushered to the adjoining Raffaele restaurant. It is an inviting spot with a terrace overlooking a picturesque canal, but reported as being not particularly good value.

Nearby Piazza San Marco (2-3 min walk).

Via XXII Marzo,
Venice 30124
Tel (041) 5207855
Location 200 m W of Piazza San Marco, in a dead-end street off Via XXII Marzo
Food & drink breakfast
Prices rooms L81,000-L165,500; meals L22,000
Rooms 25 double, 10 single; all with bath or shower; all rooms have central heating, air-conditioning (extra charge), minibar, phone
Facilities breakfast room, TV room, courtyard/patio
Credit cards AE, DC, MC, V
Children accepted **Disabled** access difficult **Pets** small ones only **Closed** never
Proprietor Giovanna Salmaso

Town hotel, near Fenice theatre

Kette

This polished little hotel can boast an excellent position – convenient for many of the major sights, but reasonably quiet.

The building dates from the the mid-18thC, and the comfortable TV room and writing-retain a period elegance, with rugs on parquet floors, and, in the latter, Regency stripes. The breakfast room has a more modern feel, emphasized by the furniture, but retaining the parquet floor and exposed beams. Bedrooms are comfortable and restrained, with simple pieces of reproduction dark-wood furniture against light wallpapers – smarter than average for Venice.

Nearby Teatro la Fenice, Piazza San Marco, Rialto.

San Marco 2053,
Venice 30124
Tel (041) 5222730
Location close to the Fenice theatre, W of St Mark's
Food & drink breakfast
Prices rooms L70,000-L180,000
Rooms 38 double, 8 with bath, 30 with shower; 9 single, 3 with bath, 6 with shower; 4 family rooms, 2 with bath, 2 with shower; all rooms have central heating, air-conditioning, colour TV, electronic safe, phone
Facilities TV room, reading-room, breakfast room
Credit cards AE, V
Children accepted
Disabled access difficult
Pets not accepted
Closed never **Proprietor** Sardo Salvatore Sutera

Venice

Town hotel, east of St Mark's

Nuovo Teson

This modest hotel is on a small, peaceful square in Castello, a stone's throw from the Riva degli Schiavoni, which will be your main route to Piazza San Marco, some five minutes' walk away.

By Venetian standards this is a modern building, and it has recently been renovated to a high standard. The compact breakfast room and bar feature rich fabrics, painted furniture and rugs on terrazzo floors. The lack of a dining-room is no problem, with two or three excellent restaurants to tempt you within easy walking distance.

The bedrooms are light and pretty, and all have reproduction Venetian painted furniture, from headboards to chairs and tables and brass and glass lamps.

Nearby Piazza San Marco, Scuola di San Giorgio.

Riva degli Schiavoni 3980, Venice 30122
Tel (041) 5229929
Location set back from the waterfront, on a small square
Food & drink breakfast
Prices rooms L57,750-L101,000
Rooms 29 double, one single, all with shower; all rooms have central heating, radio, piped music
Facilities breakfast room, conference room, bar
Credit cards AE, MC, V
Children accepted **Disabled** one ground-floor bedroom in annexe **Pets** accepted
Closed Nov to Jan
Proprietor Nicola Caputo

Town hotel, east of St Mark's

Paganelli

Most of the hotels along the Riva degli Schiavoni charge notoriously high prices for the waterfront's stunning panorama across the lagoon (and proximity to St Mark's). But the Paganelli is a modest, unpretentious hotel whose best rooms, decorated in typical 18thC Venetian style, look out across the water. Elsewhere the decoration is nothing special, either in the main hotel or in the annexe in the adjoining side street, where you will also find the modern restaurant. But it is a friendly place nevertheless, and for the position, the rooms are by Venice standards not overpriced.

Nearby Piazza San Marco.

Riva degli Schiavoni 4687, Venice 30122
Tel (041) 5224324
Location on main waterfront, close to Piazza San Marco
Food & drink breakfast, lunch, dinner
Prices rooms L57,000-L99,500; 30% reduction for young children
Rooms 12 double, 3 with bath, 7 with shower; 8 single, one with bath, 6 with shower; 3 family rooms, all with bath; all rooms have phone; 11 rooms have air-conditioning
Facilities dining-room, bar
Credit cards AE, MC, V
Children accepted **Disabled** no special facilities **Pets** not accepted
Closed restaurant only, mid-Nov to mid-Mar
Proprietor Francesco Paganelli

Venice

Town hotel, west of Accademia

Pausania

The San Barnaba area, traditionally the home of impecunious Venetian nobility, is quiet and picturesque. The Pausania is a small hotel lying close to the last surviving floating vegetable shop in Venice – a colourful barge on the San Barnaba canal. The building is quintessentially Venetian – a faintly shabby Gothic 'palazzo' with distinctive ogee windows. Inside, the timber ceiling of the breakfast room and the supporting stone columns are both features of the original building, but the rooms are far from palatial. Bedrooms, in modern and traditional styles, are simply furnished. The place's main advantages are the terrace and garden (which, although scruffy, is peaceful) and the prices, which are substantially lower than in equivalent, more central hotels.

Nearby Scuola dei Carmini, Accademia gallery.

Dorsoduro 2824, Venice 30124
Tel (041) 522 2083
Location short walk W of Grand Canal; with terrace
Food & drink breakfast
Prices rooms L80,000-L171,000
Rooms 23 double, 5 with bath, 18 with shower; 3 single, all with shower; 5 family rooms, one with bath, 4 with shower; all rooms have central heating, TV, air-conditioning, phone
Facilities breakfast room, bar, reading-room
Credit cards AE, MC, V
Children welcome **Disabled** not suitable **Pets** only small ones accepted **Closed** never
Proprietor Guido Gatto

Town hotel, on Grand Canal

San Cassiano

This small Gothic *palazzo* looks across the Grand Canal to the glorious façade of the Ca d'Oro from a quiet neighbourhood where old, slightly decayed houses line narrow streets – but the tourist-thronged Rialto is only five minutes' walk away. The inside is handsomely furnished, the timbered ceilings, Murano-glass chandeliers and period pieces preserving the authentic Venetian air. Particularly impressive is the breakfast room, with canal views through ogee arches. Bedrooms are furnished with reproduction antiques and decorated with good-quality fabrics – but the smaller ones at the back tend to be a bit gloomy.

Nearby Franchetti gallery in the Ca d'Oro.

Santa Croce 2232, Venice 30135
Tel (041) 721033
Location on Grand Canal, facing Ca d'Oro
Food & drink breakfast
Prices L115,000- L175,000
Rooms 30 double, 3 with bath, 27 with shower; 5 single, all with shower; all rooms have air-conditioning, colour TV, radio, phone, minibar, hairdrier
Facilities breakfast room, bar, writing-room, TV room
Credit cards AE, DC
Children welcome
Disabled no special facilities
Pets not accepted
Closed never
Proprietor Giancarlo Manao

Venice

Town hotel, east of St Mark's

La Residenza

This grand Gothic 'palazzo' dominates the square of Campo Bandiera e Moro. Just to enter is an experience: press the lion's nose on the right of the huge entrance doors and they swing open to reveal an ancient covered courtyard. A wrought-iron gate moves to one side to admit you up the ancient stone steps to the reception and sitting-room – a vast hall with mullioned windows looking out over the square, furnished with soft couches and antiques. The soft pastel shades of the plaster-painted walls add to the feeling of faded grandeur and immersion in Venice's Renaissance history.

Nearby Scuola di San Giorgio degli Schiavoni.

Campo Bandiera e Moro 3608, Castello, Venice 30122
Tel (041) 528 5315
Location on a small square, 100 m back from the main waterfront; nearest landing-stage Arsenale
Food & drink breakfast
Prices rooms L100,000
Rooms 14 double, 5 with bath, 9 with shower; 2 single, both with shower; all rooms have air-conditioning, phone, TV, minibar
Facilities large sitting-room
Credit cards AE, DC, MC, V
Children not accepted
Disabled not suitable
Pets not accepted
Closed Jan until carnival; end Nov to mid-Dec
Proprietor Sg Tagliapietra

Venice

Town guest-house, west of St Mark's

San Fantin

It is not easy to find cheap hotels in this fashionable area of
Venice. The San Fantin stands in a characteristic corner, next to
the ravishing little Fenice theatre, only a few minutes' walk from
San Marco. You cannot mistake its façade, the lower storey
dotted with cannon balls and the balcony above, where a lion
stands guard, flowing with geraniums and wisteria.

The interior is distinctly modest. Indeed some of the bedrooms seemed basic, dark and poorly lit when we last visited. But
it is not without charm or character and the breakfast room, with
its profusion of pictures, has a cosy atmosphere. There is no
restaurant and the taverna opposite is overpriced. But there are
plenty of cheaper alternatives in the area.

Nearby Fenice Theatre.

Campiello de la Fenice
1930/a, San Marco,
Venice 30124
Tel (041) 5231401
Location on small square in
middle of city
Food & drink breakfast
Prices rooms L43,000-
L138,000
Rooms 11 double, 9 with
shower; 3 single; all rooms
have central heating
Facilities sitting-room,
breakfast room
Credit cards not accepted
Children accepted if well
behaved **Disabled** no special
facilities **Pets** not accepted
Closed winter
Proprietor Pierina de Ghetto

Town hotel, near St Mark's

San Moisé

A couple of minutes from Piazza San Marco, bordering a quaint
canal, the San Moisè has obvious attractions. Not long ago it was
entirely restored and given a spruce new image. Rugs on wood-
block floors, elaborate chandeliers and walnut furniture create a
typically Venetian setting. Bedrooms (some rather small) are
neatly furnished, in similar style to public rooms. Anyone rich
enough to afford a gondola or a water-taxi can enjoy door-to-
door service at the San Moisè – there is a private landing-stage
just outside the hotel.

Nearby Piazza San Marco (200 m).

San Marco 2058,
Venice 30124
Tel (041) 520 3755
Location between Piazza San
Marco and the Fenice
theatre, bordering on a canal
Food & drink breakfast
Prices rooms L118,000-
L181,000
Rooms 8 double, one with
bath, 7 with shower; 2 single,
both with shower; 6 family
rooms, all with shower; all
rooms have phone, minibar,
TV, radio, air-conditioning
Facilities breakfast room,
sitting-room, bar
Credit cards AE, DC, MC, V
Children accepted
Disabled not very suitable
Pets accepted
Closed never
Proprietor Franco
Maschietto

Venice

Town hotel, west of St Mark's

San Stefano

If you follow the popular route from Piazza San Marco to the Accademia gallery you will walk across the Campo Santo Stefano (which, just to confuse you, is also called the Campo Francesco Morosini). It is a large, lively and rambling square whose best-known features are the alarmingly tilted *campanile* of the church of Santo Stefano and the café/*gelateria* Paolin, whose reputation for making the best ice creams in town is well deserved.

Close to all the activity lies the Santo Stefano, a welcoming and well-cared-for little hotel whose front rooms have views of the piazza. It is not a spacious place; downstairs there is only a modest reception area, a tiny breakfast room and an even tinier courtyard at the back; and upstairs the bedrooms are barely big enough for two. But lack of size is made up for in other ways. The decoration is exceptionally pretty – many of the bedrooms are decked out with painted furniture and pretty pink fabrics – and it is kept in immaculate condition throughout.

Finally, another bonus – for Venice the prices are low.

Nearby Accademia gallery, Grand Canal.

Campo Santo Stefano, San Marco 2957, Venice 30124
Tel (041) 5200166
Location on large square about 500 m W of Piazza San Marco; nearest landing-stage Sant'Angelo
Food & drink breakfast
Prices rooms L48,000-L135,000
Rooms 7 double, 3 single, 2 family rooms; all with shower; all rooms have phone, minibar, air-conditioning, TV
Facilities breakfast room, hall, tiny rear courtyard
Credit cards not accepted
Children accepted
Disabled not suitable
Pets not accepted
Closed never
Proprietor Dr Giorgio Gazzola

Venice

Town hotel, Venice

Scandinavia

The Campo Santa Maria Formosa is a rambling piazza with a buxom church, morning market stalls and noisy Venetian children. The Scandinavia lies just off it – a modest hotel with reception on the first floor. Despite the name, the furnishings are in 18thC Venetian style – pink Murano chandeliers, brocade chairs and floral walls, along with a mixed collection of paintings. Bedrooms are in similar style to public rooms, but perhaps over-patterned for their size, but are well cared for and comfortable. The Trattoria Pizzeria Burchiello in the square is under the same ownership, and serves both lunch and dinner; specialities are Venetian and Arab dishes.

Nearby Piazza San Marco, Rialto.

Campo Santa Maria Formosa, Castello 5240, Venice 30122
Tel (041) 5223507
Location just off Campo Santa Maria Formosa, about 5 minutes NE of San Marco
Food & drink breakfast; lunch and dinner at nearby Trattoria Al Burchiello
Prices rooms L70,000-L171,000
Rooms 25 double, 10 with bath, 15 with shower; 4 single, 2 with bath; all rooms have central heating, phone, minibar; air-conditioning, TV on request
Facilities breakfast room, sitting-room, bar
Credit cards AE, MC, V
Children accepted if well-behaved **Disabled** no special facilities **Pets** accepted
Closed never **Proprietors** Grazia and Giorgio Tinacci

Town hotel, near St Mark's

Torino

An old Venetian *palazzo*, the Torino lies only a few minutes' walk from Piazza San Marco, on a popular pedestrian thoroughfare. Neither the unprepossessing exterior nor the modest official star-rating leads you to expect an interior which is extraordinarily lavish. The reception area might be small, but all the trappings of a Venetian Gothic palace are there: an elaborate ceiling, pillars, a huge chandelier. Bedrooms too have chandeliers and other touches of grandeur along with modern comforts of private bathrooms and air-conditioning. The first-floor salon also has an air of formality, though softened by pretty modern sofas and water-colours of Venice. Breakfast is served in the bedrooms.

Nearby San Marco, Accademia gallery (5 minutes).

Calle delle Ostreghe 2356, San Marco, Venice 30124
Tel (041) 520 5222
Location San Marco, 5 min
Food & drink breakfast
Prices rooms L125,000-L180,000
Rooms 15 double, 5 single, all with shower; all rooms have central heating, air-conditioning, phone, radio, TV, minibar
Facilities sitting-room
Credit cards AE, DC, MC, V
Children accepted **Disabled** not suitable **Pets** accepted
Closed never
Proprietor Claudio Vecchiato

Venice

Town guest-house, on the Zattere

Seguso

Sitting on the wide sunny promenade of the Zattere gives you the distinct feeling of being by the seaside. The quayside is lapped by the choppy waters of the wide Guidecca canal which separates the main part of Venice from the island of Guidecca. This open setting, with a grand panorama across the lagoon, is just one of the charms of the Seguso. A *pensione* in the old tradition, it is family-run, friendly and solidly old-fashioned. And (unlike most hotels in Venice or indeed in any of the main Italian cities) it offers only half-board terms. This could be a drawback were it not for the fact that dinner, bed and breakfast combined cost no more than B&B only in hotels of similar comfort closer to the Piazza San Marco. The best bedrooms are the large ones at the front of the house, overlooking the canal – though for the privilege of the views and space you may have to forfeit the luxury of a private bathroom (only half the rooms have their own facilities). The main public rooms are the dining-room, prettily furnished in traditional style, and the modest sitting-room where you can sink into large leather chairs and peruse ancient editions of travel and guide books. Breakfast is taken on a small terrace at the front of the hotel – a prime spot for watching the ferries, launches or huge ocean-going liners plying the waters of the lagoon. Delightful.

Nearby Accademia gallery, Gesuati church.

Zattere 779, Dorsoduro, Venice 30123
Tel (041) 5222340
Location 5 minutes S of Accademia, overlooking Guidecca canal; with open-air terrace; nearest landing-stage Zattere
Food & drink breakfast, lunch, dinner
Prices DB&B L55,000-L113,000; reductions for children
Rooms 31 double, 5 single; 9 with bath, 9 with shower; all rooms have phone
Facilities dining-room, sitting-room, terrace
Credit cards AE, MC, V
Children welcome
Disabled no special facilities
Pets accepted
Closed Dec to Feb
Proprietors Seguso family

Piedmont

Area introduction

Piedmont hotels

Piedmont does, no doubt, have its attractions, but they do not impress themselves on many foreign visitors, who tend to hurry across this large region on their way to the recognised glories of Italy to the east and south. To the traveller as to the resident, the region is dominated by the city lying at its heart – Turin. And although Turin is a grandly spacious city with definite cultural attractions, the fact is that the capital of the Italian engineering industry does not attract many foreign visitors other than engineers and business people.

Although we have found a couple of recommendable hotels within easy reach of Turin, and one on the fringes of the city itself (see below), we have not found hotels in the middle of the city which deserve to be picked out in these pages. But this does not mean that the city lacks comfortable hotels: there is no shortage of swish, large impersonal places right in the heart of things. Of these, the most attractive (and not quite the most expensive) is the Jolly Hotel Ligure (Tel 55641). Of the more modest places, the Genio (Tel 650 8264) and the Victoria (Tel 553710) are smartly modern, of moderate size and central – the former particularly handy for the station. Only a little further away from the middle is the cheaper Piemontese (Tel 669 8101) – ideal for travellers on a tight budget who do not wish to be confined to the suburbs. None of these cheaper hotels has a restaurant, but there are plenty of eating places within walking distance, many accessible without even stepping outside the cover of the centre's extensively arcaded pavements.

Town villa, Turin

Villa Sassi-El Toulà

The Villa Sassi is unrivalled in Turin – a noble villa, dating from the early 17thC and retaining many of the original features – marble floors, ornately carved doors, old fireplaces, 17thC candelabra and Old Master paintings on the walls; one of the salons has a superb tapestry. The bedrooms are furnished with antiques and look out over the park, landscaped *all'inglese*.

There is also an exceptionally fine restaurant, now part of the El Toulà chain, and a famous cellar said to contain over 90,000 bottles. The Villa Sassi, if you can afford it, is very much part of the experience of visiting Turin.

Nearby sights of Turin; basilica of Superga (23 km).

Traforo del Pino 47, Turin 10132
Tel (011) 225437
Location 2 km E of city towards Superga; in grounds, with ample car parking
Food & drink breakfast, lunch, dinner
Prices rooms L240,000-L350,000
Rooms 18 bedrooms; all rooms have phone, TV, minibar
Facilities air-conditioned restaurant; sitting-rooms, bar
Credit cards AE, DC, MC, V
Children accepted **Disabled** lift/elevator **Pets** dogs not accepted in public rooms
Closed Aug; restaurant only, Sun
Manager Sga R Aonzo

Piedmont

Converted monastery, Cioccaro di Penango

Locanda del Sant'Uffizio

About 20 years ago the Firato family opened a restaurant here: it now has the reputation of being one of the best places to eat in the whole region. Bedrooms were added in the late 1980s, turning the place into a hotel of style and elegance. Some original features have been preserved and chic modern furnishings added – along with a fine collection of antiques. Bedrooms are decorated in unimpeachable taste: whitewashed walls, tiled floors, fresh fabrics and antique walnut or wroughtiron beds. A recent visitor praises the welcome, service and food, and pronounces the hotel 'very fair value for money'.

Nearby Asti (19 km); Monferrato hills; Turin within reach.

Cioccaro di Penango 14030 Asti
Tel (0141) 91271
Location 5 km SE of Moncalvo; in private grounds with car park
Food & drink breakfast, lunch, dinner
Prices DB&B L180,000
Rooms 29 double, all with shower or bath; 2 single; all rooms have central heating, minibar, TV

Facilities dining-room, billiards room, meeting-room; tennis, outdoor swimming-pool
Credit cards AE, DC, MC, V
Children welcome
Disabled no special facilities
Pets accepted if well behaved
Closed 3 weeks in both Jan and Aug
Proprietors Giuseppe Firato and Carla Comollo

Restaurant with rooms, San Giorgio Monferrato

Castello di San Giorgio

The history of the Castello goes back to the 10thC, when it was built to ward off Saracen attacks. But the building you see today – a fine pink mansion set in extensive parkland – dates from the 16thC. Thanks to expert restoration and appropriate period furnishings, the castle is now a particularly elegant hotel; but it is the superb food which attracts attention – including plenty of local dishes. The dining-room, with its crisp linen table-cloths, candelabras and Limoges porcelain, is the height of elegance; and bedrooms, furnished with antiques, and some with their own sitting areas, are unlikely to disappoint.

Nearby Monferrato massif; Asti (30 km).

Via Cavalli d'Olivola 3, San Giorgio Monferrato 15020 Alessandria
Tel (0142) 806203
Location 3 km SW of Casale, in the hills, with shady park and private car parking
Food & drink breakfast, lunch, dinner
Prices rooms L96,000-L140,000; meals about L65,000

Rooms 11 rooms, all with bath; all rooms have central heating, phone, colour TV, minibar
Facilities dining-room, bar
Credit cards AE, DC, V
Children accepted
Disabled no special facilities
Pets dogs not accepted
Closed restaurant only, Mon
Proprietor Maurizio Grossi

Emilia-Romagna

Villa Bolis

The friendly Lucchi family have recently taken over as proprietors of this lovely country house hotel which was beautifully restored and converted in the mid 1970s. Many of the original 17thC features have survived (high ceilings, stucco decorations, fireplaces) and the villa has been furnished with period antiques plus some elegant modern additions. The modern trattoria-style restaurant, which serves typical Romagnolo dishes, has a terrace overlooking the main swimming pool.

Nearby Faenza (15 km); Ravenna (30 km); Brisighella hills.

Via Corriera 5, Barbiano di Cotignola, Lugo 48010 Ravenna
Tel (0545) 78347
Location just N of village, in park; car parking in front of hotel, and garaging
Food & drink breakfast, lunch, dinner
Prices rooms L53,500-L87,000; dinner L20,000
Rooms 8 double, all with bath, one with bath and shower; 2 single, both with bath and shower; all rooms have central heating, phone, radio; TV on request
Facilities dining-room, bar, conference rooms, TV lounge; outdoor swimming-pool and tennis court available (charge made)
Credit cards AE, DC
Children welcome **Disabled** no special facilities **Pets** not accepted **Closed** Aug; restaurant only, Mon
Proprietor Nives Lucchi

Orologio

The Corona d'Oro (page 75), Commercianti (page 76) and the Orologio are all under the same management; and of the three this is the simplest and cheapest. It stands close to the main square, flanking a pedestrianized thoroughfare and facing the handsome Palazzo Communale. The interior is essentially functional and bedrooms are all alike: small, modern and reached by a tiny lift that starts from the second floor. There is no real sitting-room but the breakfast-room/bar, which has been newly decorated, is fresh and white, and the breakfasts served here are exceptional for a simple Italian hotel – freshly squeezed orange juice, yoghurts and various pastries.

Nearby Palazzo Communale, Palazzo del Podesta, basilica of San Petronio, Fontana del Nettuno.

Via IV Novembre 10, Bologna 40123
Tel (051) 231253
Location in middle of city, on pedestrian thoroughfare, with private car parking
Food & drink breakfast
Prices rooms L60,000-L100,000
Rooms 26 double, 6 with bath, 18 with shower; 6 single, 5 with shower; all rooms have central heating, phone
Facilities breakfast room, bar
Credit cards AE, DC, MC, V
Children accepted
Disabled no special facilities
Pets small ones only
Closed never
Proprietor Mauro Orsi

Emilia-Romagna

Town hotel, Bologna

Corona d'Oro 1890

Despite Bologna's many assets, which include fine medieval architecture and exceptional food, it is a city neglected by tourists. Most of the hotels cater for business travellers and fall far short of the 'small and charming'. The Corona d'Or is one of the few exceptions. It lies in the historic old city, close to the two famous leaning towers, in a cobbled street which for most of the time is closed to traffic. Enticing food shops (including a wonderful delicatessen) give you some idea of why the city is nicknamed Bologna La Grassa (the Fat) – and you certainly will not find it hard to eat well in this part of town.

The Corona d'Or became a hotel in 1890, though the original building dates back to 1300. It was here that Italy's first printing press was established and there are still a few features surviving from the original palace. In the early 1980s the hotel was bought by a packaging magnate, who elevated it from a simple hotel to four-star status, successfully combining the old features with the stylish new. The 14thC portico and Renaissance ceilings were preserved, while the plush bedrooms were provided with all modern conveniences. The showpiece was the hallway, with its fine art nouveau frieze supported on columns. Light streaming from above, fresh flowers and the central feature of lush feathery plants combined to create a cheerful, inviting entrance. In September 1989, as this edition was going to press, the hotel was undergoing a thorough process of refurbishment, which we trust will not have interfered with its existing attractions. This is not a cheap base, but for style and comfort in central Bologna, you cannot do better.

Nearby Piazza Maggiore and Piazza del Nettuno.

Via Oberdan 12, Bologna 40122
Tel (051) 236456
Location in middle, close to the two leaning towers in Piazza di Porta Ravegnana
Food & drink breakfast
Prices rooms L100,000-L250,000
Rooms 25 double one with bath, 24 with shower; 8 single; all with shower; all rooms have central heating, colour TV, minibar, phone, safe
Facilities bar, conference room, sitting area
Credit cards AE, DC, MC, V
Children accepted
Disabled no special facilities
Pets only small ones accepted
Closed Aug
Proprietor Mauro Orsi

Emilia-Romagna

Town hotel, Bologna

Dei Commercianti

As its name suggests, the Commercianti caters primarily for businessmen, but in a city with few tourist hotels it is a useful little place to know about. In the last year or two, the hotel has been given a face-lift and it is now looking spruce. Bedrooms are neat and modern, apart from the occasional old beam to remind you that you are in a medieval building. There is no restaurant – just a café-like breakfast-room. In a corner off reception is a little sitting area with pretty blue flowery sofas. The hotel has an air of efficiency and slight impersonality; but for a reasonably priced base in central Bologna it serves its purpose well.

Nearby San Petronio, Fontana and Piazza del Nettuno.

Via Pignattari 11, Bologna 40124
Tel (051) 233052
Location in middle of city, off Piazza Maggiore, with private car parking
Food & drink breakfast
Prices rooms L83,000-L134,000
Rooms 23 double, 8 single; all with shower; all rooms have central heating, TV, minibar, phone
Facilities bar/breakfast room, sitting-area
Credit cards AE, DC, MC, V
Children accepted; beds and cots available **Disabled** lift/elevator available
Pets small ones only
Closed never
Proprietor Paolo Orsi

Emilia-Romagna

I Due Foscari

The Due Foscari is a mock Gothic building in a quiet corner of this charming medieval town. It is only 25 years old, though that is hard to believe when you step inside into what appears to be an authentic medieval setting. There are handsome beamed ceilings, huge wrought-iron candelabras, tapestries, Gothic arches and heavy dark-wood antiques. You can try local specialities in the baronial splendour of the dining-room or, in summer, wine and dine on the elegant outdoor terrace. First and foremost the Due Foscari is a restaurant, but its rooms, with modest furniture in traditional style, make a more than adequate base for exploring the area.

Nearby Cremona (25 km), Piacenza (31 km), Parma (40 km), Milan (75 km).

Piazza Carlo Rossi 15, Busseto 43011 Parma
Tel (0524) 92337
Location overlooking small, grassy square in medieval town; with private car park
Food & drink breakfast, lunch, dinner
Prices rooms L50,000-L90,000; meals L28,000-L45,000

Rooms 20 rooms, all with bath or shower; all rooms have phone
Facilities 2 dining-rooms, bar
Credit cards MC, V
Children accepted **Disabled** no special facilities **Pets** dogs not accepted **Closed** Aug and Jan; restaurant only, Mon **Proprietor** Carlo Bergonzi

Ripagrande

Although this Renaissance 'palazzo' underwent major renovations in conversion to a four-star hotel, its dignity is still preserved – at least in the public rooms. The hall, with its elegant stone columns, timbered ceiling and period furniture, makes an appropriately noble entrance. And there are two Renaissance-style courtyards – one used for eating al fresco in summer. But bedrooms are surprisingly modern and stark; some have private balconies. Staff are very friendly and helpful.

Nearby Este castle and cathedral.

Via Ripagrande 21, Ferrara 44100
Tel (0532) 34733
Location in middle of city, some car parking in front
Food & drink breakfast, lunch, dinner
Prices rooms L180,000
Rooms 20 double, 2 with bath, 18 with shower; 2 single, both with shower; 20 family rooms, 2 with bath, 18 with shower; all rooms have central heating, air-conditioning, minibar, TV, phone
Facilities 2 internal courtyards, dining-room, one main sitting-room and 4 smaller ones
Credit cards AE, DC, MC, V
Children welcome **Disabled** access possible **Pets** not accepted in restaurant
Closed restaurant only, late Jul to late Aug
Proprietors Lanfranco and Roberto Viola

Emilia-Romagna

Town hotel, Parma

Torino

Most of the reasonably priced hotels of Parma are the slightly seedy ones around the station. The Torino is a notable exception: it lies in the heart of the city, just a stone's throw from the main sights (and with the bonus of a private garage). Bedrooms err towards the spartan, but are clean and well-cared for. Public rooms, in art nouveau style, are confined to the foyer and some small breakfast seating areas. Breakfast, which you may take in your room, includes cakes and local specialities. In a city of high gastronomic repute (especially for its hams and cheeses), the absence of a restaurant is no real drawback.

Nearby cathedral, baptistry and church of San Giovanni.

Via A Mazza 7, Parma 43100
Tel (0521) 281047
Location in middle of city, facing the Teatro Regio, with private garage
Food & drink breakfast
Prices rooms L60,000-L94,000
Rooms 12 double, all with shower; 15 single, all with shower; 6 family rooms, all with bath, all rooms have

central heating, piped music, TV, phone
Facilities hall, bar, conference room
Credit cards AE, DC, MC, V
Children welcome
Disabled access possible
Pets welcome
Closed first 3 weeks Aug, and Christmas
Proprietor Giulia Maria Chiri

Country hotel, Sarsina

Al Piano

The small town of Sarsina is well off the beaten tourist track, in an area of dramatic hill scenery. The Al Piano has a splendid high position, with a large grassy garden in front and a hedge hiding the industry which is beginning to encroach in the valley below. From a baronial mansion the building has been turned into a hotel with a curious mix of old and new furnishings – the bedrooms, in the annexe behind, are all very modern. For some time this has been an oasis in an area where hotels are virtually non-existent. But it has changed hands since our last visit, and to judge by an enthusiastic reader's report is now more attractive than ever: 'first-rate, with that distinctive family-run atmosphere.'

Nearby Forli (48 km), Ravenna (62 km), Rimini (66 km).

Via San Martino, Sarsina 47027 Forli
Tel (0547) 94848
Location 2 km SW of Sarsina; in own grounds with car parking
Food & drink breakfast, lunch, dinner
Prices rooms L42,000-L80,000
Rooms 13 rooms, all with bath or shower; all rooms

have phone, TV, minibar
Facilities dining-room, bar, sitting-room; swimming-pool
Credit cards DC, V
Children accepted
Disabled no special facilities
Pets dogs not accepted
Closed restaurant only, Mon
Proprietor Dr Arveda

Emilia-Romagna

Restaurant with rooms, Brisighella

Gigiolè

Brisighella is a picturesque small town 13 km south-west of Faenza. A clock tower on a rocky spur, a castle with two towers and an intriguing covered alley with arcades are the main features of the old quarter. The Gigiolè stands across from the main church – a vaguely French-looking shuttered building with a shaded terrace in front.

The French style extends to the food: Tarcisio Raccagni, the chef, has been put on a par with the famous Paul Bocuse. Like Bocuse he places great stress on using seasonal local ingredients of top quality and the results are superb: succulent meats, delicious soups and imaginative use of vegetables and herbs – top quality *nouvelle cuisine* but at prices you can afford and in helpings that don't leave you hungry. The setting is late 18thC, with stone arches, ceramics and copper pots. Table-cloths are white and crisp, and glasses gleam. Service is 'grave but efficient'.

After all this, the bedrooms come as a bit of an anti-climax; but they are adequate, and give little cause for complaint. Some of the newly decorated rooms are quite pretty, with white modern furnishings and fabrics, and good new bathrooms; others are being redecorated. Ask for a room at the back if peace is a priority. 'Excellent value; I should gladly return', says a recent visitor.

Nearby Faenza; Florence, Ravenna, Bologna, Rimini.

Piazza Carducci 5, Brisighella 48013 Ravenna
Tel (0546) 81209
Location in middle of town, 13 km SW of Faenza on S302; no private car parking, but space available in the piazza
Food & drink breakfast, lunch, dinner
Prices rooms L46,000-L60,000
Rooms 7 double, 5 single, 2 family rooms; all with bath; all rooms have central heating, phone
Facilities dining-room, bar, TV room
Credit cards AE, DC
Children welcome
Disabled access difficult
Pets welcome if clean and well behaved
Closed one week Feb, one week Mar; restaurant only, Mon
Proprietor Tarcisio Raccagni

Emilia-Romagna

Converted monastery, Portico di Romagna

Al Vecchio Convento

A sleepy medieval village, Portico di Romagna lies on the borders of Tuscany and Emilia Romagna, in the valley of l'Acquacheta. It is a beautiful unspoiled region whose praises were sung by Dante in the *Divine Comedy*.

The Vecchio Convento lies in the middle of the village in the very same street as the palace which belonged to Beatrice Portinori, muse of Dante. It was built in 1840 and converted only four years ago into a hotel by the Raggi family – and, thanks to them, it still maintains the feel of an old country house. Tiles, beams and old fireplaces create a delightfully rustic setting and the warmth and hospitality of the family is part of the great charm of the place. The husband is the chef, renowned for his expertise in the kitchen, particularly his home-made pastas served with fresh herbs or *funghi* and white truffles. The ground floor is devoted mainly to the dining area – four rooms, each with the feel of a Tuscan farmhouse, from the tiny vaulted room with a huge stone fireplace to the much larger old granary with its timber ceiling and arched windows overlooking the valley.

Many of the antiques from the original buildings are still in place, and this applies even to the bedrooms. Handsome and elaborate antique beds are features of rooms that are otherwise quite plain and simple. Even the new attic rooms at the top of the house have a certain rustic charm.

Nearby walks in the valley of l'Acquacheta; Faenza (46 km).

Via Roma 7, Portico di Romagna 47010 Forli
Tel (0543) 967752
Location 30 km SE of Forli, in village; with some private parking
Food & drink breakfast, lunch, dinner
Prices rooms L43,000-L58,000; meals L25,000-L45,000
Rooms 11 double, 9 with shower; 3 single, 2 with shower; all rooms have phone
Facilities bar, dining-room, hall/sitting-room
Credit cards AE, DC, V
Children welcome
Disabled access difficult
Pets not accepted
Closed never
Proprietors Marisa Raggi and Giovanni Cameli

Western Riviera

Villa Elisa

On the western side of the Italian Riviera (only 32 km from Monte Carlo), Bordighera is a popular family resort, famed for its flora and mild winter climate. The beach is no match for those of the French Riviera and the main coastal road and railway running parallel are a distinct disadvantage, but there is a quiet and civilized area to stay at the back of the town where hotels and villas stand among sub-tropical gardens. The Villa Elisa lies in this area – an attractive old house with a lush garden of mandarins and olive trees in front. Public rooms are peaceful and civilized, bedrooms are spacious and pleasantly old fashioned; but perhaps the biggest attraction is the prices.
Nearby San Remo (12 km), France (10 km).

Via Romana 70, Bordighera
18012 Imperia
Tel (0184) 261313
Location in residential quarter about 10 minutes' walk from beach; with garden and private parking
Food & drink breakfast, lunch, dinner
Prices rooms L63,000-L103,000
Rooms 33 double, 16 with bath, 17 with shower; 2 single, both with bath; all rooms have phone, TV
Facilities dining-room, 2 sitting-rooms, TV room, terrace; swimming-pool
Credit cards AE, MC, V
Children accepted
Disabled not suitable
Pets not accepted in public rooms **Closed** Nov to mid-Dec
Proprietor Maurizio Oggero

La Meridiana

The Meridiana is a little oasis of peace, a short drive inland from the Riviera, among woods and vines. Primarily it is a golfers' hotel, but there are plenty of other sports facilities on hand, plus lovely walks. The whole place is spacious, comfortable and quiet. Bedrooms are well equipped. Food is a cut above average – particularly the pasta (try it with the local 'pesto' sauce), the risottos and the fish.
Nearby old quarter of Alberga (12 km); Genoa (93 km).

Garlenda 17033 Savona
Tel (0182) 580271
Location one km from village of Garlenda, 12 km inland from Alberga; in spacious gardens with private car parking
Food & drink breakfast, dinner
Prices rooms L157,000-L254,000; suites L264,000-L309,000
Rooms 16 double, 14 suites; all with bath and shower; all rooms have phone, satellite TV, minibar
Facilities sitting-room, dining-room, bar, bridge room, conference room; barbecue, swimming-pool, sauna, massage, bicycles
Credit cards AE, DC, MC, V
Children welcome; special meals on request
Disabled 10 ground-floor rooms **Pets** dogs not accepted in restaurant
Closed last 3 weeks Jan, few days early Feb
Proprietor Edmondo Segre

Western Riviera

Seaside hotel, Laigueglia

Splendid

The Splendid lies in the middle of Laigueglia, not far from its private beach. The building was originally a monastery – exhibits in the ground-floor showcase and the ancient well in the dining-room testify to its age, and the vaulted ceilings have been preserved. Elsewhere furnishings and style are a happy combination of old and new – antiques and tapestries in some of the public areas, with bedrooms more modern in style, particularly the fourth-floor attic rooms. A key feature is the small garden at the back of the hotel, with an inviting pool where drinks are served.

Nearby Alassio (3 km), San Remo (44 km).

Piazza Badaro 3, Laigueglia
17020 Savona
Tel (0182) 49325
Location in middle of resort, with small garden and private parking for 30 cars
Food & drink breakfast, lunch, dinner
Prices DB&B L55,000-L88,000; 30% reduction for children under 7
Rooms 35 double, 7 single, 8 family rooms; all with bath or shower; all rooms have central heating, phone
Facilities dining-room, bar; swimming-pool, beach
Credit cards AE, DC, V
Children accepted over 2
Disabled no special facilities
Pets small ones accepted, but not in dining-room, nor on beach
Closed Oct to Mar
Proprietor Angelo Marchiano

Seaside hotel, Ospedaletti

Delle Rose

One of the more secluded and peaceful hotels of Ospedaletti, the Delle Rose lies about 400 m from the beach. The resort, like so many along this coast (commonly called the Riviera dei Fiori), is famed for its flowers – and it is the garden which is perhaps the hotel's finest feature. Sandro Colombo is a cactus expert and grows (we are told) 6,000 varieties, many of which can be admired from the shady terrace. The hotel is a modest, friendly one, with essentially modern furnishings and a fine collection of post-War landscape paintings. The bedrooms are all quite simply furnished, the dining-room more elegant – a visitor notes "silver rather than stainless steel" on the tables.

Nearby San Remo (6 km), Taggia (17 km), Baiardo (27 km).

Via De Medici 17,
Ospedaletti 18014 Imperia
Tel (0184) 59016
Location close to middle of resort; in gardens, with private car parking
Food & drink breakfast, lunch, dinner
Prices rooms L28,000-L67,000; dinner L16,000
Rooms 14 double, 13 with bath; 2 single; all rooms have central heating, phone
Facilities dining-room, TV room, sitting-room, bar
Credit cards not accepted
Children welcome
Disabled access difficult
Pets not accepted
Closed never
Proprietor Sandro Colombo

Western Riviera

Seaside villa, Finale Ligure

Punta Est

The Italian Riviera west of Genoa is for the most part disappointing: most of its resorts are dreary, and most of its hotels mediocre. Happily, both the Punta Est and Finale Ligure are exceptions. The hotel is converted from a splendid 18thC villa which stands high and proudly pink above the buzz of the main coastal road, overlooking the sea. Signor Podesta, who used to be a sculptor, has acted as resident architect since the hotel was first created in the late 1960s, and with great success. By preserving the original features of the house and adding to it in a sympathetic style, he has managed to preserve the atmosphere of a private villa. The interior is cool and elegant – all dark-wood antiques, fine stone arches, fireplaces and tiled floors. But with such an impressive setting, for most months of the year the focus is on the outdoor terraces, pool and gardens, with their pines, potted plants and lovely views.

Breakfast is taken (off Staffordshire china) in a sort of canopied greenhouse – a lovely sunny spot, surrounded by greenery. Other meals are served in a dining-room in the annexe, where stone arches and beams create a vaguely medieval setting. You can choose between international and Ligurian dishes, including bass cooked with strong aromatic local herbs.

The hotel is also very close to the beach, which is only a couple of minutes' walk down the hillside.

Nearby Finale Borgo (3 km), Alassio (26 km).

Via Aurelia 1, Finale Ligure
17024 Savona
Tel (019) 600611
Location E of the historic town, in private gardens; private car parking
Food & drink breakfast, lunch, dinner
Prices rooms L80,000-L160,000; meals L40,000-L50,000
Rooms 30 double, 4 single, 5 suites; all with bath and shower; all rooms have central heating, phone; minibar in 25 rooms, TV in 10
Facilities sitting-room, bar, TV room, conference room, piano bar; swimming-pool, half tennis court, solarium
Credit cards AE, V
Children accepted, provided they are under parents' control
Disabled lift/elevator
Pets accepted on request
Closed Oct to Easter
Proprietors Podesta family

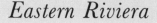

Eastern Riviera

Genio

The picturesque fishing village of Portovenere, at the tip of a peninsula which flanks the western side of the Gulf of La Spezia, is one of the most popular and fashionable excursion spots along the coast. The Genio is a tiny, simple family-run hotel partially occupying an old medieval tower at the entrance to the town. Bedrooms (of which there are only seven) are basic and there is only one with its own bathroom. But the tower and its vine-clad terraces have character, and the rooms are, after all, the cheapest in town. The only public rooms are the modest reception/bar and a games room, popular with young locals. There is no restaurant, but plenty along the waterfront.

Nearby church of San Pietro, Byron's Grotto, castle; boat trips to the Palmaria, Tino and Tinetto islands and the Blue Grotto.

Piazza Bastrieri 8,
Portovenere 19025
La Spezia
Tel (0187) 900611
Location in middle of resort, close to waterfront, with tiny garden but no private car parking
Food & drink no meals available
Prices rooms L33,000-

L49,000
Rooms 6 double, one single; all with shower; all rooms have central heating
Facilities bar, games room,
Credit cards MC, V
Children accepted
Disabled access difficult
Pets accepted
Closed Jan and half of Feb
Proprietor Laura Canese

Grand Hotel dei Castelli

Once the home of a local Tuscan noble, this is now the most luxurious hotel in Sestri Levante. It is not in itself a really remarkable hotel: the decoration is not always well co-ordinated, there are some inappropriate modern furnishings, and there are signs of wear. But all may be forgiven when you sit on the balcony and enjoy glorious views of the blue seas and boats in the harbour, or when you amble through the park.

Nearby Portofino (28 km), Santa Margherita Ligure (23 km).

Via Penisola 26, Sestri
Levante 16039 Genoa
Tel (0185) 41044
Location on promontory, surrounded by park with ample car parking
Food & drink breakfast, lunch, dinner
Prices rooms L132,000-L263,000; meals L66,000; 30% reduction for children under 6
Rooms 38 double, all with bath; 7 single, 3 with bath, 4 with shower; all rooms have

central heating, phone; air-conditioning at extra cost
Facilities 2 restaurants (one open-air), TV room, meeting-rooms; sea-water swimming-pool, bowls
Credit cards AE, DC, MC, V
Children accepted provided they stay with parents
Disabled no special facilities
Pets accepted, but not in restaurant or on beach
Closed 2nd week Oct to 2nd week May
Manager Lino Zanotto

Eastern Riviera

Seaside hotel, Sestri Levante

Helvetia

The Helvetia's claim that it has 'the quietest and most enchanting position of Sestri Levante' is no exaggeration. It stands at one end of the appropriately named Baia del Silenzio, a peaceful crescent of sands lined by mellow pink and ochre houses. The hotel is distinguished by its spotless white façade, and the yellow and white canopies that shade its balconies and terrace. Lorenzo Pernigotti devotes himself wholeheartedly to making his guests as content as possible. He provides the sort of extras – including 15 gleaming yellow bikes – that you might expect to find in a four-star hotel; but the special charm of the Helvetia is that it is small and personal.

The sitting-room/bar has the air of a private home – antiques, coffee-table books, newspapers, potted plants – and the restaurant is a lovely light room with bird's-eye views of the bay. Bedrooms are light and airy, overlooking either the bay – there are six with their own balconies – or the gardens. The day starts on the delightful terrace, with an unusually liberal help-yourself breakfast of croissants, cheese, fruit, coffee and rolls. Behind the terrace luxuriant gardens climb up the hillside, with tables in the shade of palm trees. Serious sunbathers can take to sunbeds. And there is a tiny pebble beach with private changing cabins just across the road.

Half- or full-board terms are attractive, given the high quality of food and the beautiful views from restaurant and terrace; but bed and breakfast is now available out of season.

Nearby beauty spots of the eastern Riviera, eg Portofino (28 km), Cinqueterre and Portovenere.

Via Cappuccini 43, Sestri Levante 16039 Genova
Tel (0185) 41175
Location on the Baia del Silenzio, overlooking small beach, with private paying garage
Food & drink breakfast, lunch, dinner
Prices rooms L90,000-L100,000; DB&B L90,000-L100,000; 30% reduction for children under 6 sharing parents' room
Rooms 28 double, 14 with bath, 14 with shower; all rooms have central heating, phone, hairdrier, radio, TV, video, minibar
Facilities sitting-room, TV/video room, dining-room, bar, terrace; solarium, ping-pong, free bicycles
Credit cards not accepted
Children welcome; small beds provided
Disabled no special facilities
Pets dogs accepted but not in dining-room
Closed Nov to Feb
Proprietor Lorenzo Pernigotti

Eastern Riviera

Miramare

The Miramare is one of several pink shuttered houses that line the Baia del Silenzio and date from the last century. But step inside and the hotel seems anything but old. Public rooms are cool, contemporary and elegant, with white sofas, potted plants and huge arched windows making the most of the sea views. The mini-apartments have kitchenettes as well as sitting-rooms – again in a light, modern style. The terrace makes an idyllic spot for drinks and breakfast. 'Most enjoyable', says a recent report.
Nearby Portofino (28 km); Cinqueterre, Portovenere.

Via Cappellini 9, Sestri Levante 16039 Genoa
Tel (0185) 480855
Location on waterfront, above private beach; with garden and garage
Food & drink breakfast, lunch, dinner
Prices rooms L80,000-L190,000; reduction for children
Rooms 21 rooms, 14 apartments, all with bath or shower; all rooms have cool air system, phone, colour TV, minibar; apartments have sitting-room and kitchenette
Facilities sitting-room, bar, dining-room, conference rooms, terrace, boutique
Credit cards AE, DC, MC, V
Children welcome
Disabled not suitable
Pets small ones only accepted
Closed never
Proprietor Sg Laurenzana

Portofino Vetta

A private road twists through quiet woodland to the mount of Portofino where this grandiose pink villa stands, with stunning views down to one of the loveliest stretches of the whole of the Italian Riviera.

The foyer is cool, spacious and civilized, with big windows making the most of the views; the dining and banqueting areas verge on the grand. The atmosphere is formal, even a little staid, and there is no doubt that the hotel's greatest asset is its location, providing the tranquillity you rarely find along this coast. There are lovely walks in the area and, belonging to the hotel itself, a museum with 'the most important frescoes in the world' – a claim which we have been unable to verify.
Nearby church of San Lorenzo della Costa (3 km); Portofino (17 km); Camogli (7 km).

Portofino Vetta, Ruta di Camogli 16030 Genova
Tel (0185) 772281
Location 2 km S of Ruta, in large private park with car parking in front of hotel
Food & drink breakfast
Prices B&B L72,500
Rooms 12 double, all with bath or shower; all rooms have central heating, minibar, phone
Facilities hall, sitting-room, bar, terrace
Credit cards AE
Children accepted
Disabled access difficult
Pets not accepted
Closed never
Manager Sg Capurro

Eastern Riviera

Town guest-house, Portofino

Eden

Such is the popularity of Portofino – small, chic and enchanting – that you can spend two hours waiting for car parking space in peak season; its charms are invariably spoiled by the onslaught of daytrippers. But stay the night and you see a different Portofino: you can dine on the waterfront in relative peace, and watch the early-morning fishing activities before the tourist crowds arrive.

Hotel rooms are at a premium. There is the grand (and expensive) Hotel Splendid, and a handful of much smaller, more modest hotels. The Eden is one of these – a tiny place tucked away down a narrow street a couple of minutes from the waterfront. The garden, shaded by a large palm and a mass of greenery, is a quiet enclave in the middle of the resort – all meals can be taken on the terrace here in summer. On cooler days meals are taken in the trattoria-style dining-room which overlooks the garden. The only other public area is the entrance hallway with a bar, prints of Portofino and Genoa and, at the end, a reception desk tucked under the stairs.

Bedrooms range from the spruce, newly whitewashed rooms on the upper floors to the larger doubles downstairs with floral walls; all are light and fresh, with spotless bathrooms, and we are assured that the 'signs of wear' originally noted by our inspector have been remedied.

Nearby walk to lighthouse (half-hour); fishing village of San Fruttuoso (reached by boat or 2 hr walk); Santa Margherita Ligure (5 km).

Portofino 16034 Genoa
Tel (0185) 269091
Location in middle of resort, with private garden in front; public car park only (very expensive)
Food & drink breakfast, lunch, dinner
Prices rooms L120,000-L140,000; meals L40,000-L60,000
Rooms 12 double, 6 with bath, 6 with shower; all rooms have central heating, phone; air-conditioning and TV in some rooms
Facilities dining-room with outdoor terrace, bar
Credit cards AE, DC, MC, V
Children welcome if well behaved **Disabled** no special facilities **Pets** accepted, but not in restaurant **Closed** never
Proprietor Osta Ferrucio

Tuscany

Tuscany hotels

No other region of Italy is as rich in good small hotels as Tuscany; our problem here was not the difficulty of finding hotels worthy of inclusion in the guide, but one of struggling to cut down the number of hotels which seemed to justify a full-page entry.

The greatest concentrations of hotels are naturally around the tourist highlights of Florence, Siena and San Gimignano. But on recent visits we have been struck by the momentum that tourism is gaining in the countryside between Florence and Siena – the Chianti wine region. There have been good hotels in this area for many years; but alongside the old favourites in this section of the guide there are some new discoveries, and the area also contains other promising hotels which the visitor may wish to look out for.

We have heard flattering comments about the Albergo del Chianti (Tel 055 853763), a spick-and-span little hotel close to the middle of Greve, entirely refurbished in 1986 "with great care and taste" (according to another Chianti hotelier); it has a fair-sized swimming pool in the back garden, and offers attractively modest prices. A little way outside Gaiole, on the western side of Chianti, is the Cavarchione Toscanum (Tel 0577 749550) – a highly individual old farmhouse with pool and gardens, in an elevated spot with good views, run with characteristic care by charming German owners. Only problems of space have prevented our giving this delightful spot a full entry in this edition.

An acceptable alternative to our recommendation in Volterra is the more central San Lino (Tel 0588 85250).

Paggeria Medicea

Ferdinand I of Medici was so impressed by the beauty of the hilltop village of Artimino that he built a grand villa there in the 16thC. The villa still stands today, and a few years back the smaller simpler building which used to be the servants' quarters was converted into this smart, well-equipped hotel. The furnishings are a stylish mix of new and old. Features such as old sloping wood beams, chimneys and ceilings have where possible been retained in the bedrooms and the public areas. Tuscan dishes "with a Renaissance flavour" are served in the rustic restaurant just a couple of minutes away, along with wines from the estate.

Nearby an Etruscan museum; a medieval village; Prato (18 km), Florence (25 km).

Viale Papa Giovanni XXIII, Artimino 50040 Firenze
Tel (055) 8718081
Location 25 km NW of Florence, close to village, with ample car parking
Food & drink breakfast, lunch, dinner
Prices rooms L95,000-L160,000; DB&B L100,000-L120,000
Rooms 34 double, 8 with bath, 26 with shower; 3 single, all with shower; all rooms have central heating, minibar, colour TV, phone
Facilities dining-room, reading-room, TV room; 2 tennis courts, jogging
Credit cards AE, DC, MC, V
Children accepted **Disabled** no special facilities **Pets** accepted, but not in dining-room **Closed** never
Manager Luisa Dapelo

Tuscany

Country hotel, Camaiore

Peralta

Skiers who are used to the chalet holiday may find echoes in the way Peralta is run – at least in the summer months, when it is taken over by a London-based company. They organise it informally along house-party lines, with set meals which may now be taken around big shared tables or at smaller tables for two. As in a chalet, much of the success of a holiday at Peralta depends on how you get on with fellow inmates – particularly if (as is likely) you go with the idea of spending much of your time at base.

Peralta is a tiny hamlet, high in the Tuscan hills but within sight of the sea, dating from Etruscan times and restored from ruin by the sculptress Fiore de Henriquez, who still lives there (and – if she is at home – welcomes guests herself when the place reverts to her control out of season). Its great attractions are simplicity (rough walls, beams, country furniture), peaceful seclusion (you have to walk the last few hundred yards from the end of the narrow, winding access road) and superb views from flowery terraces across woods and olive groves. Lucca, with its wealth of churches and delightful flower market, is only a short drive away.
Nearby coastal resorts; Lucca (30 km).

Pieve di Camaiore 55043
Lucca
Tel (0584) 951230
Location 10 minutes' drive
SE of Camaiore
Food & drink breakfast;
buffet lunch, dinner (except
Thu)
Prices DB&B £33-£40;
single supplement £5 (prices
apply for UK bookings)
Rooms 16 double, all with
shower; rooms spread over 5
buildings

Facilities bar, sitting-room,
dining-room, terrace;
swimming-pool, boule
Credit cards not accepted
Children welcome over 16
Disabled access difficult
Pets not advised
Closed early Oct to May –
though rooms available by
arrangement
Managers Philip Harrison
Stanton and Humphrey
Haslam

Country Inn, Pieve Santo Stèfano

Locanda Sari

The upper Tiber valley is an unjustly neglected corner of Tuscany – slightly awkward to get to from Florence, but worth the effort if you fancy a slightly Alpine change of scene, and not without cultural interest either. The area is also well placed for excursions down into Umbria, and over to the Marches.

Locanda Sari has long been run by Carmen Pierangeli's family as a local inn and convenient port of call on the road over to Ravenna; but the traffic which once passed within feet of the front door now whizzes up a neo-motorway on the other side of the narrow valley, and Carmen has seized the opportunity to turn the locanda into a place worth travelling to find. The house has been restored with real panache in classy country style. In the bedrooms, rustic antiques and painted reproduction wardrobes sit on glistening tiled floors, with creamy rugs and bedspreads woven to a special pattern; old iron bedheads are fixed to the walls, but the beds themselves are new (and splendidly firm); the shower rooms are compact but smart. The dining-room shows the same simple good taste, but the real attraction here is Carmen's exquisite country cooking, of the kind that tourists are rarely privileged to taste; even the simplest things – the daily batch of ravioli, made with local ricotta, for example, are superb.

The new road is something of an eyesore at present, but husband Pio has plans for screening trees, and we did not find noise a problem even in front rooms.

Nearby Sansepolcro (16 km); La Verna (20 km); Anghiari (20 km).

Via Tiberina km177, Pieve
Santo Stèfano, Arezzo
Tel (0575) 799129
Location in countryside 3km
N of village, on minor road;
car parking across the road
Food & drink breakfast,
lunch, dinner
Prices rooms L46,000; meals
L25,000-L30,000
Rooms 8 double, one with
bath, 7 with shower; all
rooms have central heating
Facilities dining-room,
lobby, bar; small terrace
Credit cards AE, MC, V
Children welcome
Disabled access difficult
Pets not accepted
Closed no regular times
Proprietor Carmen
Pierangeli

Tuscany

Country villa, Castellina in Chianti

Villa Casalecchi

It is not difficult to find fault with this unassuming villa immersed in woods and vineyards in the heart of Chianti. It does not set particularly high standards of decoration, hotel-keeping or cuisine, and not all of those involved in its running are notably welcoming. But Casalecchi is one of those places it is always comfortable to be going back to; perhaps the fact that it does not feel the need to try too hard is part of its charm.

The house sits high on a steepish slope. There is no clearly defined front and back, but you approach from above, and below is the fair-sized pool. Bedrooms fall into two categories: the old ones in the main house, which are lofty, fairly spacious and full of lovely antique furniture; and the ones added on to the downhill side of the house overlooking the pool, which are rather cramped, but which have the undeniable attraction of a terrace immediately outside where you can take breakfast. This last is a pleasant setting, with nothing but trees and vines in view, and a great advance on the dreary breakfast room. The sitting areas – one a sort of lobby and the other a more rustic affair looking out over the vineyards – are no more than adequately comfortable. The dining-room, in welcome contrast, boasts splendid old wood-panelled walls.

Nearby Florence, Siena, San Gimignano, Volterra, Perugia.

Castellina in Chianti 53011 Siena
Tel (0577) 740240
Location one km S of Castellina, in countryside, with adequate car parking
Food & drink breakfast, lunch, dinner
Prices DB & B L180,000; FB L205,000; 20% reduction for children under 6
Rooms 19 double, 16 with bath, 3 with shower; all rooms have central heating, phone
Facilities dining-room, breakfast room, bar, 2 sitting-rooms, open-air swimming-pool
Credit cards AE, DC, MC, V
Children accepted
Disabled access difficult
Pets accepted, but not in public rooms
Closed Oct to Mar
Proprietor Elvira Lecchini-Giovannoni

Country hotel, Castellina in Chianti

Tenuta di Ricavo

If away from it all is where you want to get – while retaining the possibility of doing some serious sightseeing – Ricavo is hard to beat. The hotel occupies an entire hamlet, deserted in the 50s when people left the land for the cities in search of work. The charming family who took it over then are there still: day-to-day running is in the hands of the third generation.

The grouping of houses along a wooded ridge in the depth of the countryside might have been conceived as a film-set replica of a medieval hamlet. The main house, facing a little square of other mellow stone cottages, houses some of the bedrooms, the no-smoking dining-room – smart and restrained with plain white walls, brick arches and tiled floor – and the several sitting-rooms, which are comfortably furnished with a pleasant jumble of antique chairs and sofas (one of them with a small library of English, Italian, French and German books).

Breakfast can be had in several spots outdoors – perhaps in the shade of linden trees. At the right time of the year the gardens are bright with flowers – one of the highlights is a grand old wisteria – and there are plenty of secluded corners, with the result that the place seems calm and quiet even when the hotel is full. The small garden pool is ideal for quiet cooling off, the larger one out of the way so that lively children are no problem.

If the 'Ricavo' has a weak spot, it may be the food, which in some eyes has lacked both choice and inspiration.

Nearby Siena (22 km); San Gimignano and Florence within a day's drive.

Localita Ricavo, Castellina in Chianti 53011 Siena
Tel (0577) 740221
Location isolated in countryside, about 3 km N of Castellina in gardens, with ample car parking
Food & drink breakfast, lunch, dinner
Prices DB&B L132,000-L175,000
Rooms 13 double, 2 single, 10 family rooms; all with bath; all rooms have central heating, phone
Facilities 3 sitting-rooms, bar, dining-room; 2 swimming-pools, table tennis, 2 'boccia' courts
Credit cards not accepted
Children welcome **Disabled** some ground-floor rooms
Pets not accepted
Closed Nov to Easter; dining-room closed Wed lunch-time
Proprietor Dr Scotoni

Tuscany

Country guest-house, Castellina in Chianti

Salivolpi

This welcome addition to the Castellina hotel establishment – open since 1983 – offers a much cheaper alternative to its two illustrious neighbours. It occupies two well restored farm buildings and one new bungalow in an open position on the edge of the village. There is a Spanish feel to the older of the houses – iron fittings, exposed beams, white walls, ochre tiles – and the spacious rooms are both neat and stylish. The garden is well cared for, with plenty of space. Breakfast (*"molto abbondante,"* claims the boss, with justice) is served in a crisp little room in the smaller of the houses.

Nearby Siena (18 km); Florence, San Gimignano and other Tuscan attractions within reach.

Via Fiorentina, Castellina in Chianti 53011 Siena
Tel (0577) 740484
Location 500 m from middle of village, on the road to San Donato, with gardens and ample open-air car parking
Food & drink breakfast
Prices rooms L52,000-L84,000
Rooms 18 double, 16 with bath; one single with bath; all rooms have central heating, phone
Facilities hall, breakfast room; swimming-pool
Credit cards not accepted
Children accepted
Disabled no special facilities
Pets not accepted
Closed never
Manager Sga Laura

Country inn, Certaldo

Osteria del Vicario

This simple inn was a monastery in the 13thC and has retained its basic structure, with a garden enclosed in a Romanesque cloister. It is a delightful place to stay; bedrooms, with leaded windows and old terracotta floors, have plenty of old-fashioned charm. Chef Ferdinando and his wife Linda look after everyone attentively and in several languages. A summer bonus is the lovely flowered terrace but game, fresh wild mushrooms and truffles are autumnal attractions.

Nearby House of Boccaccio; San Gimignano (13 km).

Via Rivellino 3, Certaldo Alto 50052 Firenze
Tel (0571) 668228
Location at top of main street of upper town; in garden, with car parking in front of hotel
Food & drink breakfast, dinner; vegetarian meals
Prices DB&B L70,000 (3 nights' stay preferred)
Rooms 10 double, 2 single, 2 family rooms, all with shower; all rooms have small TV on request
Facilities bar, 3 sitting-rooms (one with TV), 2 dining-rooms; terrace, small swimming-pool
Credit cards AE, DC, V
Children welcome if well behaved
Disabled not suitable
Pets small ones only accepted
Closed mid-Jan to end Feb
Proprietors Ferdinando and Linda Steyn Ulivieri

Town guest-house, Fiesole

Villa Bonelli

The friendly and helpful Boninsegni brothers have run this appealing little hotel since 1972. Bedrooms are simple but pleasant, public rooms rather cramped, except for the restaurant – a beamed room on the top floor which enjoys marvellous picture-window views of the countryside, especially when candle-lit at night. There is also a pleasant terrace. Regional specialities and local wines are served and you are expected to take at least half-board, except in low season; this is no disadvantage, as the food is excellent and varied. The approach to the hotel is narrow and steep, but well signed.

Nearby cathedral, Roman theatre; Florence (10 km).

Via Francesco Poeti 1, Fiesole, Florence 50014
Tel (055) 59513
Location 10 km N of Florence; ample car parking, and garaging for 8 cars
Food & drink breakfast, dinner
Prices rooms L48,600-L87,500; DB&B L84,000-L157,000
Rooms 15 double, one with bath, 12 with shower; 7 single; one family room, with shower; all rooms have central heating, phone
Facilities dining-room, bar/TV room, terrace
Credit cards AE, DC, MC, V
Children welcome **Disabled** bedrooms on ground floor
Pets dogs accepted in bedrooms
Closed restaurant only, Nov to mid-Mar
Proprietors Andrea and Silvano Boninsegni

Country villa, Colle di Val d'Elsa

Villa Belvedere

Though it calls itself a hotel, this handsome, weathered villa standing in open countryside a few miles from Siena is perhaps better thought of as a elegant restaurant with rooms; although there is a grand first-floor salon, it is often taken over as a function room, and the stylish dining-room – with its bentwood cafe chairs, white walls and low, vaulted ceiling – is very much the heart of the place. The food here enjoys a high reputation in the locality. Bedrooms are similarly restrained in decoration, but some do contain amusingly ornate antique furniture.

Nearby San Gimignano (14 km), Siena (25 km); Florence and other Tuscan attractions within reach.

Localita Belvedere, Colle di Val d'Elsa 53034 Siena
Tel (0577) 920966
Location 2 km E of Colle di Val d'Elsa, in countryside, with large garden and ample car parking
Food & drink breakfast, lunch, dinner
Prices rooms L100,000; DB&B L180,000; FB L250,000
Rooms 15 double, all with bath; all rooms have phone
Facilities 2 sitting-rooms, TV room, bar, dining-room
Credit cards AE, DC, MC, V
Children welcome if not too noisy
Disabled no special facilities
Pets not accepted
Closed never
Proprietor Daniele Conti

Tuscany

Country guest-house, Fiesole

Bencista

"Don't send us too many tourists," the smooth Simone Simoni begged our inspector – and he genuinely meant it. It is easy to see why the Bencista is so popular. The *pensione* stands on a hillside overlooking Florence and the Tuscan hills; views from the terrace and many of the bedrooms are unforgettable. Added to this are the charms of the building, once a monastery: a handsome hallway, three salons almost entirely furnished with antiques (including a little reading-room with shelves of old books and a cosy fire), plus plenty of fascinating nooks and crannies.

No two bedrooms are alike and each one has some captivating feature – perhaps a beautiful view, a fine piece of furniture, a huge bathroom or, in some, a private terrace. They are nearly all old-fashioned, with plain whitewashed walls and solid antiques, and the accent is more on character than luxury.

The dining-room is simple, light and spacious, overlooking gardens where olives, roses and magnolia flourish. Breakfast is taken *al fresco* on the terrace – a glorious spot to start (and end) the day. Meals offer no choice, but are well cooked; puddings are 'superbly wicked', and the house wine excellent.

Nearby Roman theatre, cathedral and monastery of San Francesco, all at Fiesole.

Via B da Maiano 4,
Fiesole 50014
Tel (055) 59163
Location 2.5 km S of Fiesole on Florence road, set in private park overlooking city; garage and ample open-air car parking
Food & drink breakfast, lunch, dinner
Prices DB & B L57,000-L74,000; FB L71,000- L88,000

Rooms 27 double, 15 with bath, 9 with shower; 8 single, 2 with bath; all rooms have central heating
Facilities 3 sitting-rooms, dining-room
Credit cards not accepted
Children accepted
Disabled no special facilities
Pets no dogs in restaurant
Closed never
Proprietor Simone Simoni

Tuscany

Country villa, Fiesole

Villa San Michele

According to its brochure the Villa San Michele was designed by Michelangelo – which perhaps accounts in part for the high prices. Rooms here cost roughly the same as a five-star hotel in central London and only a fraction less than the San Michele's more swanky sister, the Cipriani in Venice. Prices like these are difficult to justify; but the guide would be incomplete without this little gem on the peaceful hillside of Fiesole. The villa was originally a monastery, built in the early part of the 15thC and substantially enlarged towards the end of it.

The views from the villa are exceptional. One of the great delights of the place is to lunch or dine *al fresco* in the loggia, gazing down slopes of olives and cypresses to the city below.

There is nothing extravagant about the decoration. The elegance of the public rooms is very discreet, and for the price some of the bedrooms seem surprisingly unluxurious, with solid antique furniture and tiled floors. But the bathrooms are appropriately impressive (most have jacuzzis), and the simple, almost rustic elegance is part of the charm. If a luxury room is a priority, you can always opt for one of the distinguished suites.

The latest addition to the hotel is a panoramic pool whose terraces overlook the gardens and city below.

Nearby Roman theatre, cathedral and monastery of San Francesco at Fiesole.

Via Doccia 4, Fiesole 50014
Tel (055) 59451
Location on Florence-Fiesole road, in private grounds with car parking available
Food & drink breakfast, lunch, dinner
Prices DB&B L330,000-L560,000
Rooms 24 double, 2 single, and 2 suites; all with bath and shower; all rooms have central heating, air-conditioning, music, phone; TV and minibar on request
Facilities reading-room/bar, piano bar, dining-room with loggia/terrace; heated swimming-pool
Credit cards AE, DC, MC, V
Children accepted
Disabled access difficult
Pets small dogs accepted, but not in dining-room
Closed mid-Nov to mid-Mar
Manager Maurizio Saccani

Tuscany

Country villa, Candeli

Grand Hotel Villa la Massa

The three villas making up this sumptuous (and expensive) hotel date from the 17thC – and the old dungeons now serve as the piano bar and discothèque. Bedrooms are the height of luxury, combining antique-style furniture with modern high-quality fabrics. Public rooms have a formal atmosphere, particularly the rather grand room beyond reception, with its lofty ceiling, pillars and arches, and the ornate bar to one side. More relaxing is the riverside restaurant, where you can dine outside at elegantly laid tables.

Nearby Florence (7 km).

Via La Massa 6, Candeli, Florence 50010
Tel (055) 630051
Location 7 km E of Florence, on bend of Arno in extensive grounds with abundant car parking
Food & drink breakfast, lunch, dinner
Prices rooms L198,000-L452,000; DB&B L253,000-L275,000
Rooms 32 double, 3 single, 6 suites; all with bath; all rooms have central heating, air-conditioning, colour TV, minibar, phone
Facilities dining-room, bar, piano bar, sitting-room; tennis, swimming-pool
Credit cards AE, DC, MC, V
Children accepted
Disabled no special facilities
Pets not accepted in dining-room **Closed** never
Manager Carlo Grillini

Converted castle, Gaiole in Chianti

Castello di Spaltenna

The Castello sits romantically at the top of a hill above Gaiole, a group of ancient rustic buildings in green surroundings. Beyond a grassy courtyard is the high-ceilinged dining-room – impressively medieval, with huge beams and gallery. Candles and a log fire at one end contribute further to the atmosphere. The bedrooms are spacious, with simple antique furniture; if planning a visit late or early in the year, be warned that there is no heating in them at all. Sadly, the new British proprietor has raised prices considerably – and introduced what a reporter calls 'over-ambitious, nouvelle-cosmopolitan cuisine'.

Nearby Siena (28 km), Arezzo (56 km), Florence (69 km).

Gaiole in Chianti 53013 Siena
Tel (0577) 749483
Location on hilltop close to middle of Gaiole, 28 km NE of Siena
Food & drink breakfast, lunch, dinner
Prices rooms L120,000-L200,000; meals L40,000-L60,000
Rooms 15 double (2 twin), all with bath and shower; all rooms have phone, TV, minibar
Facilities dining-room, 2 sitting-rooms, wine bar, terrace bar; swimming-pool
Credit cards AE, DC, MC, V
Children welcome
Disabled no special facilities
Pets accepted, with small charge
Closed mid-Jan to Feb
Proprietor Seamus de Pentheny O'Kelly

Tuscany

Converted castle, Leccio

Castello di Sammezzano

Once a princely Renaissance residence, the Castello was rebuilt in the mid-1850s by the eccentric Marquis of Aragona. The exotic first-floor apartments and hallways are stunning: every inch of wall and ceiling is decorated with Saracen, Arabic or Indian motifs. Bedrooms are less lavish and the downstairs public rooms are restrained and simple in comparison. The main area is the dining-room, which is cool-trattoria-style. Meals draw on the produce of the castle farm. The huge park, planted with exotic shrubs and trees, is open to the public.

Nearby walks in the park; Florence (half-hour drive); Arezzo, Siena within reach.

Leccio, Rignano sull'Arno 50067 Florence
Tel (055) 8657911
Location in town, 10 km S of Pontassieve, 30 km SE of Florence; in huge park with ample car parking space
Food & drink breakfast, lunch, dinner
Prices rooms L145,000-L195,000
Rooms 15 double, 5 with bath, 10 with shower; all rooms have central heating, minibar, TV, sitting-room, phone
Facilities dining-room, sitting area, bar
Credit cards AE, DC, MC, V
Children accepted
Disabled access difficult
Pets not accepted
Closed never
Proprietor Narciso Brunori

Country villa, Lucca

Villa la Principessa

La Principessa was once occupied by the last Dukes of Bourbon-Parma and still has a somewhat French feel in the furnishings and the formal park. The bedrooms have bold colour schemes and modern comforts, the public rooms rather more character – notably the grand central sitting-room, with its painted beams, and rugs on a marble floor. The restaurant is elegant but relatively informal, the food excellent. The pool, behind the house, is a pleasant place to relax. With easy access from Pisa airport, La Principessa makes a comfortable base, ideal for those who want to be looked after by English-speaking staff.

Nearby Pisa (18 km).

Massa Pisana, Lucca 55050
Tel (0583) 370037
Location 4 km S of Lucca on SS12r towards Pisa
Food & drink breakfast, lunch, dinner
Prices rooms L190,000-L360,000; meals from L45,000
Rooms 32 double, 5 single, 5 suites; all with bath or shower; all rooms have phone, air-conditioning, TV
Facilities sitting-room, bar, TV room, breakfast room, dining-room, banquet and congress room; outdoor swimming-pool
Credit cards AE, DC, MC, V
Children accepted **Disabled** no special facilities **Pets** small dogs accepted, but not allowed in restaurant
Closed early Jan to mid-Feb; restaurant only, Wed
Proprietor Sg M G Mugnani

Tuscany

Converted castle, Monte San Savino

Castello di Gargonza

Gargonza is not so much a castle as a whole village, perfectly preserved in a typically Tuscan landscape, surrounded by cypresses. The various houses, each with its own character and name (the farmer's house, the guard's house, Lucia's house) are let individually, some on a long-term basis, but usually by the week. Mostly dating from the 18thC, they have been restored and comfortably furnished. All have kitchens but there is also a restaurant just outside the walls (specialities include spinach and ricotta roulade and wild boar) and you can take breakfast in the old oil-pressing house ('il frantoio'). In the main guest-house ('la forestiera') you can stay for a few nights on bed-and-breakfast terms.

The English-speaking Count is both efficient administrator and charming host. Keen to preserve the sense of community in his village, he organizes concerts and other evening entertainment from time to time.

Nearby Arezzo (25 km); hills and vineyards of Chianti, Val di Chiana.

Gargonza, Monte San Savino 52048 Arezzo
Tel (0575) 847021
Location 35 km E of Siena on SS73, 7 km W of Monte San Savino; walled village of 18 houses with garden; ample car parking outside village walls
Food & drink breakfast, lunch, dinner
Prices rooms L80,000-L126,000 in main guest-house; meals L28,000-L35,000
Rooms 7 double in main guest-house; 30 double in 18 self-catering houses; all rooms have phone, central heating; main guest-house rooms have minibar
Facilities 4 sitting-rooms (2 available for meetings), TV room; ping-pong, bowls
Credit cards AE
Children accepted
Disabled not suitable
Pets small dogs only accepted
Closed Jan
Proprietor Conte Roberto Guicciardini

Tuscany

Villa le Barone

Le Barone, the attractive 16thC country house of the della Robbia family, became a hotel in 1976, and still feels very much like a private home. The bedrooms mostly contain antique furniture. There are always fresh flower arrangements in the elegant little sitting-rooms, and guests who are not out on sightseeing excursions have plenty of space to themselves in the peaceful garden or by the lovely pool. The minimum stay of three nights contributes to a low-key house-party atmosphere.

Nearby Siena (31 km), Florence (31 km).

Via San Leolino 19, Panzano in Chianti 50020 Siena
Tel (055) 852215
Location 31 km S of Florence off SS222; covered car parking
Food & drink breakfast, lunch, dinner
Prices DB&B L130,000-L150,000 (min 3 nights); reductions for children
Rooms 25 double, 20 with bath, 5 with shower; one single, with shower; 5 rooms have air-conditioning, 5 rooms have tea-makers
Facilities self-service bar, TV room, 3 sitting-rooms, dining-room, breakfast room; ping-pong, swimming-pool
Credit cards AE
Children welcome
Disabled not suitable
Pets not accepted
Closed Nov to Mar
Proprietor Marchesa Franca Viviani della Robbia

Il Convento

A converted monastery in the verdant hills of Pistoia sounds like quite a find. Inside, Il Convento is not all that you might expect – bedrooms are uncompromisingly modern, with the emphasis firmly on efficient facilities rather than on individual character. But the public rooms are more in sympathy with their surroundings – particularly the restaurant, where the cells have been converted into tiny, intimate dining-rooms, and the food and wines (many of them vintage) are above average. Service is always smiling and professional, but what impresses visitors most is the delightfully peaceful setting, and the glorious views down to Pistoia from the lush garden.

Nearby sights of Pistoia; Prato, Florence within reach.

Via San Quirico 33, Pontenuovo, Pistoia 51100
Tel (0573) 452652
Location 4 km E of Pistoia in Pontenuovo area, on hillside overlooking city; with car parking space
Food & drink breakfast, lunch, dinner
Prices rooms L63,000-L95,000
Rooms 20 double, 4 single; all with bath; all rooms have central heating, phone
Facilities dining-room, sitting-area, bar, games room; swimming-pool
Credit cards MC, V
Children accepted
Disabled access difficult
Pets not accepted
Closed restaurant only, Mon
Proprietor Paozo Petrini

Near Florence

Country villa, Pistoia

Villa Vannini

Here is a real little gem, lying in an area which has surprisingly few small, charming places to stay – in a remote and delightfully quiet setting, high on a hill about 2 km above the small village of Piteccio and not far from the lively little city of Pistoia. To get there, you wind your way up a narrow, roughly surfaced road through unspoiled countryside. The congenial Signora Vannini offers a particularly warm welcome, and looks after her house with loving care. There are various little sitting areas with large vases of flowers, chintz or chunky modern seats, prints and water-colours, and the sort of antiques that complete an elegant family home. The dining-room, with its whitewashed walls, polished parquet floor and marble fireplace, makes an elegant setting for the excellent Tuscan specialities that are served here.

Bedrooms are beautifully and individually furnished – many of them in flowery fabrics and with fine antiques.

In front of the house a simple terrace provides a haven after a hard day's sightseeing in Florence, Lucca or even Bologna.

Sadly, we have to report that a recent visitor was double-booked by Signora Vannini. Even if you have a confirmed reservation, get there early.

Nearby cathedral, Ospedale del Ceppo and church of Sant' Andrea at Pistoia.

Villa di Piteccio, Pistoia
51030 Pistoia
Tel (0573) 42031
Location 6 km N of Pistoia on hillside, in private garden, with car parking
Food & drink breakfast, lunch, dinner
Prices rooms L60,000; DB&B L55,000
Rooms 6 double, 3 with bath, one with shower; 3 single, all with bath
Facilities 2 sitting-rooms, games room, 2 dining-rooms
Credit cards AE (surcharge)
Children not very suitable
Disabled no special facilities
Pets not accepted
Closed never
Proprietor Maria-Rosa Vannini

Tuscany

Country hotel, Radda in Chianti

Relais Fattoria Vignale

This is a rare example of the hotel-guide editor's dream: an exquisite new establishment, so far entirely undiscovered by rival publications. Our inspector, who was touring Chianti in 1987, came upon it by chance and was immediately captivated by the taste and style with which this manor-house has been converted to a hotel.

The house is built on a slope down from the middle of the village. On the main 'ground' floor are four interconnecting sitting-rooms, each on a domestic scale and beautifully furnished with comfy sofas, antiques, muted rugs on polished terracotta floors, walls either white and dotted with paintings or covered by murals – and one or two grand stone fireplaces. The bedrooms above are similarly classy, with waxed wooden doors, white walls, antique beds.

There is a neat breakfast-room in a brick vault beneath the hotel, where an excellent buffet is set out, and coffee and extras are served by friendly waitresses. The proprietors have arranged for the best-known local restaurant (300 m away) to operate under the Vignale name, and will make reservations for you.

Back bedrooms, some of the sitting-rooms and the moderate-sized pool all share a grand view across the Radda valley.

Nearby Siena, Florence, Arezzo all within reach.

Via Pianigiani 15, Radda in Chianti 53017 Siena
Tel (0577) 738300
Location in middle of village, 31 km N of Siena, with private gardens and ample car parking
Food & drink breakfast, snacks
Prices rooms L110,000-L200,000
Rooms 17 double, 2 with bath, 15 with shower; 4 single, all with shower; 3 family rooms, 2 with bath, one with shower; all rooms have central heating, phone
Facilities 3 sitting-rooms, breakfast room, indoor and pool bars, 2 conference rooms
Credit cards AE, V
Children accepted, but prefer quiet ones
Disabled access difficult
Pets not accepted
Closed Jan to mid-Mar
Manager Silvia Kummer

Tuscany

Country villa, Rigoli

Villa di Corliano

A sweeping, tree-lined drive leading through lawns with lofty palms to a fine late Renaissance mansion set against thickly wooded hills; then, an interior no less splendid – frescoes embellishing every inch of wall and ceiling, handsome classical busts on ornate stands, antiques, chandeliers and, from the 16thC salon and its balcony, a beautiful view of the sloping lawns below. Ruinously expensive? For once, no: all this comes for less than you pay for some seedy station hotel in Pisa.

The bedrooms are not quite so grand, which accounts for the ludicrously cheap prices. In fact the cheapest are bordering on the basic, with a basin and portable bidet (hidden discreetly behind decorative screens), creaky beds and possibly a long walk to the public bathroom. But there is compensation in the sheer size of the bedrooms (most are huge, with big 1920s wardrobes). The best doubles have touches of grandeur, and their own bathrooms; and the only rooms that could be described as small are the three in the 'tower' at the top.

The old cellars serve as the breakfast room, where framed awards and the colossal terracotta urn are clues to the basis of the 19thC success of the estate: top-quality olive oil.
Nearby Pisa (10 km), Lucca (15 km).

Rigoli, San Giuliano Terme
56010 Pisa
Tel (050) 818193
Location 2.5 km NW of San Giuliano Terme at Rigoli; in large park with ample car parking
Food & drink breakfast
Prices rooms L63,000-L96,000
Rooms 18 double, 6 with bath, 4 with shower; all rooms have central heating; 6 rooms have phone
Facilities sitting-rooms, bar, breakfast room, conference room
Credit cards V
Children accepted **Disabled** no special facilities **Pets** accepted **Closed** never
Proprietor Conte Ferdinando Agostini della Seta

Tuscany

Country hotel, San Gimignano

Pescille

Until 1987 the Pescille was difficult to recommend whole-heartedly. It is a rambling hilltop manor house a couple of miles out of San Gimignano, converted with great taste and care, and with sufficient diversions to keep you there all day if sightseeing seems too strenuous – and yet it has until now lacked a restaurant. This has been remedied in no uncertain fashion by the creation of a big, spanking-new dining-room, decorated in a cool, modern, grey-and-white style with cane chairs on a tiled floor. We saw it the day before it opened, and have not yet sampled the food – but it is reported to be 'excellent', and breakfast has traditionally been good.

Meanwhile, the hotel in general remains a peaceful and relaxing haven. The rustic terraced garden leading down to the vineyards beyond has plenty of secluded spots, while indoors there are several little sitting areas, trendily mixing smart modern furniture and antique agricultural clutter. Bedrooms are simple, stylish and moderately spacious, with enchanting views of open countryside or towards the distinctive skyline of San Gimignano. The pool is less than ideal – it has a raised lip about a foot high, which makes it seem utilitarian.

Nearby San Gimignano (3 km); Florence, Siena, Volterra, Pisa all within reach.

Localita Pescille, San Gimignano 53037 Siena
Tel (0577) 940186
Location 3 km SW of San Gimignano, in large gardens with private car parking
Food & drink breakfast, lunch, dinner
Prices rooms L51,800-L92,800
Rooms 28 double, 4 single, one family room; all with bath; all rooms have central heating, phone
Facilities sitting-room, TV room, breakfast room, 2 bars, dining-room; swimming-pool, tennis, bowls
Credit cards AE, DC, MC, V
Children accepted, provided they are quiet
Disabled access difficult
Pets not accepted
Closed Jan and Feb
Proprietors Gigli brothers

Tuscany

Bel Soggiorno

Just inside the walls of the extraordinary town of San Gimignano, the Bel Soggiorno is a simple hotel in a 13thC house. Inside it has mostly been unimaginatively modernized and there is little space or comfort, although on our last visit there were some improvements in progress. But despite these disadvantages, one major feature makes this the best-value base in town: the excellent food served in the attractive restaurant, with a wall of windows overlooking the hills and olive groves. The menu varies little; constant favourites are a creamy house risotto and pasta *all' lepre* (with hare sauce, a Tuscan speciality). Many of the ingredients come from a farm belonging to the owners, perhaps a factor in the surprisingly low prices.

Nearby sights of San Gimignano; Siena, Florence within reach.

Via San Giovanni 91, San Gimignano 53037 Siena
Tel (0577) 940375
Location inside Porto S Giovanni, at S end of town, park outside town gates
Food & drink breakfast, lunch, dinner
Prices rooms L57,000-L82,000; DB&B L64,000
Rooms 23 double, 2 single; all with bath; all rooms have central heating, phone
Facilities TV/sitting-room, bar, dining-room
Credit cards AE, DC, MC, V
Children accepted
Disabled not suitable
Pets not accepted
Closed mid-Oct to end Nov; restaurant only, Mon and mid-Jan to mid-Feb
Proprietors Gigli brothers

Leon Bianco

Directly opposite the Cisterna (page 107) in the main square of San Gimignano, the Leon Bianco is not so well known and has fewer pretensions (and no views to speak of), but it offers considerably better value. The receptionist may be watching TV, but the visitor's eye will be caught by the fresco on the wall behind her; pictures and antiques are dotted around the corridors; rooms are generally spacious, decorated with restraint and furnished with a bit of panache, and everything is spick and span. The bar/breakfast-room is neat, but apart from that there is only a small sitting area in reception.

Nearby Piazza del Duomo, civic museum, church of Sant' Agostino; Florence, Pisa, Volterra, Siena all within reach.

Piazza del Cisterna 13, San Gimignano 53037 Siena
Tel (0577) 941294
Location in main square
Food & drink breakfast
Prices rooms L51,000-L91,000
Rooms 20 double, 8 with bath, 12 with shower; 2 single with shower; 3 family rooms with shower; all rooms have phone
Facilities bar/breakfast room, sitting-room, terrace
Credit cards AE, DC, MC, V
Children accepted
Disabled no special facilities
Pets not accepted
Closed Jan and Feb
Proprietor Sg Galgani

Country hotel, San Gimignano

Le Renaie

A simple country hotel – built up over the years by the present owners from a simple bar and restaurant – which makes a respectable base for a few nights' stay. Outside, Le Renaie looks fairly unprepossessing: just a simple modern villa set back from a rural lane. Inside, it is cool and pretty with freshly painted walls, rattan furniture and traditional polished brick floors; bedrooms are spacious and immaculate, some with individual terraces. The restaurant, Da Leonetto, is a fairly sophisticated trattoria which is popular with locals and serves honest Tuscan fare; on fine days you can eat outside on the veranda. For most holidaymakers the chief attractions are the small swimming-pool, the tranquil location ('a guest can live peaceful hours or repose', promises the brochure) and the reasonable prices.

Nearby sights of San Gimignano; hills and vineyards of Chianti; Volterra, Siena, Florence within reach.

Localita Pancole, San Gimignano 53037 Siena
Tel (0577) 955044
Location 6 km N of San Gimignano, off road to Certaldo; private car parking
Food & drink breakfast, lunch, dinner
Prices rooms L45,000-L75,000; meals L20,000-L30,000
Rooms 24 double, 2 single; all with bath; all rooms have phone
Facilities hall, TV room, dining-room, bar; swimming-pool, tennis
Credit cards AE, DC, MC, V
Children accepted, but must be accompanied by parents at swimming-pool
Disabled access difficult
Pets accepted in bedrooms
Closed last 3 weeks Nov
Proprietor Leonetto Sabatini

Tuscany

Town hotel, San Gimignano

La Cisterna

This very well-known and indeed long-established hotel has three things in its favour: its position on the (virtually) car-free central square, the views away from the town shared by the two dining-rooms and some of the better bedrooms, and a splendid stone-arched sitting-room just off reception. In other respects it seemed to our inspector to be over-rated. The famous 14thC Loggia Rustica dining-room is certainly rustic but is crammed with too many tables. Service and cooking are satisfactory, but nothing more. And the worst bedrooms are very ordinary indeed.

Nearby Piazza del Duomo, civic museum, church of Sant' Agostino; Florence, Pisa, Volterra, Siena all within reach.

Piazza della Cisterna 24, San Gimignano 53037 Siena
Tel (0577) 940328
Location in middle of town, on main square; car park 200 m away
Food & drink breakfast, lunch, dinner
Prices rooms L52,500-L91,500; DB&B L71,000-L81,000
Rooms 40 double, 19 with bath, 21 with shower; 6 single, 2 with bath, 4 with shower; all rooms have central heating, phone
Facilities 2 dining-rooms, bar, 2 TV/reading-rooms
Credit cards AE, DC, MC, V
Children accepted
Disabled no special facilities
Pets accepted, but not in restaurant
Closed 10 Nov to 10 Mar
Proprietors Salvestrini family

Town villa, Siena

Villa Patrizia

We can imagine this plain-looking villa just to the north of central Siena making a truly excellent small hotel one day – the house has just a bit of aristocratic style, its setting in a small wooded garden (although uncomfortably close to the main road north) is relaxed and dignified, and the dining-room is pleasantly light, overlooking the garden along its length. (We're told another restaurant has been created in the 'Limonaia', too.) What it lacks is an appropriate sitting-room, and some character in the bedrooms, which are quite plush but sadly routine in their furnishings. Breakfast is an adequate self-service buffet.

Nearby sights of Siena, Chianti wine country.

Via Fiorentina 58, Siena 53100
Tel (0577) 50431
Location on N fringe of city, on road to Florence; private car parking
Food & drink breakfast, lunch, dinner
Prices rooms L200,000-L300,000
Rooms 32 double, all with bath and shower; all rooms have central heating, phone, minibar, TV
Facilities restaurant, dining-room/bar, sitting-room; outdoor swimming-pool, tennis
Credit cards AE, DC, MC, V
Children welcome **Disabled** no special facilities **Pets** small ones only and not accepted in dining-room **Closed** never
Manager Sg Broge

Tuscany

Town villa, Siena

Villa Scacciapensieri

This modest hilltop villa dating from the early 1900s has been in the Nardi family since it ceased to be a private house in the 1930s. In that time the tentacles of suburban Siena have reached out to surround it; but if the villa can no longer claim to be in the country it is certainly on the edge of it, and it is still a calm and gracious retreat from the bustle of the city.

The garden is a great asset – a neat, formal, flowery area in front of the house, and a more rustic area to the side including the swimming-pool and a leafy terrace where meals are served in summer. Inside, beyond the cool entrance hall, the dining-room is smartly traditional in style; the sitting-room is something of a disappointment, with modern furniture which is neither stylish nor comfortable – though in cooler weather there is the attraction of a roaring log fire in the grand modern fireplace. Bedrooms are spacious and solidly furnished, with views either of the roof-tops and towers of Siena or, in the opposite direction, of vineyards, olive groves and the hills beyond. Reports of the Tuscan and international cooking are consistently encouraging.

Nearby sights of Siena; Florence within reach.

Via di Scacciapensieri 10, Siena 53100
Tel (0577) 41442
Location 2 km NE of middle of city, on hill; in private gardens with car parking
Food & drink breakfast, lunch, dinner
Prices rooms L132,500-L250,000; 20% reduction for children under 6
Rooms 21 double, 13 with bath, 8 with shower; 6 single, 2 with bath, 4 with shower; 2 suites, both with bath; all rooms have central heating, minibar, colour TV, phone; 10 rooms have air-conditioning
Facilities dining-room, hall, bar, TV room; open air swimming-pool, tennis
Credit cards AE, DC, MC, V
Children welcome
Disabled lift/elevator
Pets small ones only accepted, but not allowed in public rooms or at pool
Closed Nov to Mar; restaurant only, Wed
Proprietors Emma, Riccardo and Emanuele Nardi

Tuscany

Converted monastery, Siena

Certosa di Maggiano

If you are looking for an exclusive but unostentatious hotel in Siena, this is probably it. La Certosa is a former Carthusian monastery – the oldest in Tuscany – secluded in a large park (yet only minutes from the enchanting old city) with just 14 bedrooms of which the majority are suites. Although it is extremely expensive, this is not a swanky place: the calm good taste, the atmosphere of a delightful country house and the discreet service appeal mainly to those in search of peace and privacy.

Meals are served in an exquisite dining-room, in the tranquil 14thC cloisters or under the arcades by the swimming-pool. Guests can help themselves to drinks in the book-lined library, play backgammon or chess in a little ante-room, or relax in the lovely sitting-room. Flower arrangements are just about everywhere and bowls of fresh fruit in the bedrooms add a personal touch. Bear in mind that exploration of Siena will have to be by taxi or bus – it's too far to walk, and parking is almost impossible in the centre. You may however, wish to stay put and enjoy the beauty of this place – you will have paid for the privilege after all.

Nearby sights of Siena; hills and vineyards of Chianti; San Gimignano, Florence, Arezzo within reach.

Via Certosa 82, Siena 53100
Tel (0577) 288180
Location 1 km SE of middle of city and Porta Romana; in gardens, with car parking opposite entrance and garage available
Food & drink breakfast, lunch, dinner
Prices rooms L160,000-L.530,000; meals about L80,000
Rooms 5 double, 9 suites; all with bath; all rooms have central heating, TV, phone, radio
Facilities dining-room, bar, library, sitting-room; tennis, heated outdoor swimming-pool, heli-port
Credit cards AE, DC, V
Children accepted
Disabled access possible – 3 rooms on ground floor
Pets accepted, but not allowed in public areas
Closed never
Manager Anna Recordati

Tuscany

Town guest-house, Siena

Palazzo Ravizza

We found the welcome *sotto* to say the least, but when you see your room and begin to let the Ravizza's atmosphere sink in, even the deadpan nature of the staff seems in keeping – and a recent visitor was received 'with great charm and good humour'. Owned by the same noble Siennese family for the past 200 years, it has been a hotel for most of this century (the card table was their undoing) and it positively oozes that elusive, faded charm which makes for a memorable stay.

Bedrooms vary – all are rather sombre – but the best have views over the Tuscan countryside, quirky pieces of period furniture, comfy beds and huge modern bathrooms (though awful bath towels, like table-cloths). Downstairs there is a little sitting area with bookshelves or the leather-bound visitors' books to browse through, as well as a large shady terrace (with a magnolia tree which is magnificent in spring) and a well-kept dining-room with ravishingly pretty ceilings. The food fits exactly – unpretentious but perfect home cooking (pasta in brodo, roast veal with artichokes, cold meats, lovely ice creams and so on). For breakfast there are croissants filled with apricot jam, a welcome change from the usually hard rolls on offer.

Nearby cathedral, Piazza del Campo.

Pian dei Mantellini 34,
Siena 53100
Tel (0577) 280462
Location inside city walls,
close to heart of city; public
car parking opposite
Food & drink breakfast,
optional picnic lunch, dinner
Prices DB&B L83,000
Rooms 25 double, 15 with
bath, 3 with shower; 2 single;
3 family rooms; all rooms
have central heating, phone

Facilities dining-room,
library, bar, garden terrace;
sightseeing mini-bus
Credit cards AE, DC, MC, V
Children welcome **Disabled**
level access to ground floor,
small lift/elevator to
bedrooms **Pets** small dogs
and cats only accepted
Closed restaurant only, Jan
and Feb
Proprietor Giovanni
Iannone

110

Tuscany

Restaurant with rooms, Strove

Casalta

Only a couple of miles from the San Luigi (below), but far removed in style and atmosphere, this tiny and intimate hotel is tucked away in the middle of the sleepy hilltop village of Strove. It is categorized as a restaurant with rooms by Michelin despite its civilized first-floor sitting-room. The restaurant is cool and relaxed – arches, white walls, tiled floor – and specializes in fish dishes, though we can also recommend the spicy *pasta Strovese* and the *gnochetti*. Bedrooms, reached via corridors off the sitting-room, are confidently simple: bare floors, brass bedsteads, smart little bathrooms. The gently good-humoured *padrone* oversees the whole operation with an eagle eye.

Nearby Colle Val d'Elsa (7 km), Siena (16 km), San Gimignano (15 km), Volterra (37 km), Florence (45 km).

Strove 53035 Siena
Tel (0577) 301002
Location 4 km SW of Monteriggioni
Food & drink breakfast, lunch (Sat and Sun only), dinner
Prices rooms L36,500-L78,000; DB&B L64,000
Rooms 8 double, one single, one family room, all with bath and shower; all rooms have central heating
Facilities dining-room, sitting-room; tennis
Credit cards not accepted
Children accepted **Disabled** no special facilities **Pets** not accepted **Closed** mid-Nov to Feb; restaurant Wed
Proprietor Sg Cellerai

Country hotel, Strove

San Luigi Residence

The San Luigi earns its place here by offering a formula which suits families who want access both to the sights of Tuscany and to the kind of outdoor activities which appeal to children. It is a polished conversion of a sizeable old house and its outbuildings, which are separated by expansive lawns from a very big pool. With its adjacent restaurant, this can be a hubbub of activity – though there is plenty of space in which to escape from the fun and games if you want. Food is limited ('steak is the highlight').

Nearby Siena (25 km), Florence (52 km).

Via della Cerreta 38, Strove, Monteriggioni 53030 Siena
Tel (0577) 301055
Location 2 km W of Strove; in large park with private car parking
Food & drink breakfast, lunch, dinner
Prices rooms L200,000-L250,000; meals about L45,000
Rooms 43 apartments (for 2, 2-4, 2-5 people), all with bath or shower; all have central heating, kitchenette, fridge, dishwasher, phone, radio, TV
Facilities dining-room, bar, sitting areas; volley and basket ball, swimming-pool, tennis, sauna, 'boccia', table tennis
Credit cards AE, MC, V
Children welcome; separate pool and games **Disabled** ground-floor bedrooms **Pets** small animals accepted
Closed Nov to mid-Mar
Manager Carlo Prodi

Tuscany

Town villa, Sesto Fiorentino

Villa Villoresi

The aristocratic Villa Villoresi looks rather out of place in what is now an industrial suburb of Florence, but once in the house and gardens you suddenly feel a million miles away from modern, bustling Florence.

Contessa Clarissa Villoresi is a warm hostess who has captured the hearts of many transatlantic and other guests. It is thanks to her that the villa still has the feel of a private home – all rather grand, if a little faded – and reasonable prices.

You could spend hours just exploring the house. As you make you way through the building, each room seems to have some curiosity or feature of the past. The entrance hall is a superb gallery of massive chandeliers, frescoed walls, antiques and lofty potted plants. Then there are the beautiful frescoes on the first-floor landing, the family tree in reception, the sober looking Tuscan nobility in the dining-room, the leather-bound novels and back numbers of National Geographic magazine in the sitting-room. Bedrooms are remarkably varied – from the small and quite plain to grand apartments with frescoes and Venetian chandeliers. Some overlook an inner courtyard, others look out on to the pool and garden.

Half- or full-board terms at the Villa Villoresi are so reasonable they are hard to resist. Unfortunately the same cannot be said about the food.

Nearby Florence (8 km).

Via Ciampi 2, Colonnata di Sesto Fiorentino, Florence 50019
Tel (055) 443692
Location 8 km NW of Florence; adequate car parking; follow signs to Sesto Fiorentino from Florence, then turn right to Colonnata – hotel is signposted from bridge
Food & drink breakfast, lunch, dinner
Prices rooms L113,000-L190,000, suites L270,00; DB&B L140,000-L180,000;
dinner L45,000
Rooms 18 double, 3 single, 7 suites, all with bath or shower; all rooms have central heating, phone
Facilities sitting-rooms, bar, dining-room, veranda; swimming-pool, ping-pong
Credit cards AE, DC, V
Children welcome
Disabled no special facilities
Pets not accepted in public rooms
Closed never
Proprietor Contessa Clarissa Villoresi

Tuscany

Country hotel, Volterra

Villa Nencini

Volterra is a severely impressive hilltop town in glorious, sweeping hill country to the west of Chianti. The Villa Nencini, in contrast, is anything but severe – a captivating, mellow stone house not far outside the town walls, with a jolly garden and long views. Bedrooms are compact but simply smart and light, and there is a neat breakfast room. The *padrone* likes to play it cool, but is easily disarmed by smiles or any sign of interest in his house, of which he is naturally proud. Readers report favourably on the rooms, service and breakfast.

Nearby Siena and San Gimignano within easy reach.

Borgo Santo Stefano 55,
Volterra 56048 Pisa
Tel (0588) 86386
Location outside city walls, in small park about 500 m from heart of city, with private car parking
Food & drink breakfast
Prices rooms L40,000-L82,000
Rooms 13 double, 10 with shower; one single with shower; all rooms have central heating, phone; TV on request
Facilities sitting-room with bar, TV room, hall, terrace, breakfast room
Credit cards MC, V
Children welcome
Disabled no special facilities
Pets small ones only
Closed never
Proprietor Mario Nencini

Country villa, Trespiano

Villa le Rondini

The great attraction of this villa is its secluded grounds and their beautiful views of the city and Arno valley. The hotel dates back to the 16thC though it looks quite new. There are three buildings; some of the rooms in the main house are exceptionally spacious and beautifully furnished in traditional style, some of those in the annexes are rather simpler. The main sitting-room is split-level, providing two comfortable areas where beams and an antique fireplace lend an old-fashioned atmosphere. It is a pity that the food could be better.

Nearby walks in the park.

Via Bolognese Vecchia 224,
Florence 50139
Tel (055) 400081
Location 7 km N of Florence; in park with ample car parking
Food & drink breakfast, lunch, dinner, snacks
Prices rooms L83,500-L130,500; suites L208,500
Rooms 39 double, 2 suites, all with bath or shower; 4 single, one with bath, one with shower; all rooms have central heating, minibar, phone
Facilities 4 sitting-rooms, 2 bars, piano bar, restaurant, TV room, 4 conference rooms; fashion shows, illuminated tennis court, swimming-pool, sauna, gym
Credit cards AE, DC, MC, V
Children accepted if well behaved **Disabled** no special facilities **Pets** accepted
Closed never
Proprietor Francesca Reali

Tuscany

Country inn, Sinalunga

Locanda dell'Amorosa

The Locanda dell'Amorosa is as romantic as it sounds. An elegant Renaissance villa-cum-village, within the remains of 14thC walls, has been converted into a charming country inn. The old stables, beamed and brick-walled, have been transformed into a delightful rustic restaurant serving refined versions of traditional Tuscan recipes, using ingredients from the estate, which also produces wine. The restaurant, which has earned the coveted array of chefs' hats in several Italian guides, can serve up to 80 people and is often full.

Only a fortunate few can actually stay at the Locanda – either in apartments in the houses where peasants and farmworkers once lived, or in ordinary bedrooms in the old family residence. The bedrooms we saw were cool, airy and pretty, with white-washed walls, wood-block floors, wrought-iron beds and flowery cotton curtains and bedspreads – and immaculate bathrooms. To complete the village there is a little parish church with lovely 15thC frescoes of the Sienese school. The Locanda is a paradise for connoisseurs of Tuscany, for gourmets and for all romantics.

Nearby Siena (45 km), Arezzo (45 km); Chianti wine country.

Sinalunga 53048 Siena
Tel (0577) 679497
Location 2 km S of Sinalunga; ample car parking
Food & drink breakfast, lunch, dinner
Prices rooms L290,000
Rooms 8 double, all with bath; all rooms have central heating, phone, colour TV, minibar

Facilities dining-room, sitting-room
Credit cards AE, DC, MC, V
Children accepted
Disabled access difficult
Pets not accepted
Closed mid-Jan to end Feb; restaurant only, Mon, Tue midday
Proprietor Carlo Citterio

Florence

Town hotel, near the station

Alba

A complete renovation in 1985 transformed the Alba into a spruce new hotel. The Via della Scala is not one of the most desirable streets of the city but it is handy for the station and only a few minutes' walk from the heart of the city. The bedrooms have all been entirely modernized and equipped with bathrooms and double glazing. Downstairs the main public area is the prettily decorated breakfast-room. The building may be short on charm, but the reception is smiling and friendly – which is more than can be said for many nearby hotels.

Nearby church of Santa Maria Novella (three minutes' walk); duomo (ten minutes' walk).

Via della Scala 22-38,
Florence 50123
Tel (055) 211469
Location on busy street,
about 2 minutes from
station; car parking awkward
Food & drink breakfast
Prices rooms L85,500-
L135,000
Rooms 20 double, 4 single;
all with bath or shower; all
rooms have air-conditioning,
central heating, double
glazing, phone, TV, minibar
Facilities breakfast room/
bar, TV room
Credit cards MC, V
Children accepted
Disabled not suitable
Pets not accepted
Closed never
Proprietors Caridi family

Town guest-house, near the Boboli gardens

Annalena

This 15thC *palazzo* is one of those typically Florentine places where you ring a bell and a large creaky door slowly opens to let you in to a courtyard. A wide flight of stone stairs brings you to the first floor where reception, breakfast room and sitting-room are all combined in a huge, high-ceilinged hall filled with fine antiques, paintings and sculpture. Bedrooms lead off white-washed galleries of drawings and prints; the majority are spacious and handsomely furnished with solid antiques or painted furniture, but otherwise quite simple.

Nearby Pitti Palace, Boboli Gardens, church of Santo Spirito

Via Romana 34, Florence
50125
Tel (055) 222402
Location S of the Arno, on
fairly busy street; several
paying garages in the vicinity
Food & drink breakfast
Prices rooms L82,500-
L128,500
Rooms 17 double, 3 single;
all with bath or shower; all
rooms have central heating,
phone
Facilities breakfast and
sitting area, bar
Credit cards AE, DC, MC, V
Children accepted
Disabled no special facilities
Pets dogs and small animals
accepted
Closed never
Proprietors Salvestrini and
Salimbeni families

Florence

Aprile

The station area of Florence is liberally endowed with hotels but there are few with any charm. The Aprile is one of the exceptions, converted from a 15thC Medici palace and retaining original, well kept features such as frescoes, and vaulted and painted ceilings. Downstairs there are chandeliers and indeed a few old master reproductions, but the hotel as a whole is unpretentious, and some of its bedrooms are surprisingly simple and in need of decoration. They vary from large (sometimes rather gloomy) rooms with antiques, through light, flowery rooms with painted furniture to simple modern ones with basic fittings. Back rooms away from the busy street are definitely to be preferred.

Nearby church of Santa Maria Novella.

Via della Scala 6,
Florence 50123
Tel (055) 216237
Location close to Piazza
Santa Maria Novella and
station, on fairly busy street
with no car parking facilities
Food & drink breakfast
Prices rooms L77,000-
L117,000
Rooms 25 double, 21 with

bath or shower; 4 single, one
with bath; all rooms have
central heating, phone; some
have minibar
Facilities breakfast room,
bar/sitting-room, patio
Credit cards AE, MC, V
Children accepted **Disabled**
access difficult **Pets** accepted
Closed never
Proprietor Valeria Cantini

Cestelli

Only a tiny plaque on the front door reveals that this typically Florentine *palazzo* contains a hotel. Once inside, first impressions are not good. But after you have climbed two rather gloomy flights of stone stairs confidence is restored by the delightful little entrance hall, furnished with immaculate small antiques and a few lovingly kept curiosities. This is a family hotel, run with great pride like a home by Signora Ada Cestelli.

The bedrooms range from a huge high-ceilinged room with big antiques, candelabra and sofa, down to the simple and slightly shabby – but none is without character. There is only one private bathroom, but prices are remarkably low. Book six months ahead to be sure of a room.

Nearby Ponte Vecchio, Uffizi Gallery, Palazzo Strozzi, Duomo.

Borgo SS Apostoli 25,
Florence 50123
Tel (055) 214213
Location in heart of city,
close to Piazza della Signoria;
car parking awkward
Food & drink breakfast
Prices rooms L30,000-
L58,000
Rooms 6 rooms, one with
bath

Facilities tiny breakfast
room
Credit cards not accepted
Children not very suitable
Disabled not suitable
Pets accepted
Closed never
Proprietor Ada Cestelli

Florence

Town hotel, north of the *Duomo*

Loggiato dei Serviti

One of Florence's newest charming hotels is in one of its loveliest Renaissance buildings, designed (around 1527) by Sangallo the Elder to match Brunelleschi's famous Hospital of the Innocenti, which stands opposite. Until a few years ago the arcades were dilapidated, the building housed a modest *pensione* and the beautiful square was a giant car park. But, thanks to the loving restoration of the Budini-Gattai family, the Loggiato is now an elegant place to stay and, thanks to the city council's change of heart, it is also one of the most tranquil in Florence.

The decoration is a skilful blend of old and new, all designed to complement the original vaulting and other features with a minimum of frill and fuss. Floors are terracotta tiled, walls rag painted in pastel colours. Furniture and paintings are mostly, but not exclusively, old. There is a small, bright breakfast room in which to start the day (with fruit juice, cheese and ham, brioches, fruit and coffee) and a little bar where you can recover from it, browsing glossy Italian magazines and sipping a Campari and soda.

Sadly, one visitor felt misled by our description, complaining of dirty rooms and unhelpful staff. However, others have been quite happy. More reports please.

Nearby church of Santissima Annunziata and Foundlings' Hospital; duomo, church of San Marco, Accademia gallery.

Piazza SS Annunziata 3, Florence 50122
Tel (055) 219165
Location a few minutes' walk N of the Duomo, on W side of Piazza SS Annunziata; garage service on request
Food & drink breakfast
Prices rooms L95,000-L150,000
Rooms 19 double, 9 with bath, 10 with shower; 6 single, all with shower; 4 suites, all with bath; all rooms have phone, minibar, piped music; colour TV on request
Facilities breakfast room, bar
Credit cards AE, DC, MC, V
Children welcome
Disabled not suitable
Pets accepted
Closed never
Proprietor Rodolfo Budini-Gattai

Florence

Town hotel, west of the station

Ariele

Lovers of music are likely to appreciate the location of this pleasant small hotel: it lies just a stone's throw from the Teatro Communale – main Florentine venue for concerts, opera and ballet. It is so close, in fact, that you can sometimes hear the music when you are sitting in the small garden of the hotel. Inside, the Ariele has the charm of a private Florentine home, with modestly elegant public rooms and a friendly, distinctly Italian atmosphere. Bedrooms are somewhat spartan, but any lack of furnishings is outweighed by more than ample space and very reasonable prices.

Nearby Teatro Communale (concerts, opera etc), banks of river Arno; historic heart of city about 15 minutes' walk.

Via Magenta 11, Florence 50123
Tel (055) 211509
Location between station and the Arno, about one km W of *Duomo*; with private garden and car parking
Food & drink breakfast
Prices rooms L70,000-L101,000
Rooms 36 double, 4 single, all with bath or shower; all rooms have central heating
Facilities breakfast room, 4 sitting-rooms, bar, terrace
Credit cards AE, MC, V
Children accepted
Disabled lift-elevator
Pets accepted
Closed never
Proprietors Bartelloni family

Town hotel, north of the Ponte Vecchio

Hermitage

Everything about the Hermitage is small-scale, like a doll's house – only upside down, with the old-fashioned bedrooms on the lower floors while the reception desk and public rooms are on the fifth floor, with views of the Arno. Right at the top is the charming roof terrace, with more wonderful views and overflowing with greenery and flowers. The place does not have a period look, but it has a definitely Forsterian feel, and the owners are charming. The one drawback (common to many Florentine hotels) is noise from the night-time traffic on the Lungarno, though front bedrooms do have double glazing.

Nearby Uffizi gallery, Ponte Vecchio

Vicolo Marzio 1, Piazza del Pesce, Florence 50122
Tel (055) 287216
Location in heart of city, facing the river; car parking difficult
Food & drink breakfast, snacks
Prices rooms L96,000-L135,000
Rooms 20 double, 15 with bath, 3 with shower; 2 single with shower; all rooms have central heating, phone
Facilities breakfast room, sitting-room with bar, roof terrace
Credit cards not accepted
Children welcome
Disabled access difficult
Pets small dogs only
Closed never
Proprietors Vincenzo Scarcelli and Paolo Pietro

Florence

Ariele (see opposite)

Town villa, east of the *Duomo*

Monna Lisa

Despite other challengers, the Monna Lisa remains Florence's most charming small hotel – an unusual combination of comfort without pretention. Five minutes' walk from the *Duomo*, the Monna Lisa is an elegant Renaissance *palazzo* around a small courtyard set back from the unprepossessing street façade. The main rooms, on the ground floor, have polished brick floors with Oriental carpets and beamed or vaulted ceilings, plus a very individual collection of antique furniture, paintings and sculpture. In the cosy little salon is the first model for Giambologna's famous Rape of the Sabines, and there is also a collection of drawings and statues by Giovanni Dupre, the neo-classical sculptor, from whom the owner's family is descended. The best bedrooms are huge and high-ceilinged, with old furniture, although when we visited (a few years ago) some others seemed rather dark. The quietest rooms overlook the lovely garden, a rare bonus in Florence. The Monna Lisa is not cheap, but it is both a polished and a relaxing place to stay.

Nearby *Duomo* (about five minutes' walk), Santa Croce, Bargello, Uffizi all within easy walking distance.

Borgo Pinti 27, Florence 50121
Tel (055) 2479751
Location about 5 minutes' walk E of the Duomo; with garden and private car parking
Food & drink breakfast
Prices rooms L160,000-L230,000
Rooms 15 double, 5 single; all with bath or shower; all rooms have central heating, air conditioning, phone, minibar, colour TV
Facilities sitting-rooms, bar
Credit cards AE, DC, V
Children accepted
Disabled no special facilities
Pets accepted
Closed never
Manager Riccardo Sardei

Florence

Town guest-house, on the Arno

Rigatti

With its stone-arched entrance and heavy wooden doors, the Rigatti looks a cut above your average *pensione*, and so it is. It occupies the two upper floors of the 15thC Palazzo Alberti, and is furnished in sympathetically Florentine style throughout. Polished antiques stand on wood-block floors, gilt mirrors and portraits in oils hang on whitewashed walls, and the atmosphere is civilized without being formal: like her parents and grand-parents before her, the charming Signora di Benedetti and her brother-in-law (both of them now getting on in years) manage to preserve that elusive private-home feeling, despite the comings and goings of their international (largely English-speaking) clientele.

The bedrooms are comfortably but simply furnished; most are fair-sized, but some are on the small side. Most visitors, whether Forster fans or not, prefer A Room With A View, despite the noise from the traffic roaring along the riverside Lungarno (an undeniable drawback common to many central hotels in Florence). But the quieter rooms at the back overlook the court-yard garden and you can always enjoy the views from the roof-top terrace and from the tiny side terrace.

The Rigatti won't last forever: catch it while you can.

Nearby Uffizi gallery, Santa Croce, Ponte Vecchio, *Duomo* – all within easy walking distance.

Lungarno Generale Diaz 2, Florence 50122
Tel (055) 213022
Location on the Arno, a few minutes' walk E of the Ponte Vecchio; with river-view roof garden
Food & drink breakfast
Prices rooms L42,000-L81,000

Rooms 28 rooms, 14 with bath or shower
Facilities 3 sitting-rooms, breakfast room, terrace
Credit cards not accepted
Children accepted
Disabled no special facilities
Pets not accepted
Closed never
Proprietor Sga di Benedetti

Residenza (see opposite)

Florence

Liana

Via Alfieri lies a good 15 minutes' walk from the *Duomo* and it is not one of the most interesting parts of the city. But prices at the Liana are low in comparison to more central hotels, and the rooms are quieter. For a brief period in the late 19thC the building served as the British Embassy and there are still a few touches of grandeur about it, such as the painted ceiling in the breakfast-room. Bedrooms are a little gloomy and faded though the biggest rooms at the back (which include the Consul's Room) overlook a small garden belonging to the hotel. Breakfasts at the Liana are rather better than you expect from a simple hotel. You get ham, cheese and juice in addition to the usual coffee and rolls.

Nearby Duomo (15 minutes' walk).

Via Alfieri 18,
Florence 50121
Tel (055) 245303
Location 15 minutes E of duomo; car parking
Food & drink breakfast
Prices rooms L65,000-L79,000
Rooms 19 double, 8 with bath, 4 with shower; one single; 2 suites, one with bath, one with shower; all rooms have central heating, phone
Facilities breakfast room, reading-room
Credit cards AE, V
Children accepted
Disabled no special facilities
Pets small ones only accepted **Closed** never
Proprietor Sg Spina

Residenza

Despite its smart location, the Residenza is a good-value *pensione*; it occupies the top four floors of an old *palazzo* – reached by an old-fashioned, creaky lift. The sitting-room has blue velour sofas and potted plants, the simple dining room a cheerful array of wine bottles, jars and ceramics. There are pictures everywhere, some of them the work of guests. Bedrooms range from the rustic to the modern, all quite simple. Upper ones have their own sitting-room and a delightful terrace with a cluster of plants. Recent visitors suggest that the Residenza is less cosy than it once was, and now in need of redecoration.

Nearby Palazzo Strozzi, Palazzo Rucellai, church of Santa Trinita.

Via Tornabuoni 8,
Florence 50123
Tel (055) 284197
Location on smart central shopping street; private paying garage nearby
Food & drink breakfast, dinner
Prices B&B L78,500-L120,500; DB&B L95,250-L113,500
Rooms 18 double, 11 with bath, 6 with shower; 7 single, one with bath, 3 with shower; all rooms have central heating, phone; 7 rooms have air-conditioning
Facilities sitting-room, bar, dining-room, roof terrace
Credit cards AE, DC, V
Children accepted
Disabled no special facilities
Pets small, friendly ones accepted **Closed** never
Proprietor Giovanna Vasile

Florence

Town guest-house, south of the Ponte alle Grazie

Silla

Set back from the south bank of the Arno in a relatively quiet position, the Silla is a solid Florentine *palazzo* with a handsome inner courtyard. But what really distinguishes it from other *pensioni* is its spacious terrace where you can take drinks under the shade of gaily coloured parasols and enjoy river views. Reception (where recent visitors have had a 'very friendly' welcome) has some pretty Venetian 18thC furnishings, while the breakfast room is simply decorated with copper pots and ceramics. Bedrooms, with dark walnut furniture and flowery tapestries, provide adequate comfort and good value.

Nearby Santa Croce, Uffizi, Ponte Vecchio, Pitti Palace all within walking distance.

Via dei Renai 5,
Florence 50125
Tel (055) 2342888 84810
Location on left bank of Arno, near Ponte alla Grazie; small private garage
Food & drink breakfast
Prices rooms L59,300-L103,500
Rooms 18 double, 6 with bath, 8 with shower; 4 single, 3 with shower; 10 family rooms, 6 with bath, 3 with shower; all rooms have central heating, TV, phone
Facilities breakfast room, reading-room, bar, large terrace
Credit cards AE, DC, MC, V
Children accepted if under supervision of parents
Disabled no special facilities
Pets small ones only accepted
Closed 2 weeks Dec
Proprietor Avellino Silla

Town guest-house, south of Ponte Vecchio

Pitti Palace

A popular Florentine *pensione*, run by the very helpful Amedeo Pinto and his friendly American wife. The main attractions are the pretty roof terrace and elegant drawing room. Bedrooms vary from light and bright to plain and rather spartan (especially the singles) and almost all suffer from traffic noise – the price you pay for the convenient location just south of the Ponte Vecchio. In the entrance hall the English-speaking staff are always on hand to book taxis or lend guide-books; on the walls are signed photographs of famous guests and current lists of museum opening hours, and so on.

Nearby Pitti Palace and Boboli gardens, Ponte Vecchio, Uffizi.

Via Barbadori 2,
Florence 50125
Tel (055) 282257
Location just beyond the S end of the Ponte Vecchio
Food & drink breakfast
Prices rooms L80,000-L120,000
Rooms 28 double, 22 with bath; 12 single, 6 with bath, one with shower; all rooms have central heating, phone
Facilities sitting-room, breakfast room, TV room
Credit cards AE, V
Children accepted
Disabled no special facilities
Pets accepted if well behaved
Closed never
Manager Amedeo Pinto

Florence

Town guest-house, in shopping district

Tornabuoni Beacci

Via Tornabuoni is one of the most desirable streets of Florence, renowned for the elegance of its shops, and the Tornabuoni Beacci is one of the most desirable hotels in the area.

The hotel used to be a *de luxe pensione* and it still has the feel of a family home rather than a hotel – largely due to the warm personality of Signora Beacci, who has run the place since 1954. In fact there has been a Beacci here since 1900 when her mother first established the hotel at a nearby location. The present hotel occupies the third and fourth floors of a fine old *palazzo*.

The rather gloomy ground floor entrance gives no hint of the charming interior of the hotel, where prints and paintings, patterned carpets on wood block floors and classic antiques all create an elegant, yet welcoming atmosphere. The sitting-room is exceptionally comfortable and well furnished – the sort you rarely find in a small central city hotel. The bedrooms are comfortable and classically furnished. And there is a delightful roof-top terrace, cluttered with potted plants, flowers, creepers and tables where you can have breakfast or evening drinks.

The volumes of visitors' books, which date back to the 1920s, are full of glowing praise from famous travellers who have been captivated by this little 'home from home' hotel.

Nearby Palazzo Strozzi, Palazzo Rucellai, church of Santa Trinita.

Via Tornabuoni 3, Florence 50123
Tel (055) 268377
Location at N end of busy central street, with car parking in paying garage
Food & drink breakfast, lunch, dinner
Prices DB&B L105,000-L240,000
Rooms 21 double, 18 with bath or shower; 10 single, 7 with bath or shower; all rooms have central heating, air-conditioning, minibar, phone; colour TV in some rooms
Facilities sitting-room, bar, restaurant, roof terrace
Credit cards AE, DC, V
Children accepted **Disabled** lift/elevator **Pets** accepted
Closed never
Proprietor Sga Beacci

Florence

Villa Belvedere

This modern house with modern furnishings might be anywhere in Europe – except that it stands on a peaceful hillside giving unsurpassed views across Florence. Everything is spotlessly clean and well cared for, with light, sunny rooms and plenty of potted plants and freshly cut flowers. All bedrooms except two have a full-size bath, and breakfast is taken in a glassed-in room overlooking the immaculate garden. The Ceschi-Perotto family extend a warm welcome.

Nearby Pitti Palace, Boboli gardens.

Via Benedetto Castelli 3, Florence 50124
Tel (055) 222501
Location 3 km S of city, in gardens with some private car parking
Food & drink breakfast, snacks
Prices rooms L140,000-L210,000
Rooms 24 double, 22 with bath, 2 with shower; 3 single, 2 with bath, one with shower; all rooms have central heating, air-conditioning, phone, colour TV, safe
Facilities breakfast room, 2 sitting-rooms, bar, TV room, veranda; swimming-pool, tennis
Credit cards AE, DC, MC, V
Children welcome
Disabled no special facilities
Pets not accepted
Closed Dec to Mar
Proprietors Ceschi-Perotto family

Splendor

Many of the *pensioni* in central Florence have become so expensive that they are now beyond the means of the average tourist. The Splendor, north of the *Duomo* and close to the Accademia, is a happy exception. It occupies part of a typically Florentine rusticated building. Painted ceilings, frescoes and antiques are part of its appeal, though modern seating and other newer additions are not altogether sympathetic to their surroundings. Perhaps the most charming feature of all is the terrace with its cluster of potted plants. The bedrooms are remarkably varied – some with chandeliers and painted furniture, others with modern vinyl and no atmosphere – but the majority are large.

Nearby church of San Marco, Accademia gallery.

Via San Gallo 30, Florence 50129
Tel (055) 483427
Location 50 m from Piazza San Marco; car parking in paying garage or on street
Food & drink breakfast
Prices rooms L60,000-L95,000.
Rooms 25 double, 16 with bath or shower; 6 single, all rooms have central heating
Facilities sitting-room, 2 breakfast rooms, terrace
Credit cards not accepted
Children accepted **Disabled** access difficult **Pets** accepted if small and well behaved
Closed never
Proprietor Masoero Vincenzo

Florence

Town villa, south of Boboli gardens

Villa Carlotta

A gracious 19thC patrician house, the Villa Carlotta was one of several mansions built on the south-east slopes of Florence in the days when they were almost open countryside. Today the villa stands on a quiet tree-lined street in a residential area.

The hotel has recently been upgraded to four stars and rooms have been revamped – but without sacrificing the oldest and finest features of the building. Moulded ceilings and stucco bas-reliefs in the forms of garlands and flower-filled baskets still embellish the public rooms. Oriental rugs and Tuscan furnishings (mainly reproduction antiques) create an elegant and impeccable setting. Bedrooms are furnished in sophisticated style with silk-like wall fabrics in blue or pink, wall-to-wall carpeting, woven floral bedspreads and linen sheets – plus of course all the extras you would expect in a four-star hotel. The rooms are delightfully quiet, overlooking the hills or the hotel's small garden.

Breakfast is copious, with fruit juice, yoghurts, porridge, cereal, eggs, bacon, cheese and ham – in addition to coffee, rolls and croissants. It is served in a glazed veranda – or in fine weather outside on the terrace, around the stone fountain.

Nearby Pitti Palace, Boboli Gardens, Piazzale Michelangelo.

Via Michele di Lando 3, Florence 50125
Tel (055) 220530
Location on SE side of city, close to Porta Romana on quiet street, with small garden and private garage
Food & drink breakfast, dinner
Prices rooms L127,000-L294,000
Rooms 17 double, 6 with bath, 11 with shower; 7 single, all with shower; 3 family rooms, all with bath; all rooms have central heating, air-conditioning, minibar, room safe, colour TV, phone
Facilities bar, sitting-rooms, 2 dining-rooms, breakfast room, conference room
Credit cards AE, DC, MC, V
Children accepted
Disabled access difficult
Pets small, clean ones accepted, except in dining-rooms
Closed never
Proprietor Evelina Pagni

Tuscan coast

Area introduction

Tuscan coast hotels

The Versilian Riviera begins its long sweep of resorts only a little way north-west of Lucca and Pisa, so the visitor to Tuscany should have no difficulty in combining sightseeing with seaside sunbathing. Finding notably welcoming places to stay is not so easy – although many of the better hotels in resorts such as Forte dei Marmi and Marina di Pietrasanta have attractive shady gardens, few have any other distinguishing features.

The Tuscan island of Elba is big enough to absorb the many summer visitors it attracts without being swamped in the way that some of the smaller and more southerly islands have been. We have one clear recommendation on the island, but in general Elba presents us with a problem, which is that its small hotels are, to be honest, less attractive than many of the bigger ones which cannot properly be given full entries here.

There is a handful of charming and comfortable (but not cheap) hotels with 60 to 100 rooms within a few miles of the port of arrival, Portoferraio. High in the hills to the south, with wonderful views from its terraces and pool, is the Picchiaie (Tel 0565 969932). Across the bay from Portoferraio, in leafy grounds close to the sea, is the polished Villa Ottone (Tel 0565 966042). In the opposite direction, to the west, is the excellent sandy beach of Biodola, shared by the delightful but expensive Hermitage (Tel 0565 969932), with most of its rooms in bungalows dotted among pines, and the more modest Biodola (Tel 0565 969966).

Resort village, Lacona, Elba

Capo Sud

More of a village than a hotel, the Capo Sud is a complex of little villas in a quiet, rather remote spot with plenty of activities on hand. Rooms are modern and quite simple, scattered among trees and 'macchia', none of them very far away from the focal area of the restaurant, bar, sitting-room and open-air terrace with fine views of the bay. The hotel has its own vineyard, and most fruit served here comes straight from the private orchards. There is a special weekly menu of dishes which are exclusive to the island.

Nearby Portoferraio (14 km).

Lacona, Portoferraio
57037 Livorno
Tel (0565) 964021
Location 11 km NW of Capoliveri on Golfo Stella, in grounds sloping down to sea; ample car parking
Food & drink breakfast, lunch, dinner
Prices rooms L40,000-L111,000; meals L40,000
Rooms 37 double, 2 with bath, 35 with shower; 2 single, both with shower; all rooms have phone; 20 rooms have minibar
Facilities TV room, bar, dining-room; beach, tennis, bowls, rowing, sailing, windsurfing
Credit cards DC
Children accepted
Disabled no special facilities
Pets not accepted
Closed Oct to Apr
Proprietor Enzo di Puccio

Tuscan coast

Converted castle, Giglio Porto

Castello Monticello

The pretty little island of Giglio (particularly its smart little port) attracts many day-trippers; but the island is also an attractive place to stay if good beaches are not your priority. Built as a private house in the style of a castle, the Castello Monticello lies on an unspoilt hillside. Perhaps it looks austere, but inside it is cosy and welcoming – more like a villa than a castle. Furnishings are relatively simple but any lack of luxury here is more than outweighed by the fine location. From the shady gardens, the terrace and most of the bedrooms there are splendid views of sea and coast.

Nearby Giglio Porto; Giglio Castello (4 km).

Via Provinciale per il Castello
Giglio Porto, Isola del Giglio
58013 Grosseto
Tel (0564) 809252
Location about 2 km from
port on hillside, with car
park
Food & drink breakfast,
lunch, dinner
Prices rooms L44,000-
L85,000
Rooms 27 double, 4 single,
and 6 family rooms, all with
shower; all rooms have
central heating, phone
Facilities dining-room,
breakfast room, bar, TV
room, terrace
Credit cards MC, V
Children accepted **Disabled**
no special facilities **Pets** not
in dining-room **Closed** mid-
Nov to mid-Mar
Manager Sergio Chiucini

Seaside hotel, Punta Ala

Piccolo Hotel Alleluja

Fine white sands bordered by pine woods, a variety of sports (including riding and an excellent 18-hole golf course) and a marina lure the wealthy from Florence, Milan and Rome to Punta Ala, to stay in second homes or in one of the four prestigious hotels. Of these, the Piccolo Alleluja is perhaps the most inviting. It is small, stylish and intimate, in surroundings of Mediterranean 'macchia', aromatic herbs, lawns, and flowering shrubs. Inside, rustic chic prevails. Designs and furnishings are simple, the colours are light and the atmosphere cheerful. Bedrooms are some with their own sitting-rooms.

Nearby Grosseto (41 km).

Punta Ala 58040 Grosseto
Tel (0564) 922050
Location near middle of
resort, 7 minutes from
private beach; with large
park and ample car parking
Food & drink breakfast,
lunch, dinner
Prices DB&B L130,000-
L250,000
Rooms 42 rooms, all with
bath or shower; all rooms
have air-conditioning,
phone, TV, minibar, radio
Facilities bar, 2 sitting-
rooms, bridge room;
restaurant/bar on beach;
swimming-pool, tennis
Credit cards AE, DC, MC, V
Children accepted
Disabled lift to first-floor,
but not wide enough for
some wheelchairs
Pets dogs not accepted
Closed never
Proprietor Renato Nutti

127

Tuscan coast

Seaside hotel, Porto Ercole

Il Pellicano

Porto Ercole is one of those fashionable little harbours where wealthy Romans moor their boats at weekends. Il Pellicano is a russet-coloured vine-clad villa with gardens tumbling down to the rocky shoreline, where the flat rocks have been designated the hotel's 'private beach'. It was built in the mid-1960s with only nine rooms. Today it has grown to over three times the size, and provides all the luxuries you might expect from a very expensive four-star seaside hotel. However, it manages at the same time to preserve the style of a private Tuscan villa – and the exposed beams, stone arches and antique features make it feel much older than it really is. Antique country-house furnishings are offset by whitewashed walls, brightly coloured stylish sofas and large vases of flowers.

Fish and seafood are the best things in the restaurant – if you can stomach the prices. Meals in summer are served on the delightful open-air terrace in the garden, or beside the pool where the spread of *antipasti* is a feast for the eyes.

Peaceful bedrooms, many of them in two- or three-storey cottages, combine antiques and modern fabrics. The majority are cool and spacious, and all of them have a terrace or balcony.
Nearby Orbetello (16 km).

Cala dei Santi,
Porto Ercole 58018 Grosseto
Tel (0564) 833801
Location 4 km from middle of resort, in own gardens overlooking the sea; private car parking
Food & drink breakfast, lunch, dinner
Prices rooms L230,000-L545,000; DB&B L185,000-L342,500; extra bed in room L85,000-L105,000
Rooms 30 double, 4 suites, all with bath, and shower; all rooms have central heating, air-conditioning, minibar, phone
Facilities indoor and outdoor restaurants and bars, sitting area, terrace; swimming-pool, private beach, tennis, riding, water-skiing, clay-pigeon shooting
Credit cards AE, DC, V
Children accepted over 14
Disabled access difficult
Pets not accepted
Closed Nov to Mar
Managers Sg and Sga Emili

Umbria

Umbria hotels

Visitors are increasingly discovering that there is more to Umbria than Assisi; but it remains the main tourist highlight of the region, and its popularity is such that a visit must be timed with care: arrive on a local holiday, and you may have difficulty getting accommodation at all. Choice of hotel is tricky too: there are many which are mediocre, and two of the more comfortable hotels are too big for a full entry here; of these, the Subasio (Tel 075 812206) is a polished, rather formal place, but notable for the views from its better bedrooms and beautiful flowery terraces.

One other out-of-town hotel is worth bearing in mind in addition to those we have featured. The Castel San Gregorio (Tel 075 803 8009) is about 10 km north-west of Assisi, up a winding dead-end track; it enjoys a splendid secluded position in gardens on a hilltop, with glorious views across a broad valley, but reports are divided on its decorative state: the felt-lined walls of its public rooms reminded one observer of "the very worst pretentious French chateaux".

Perugia is not nearly so well known as Assisi, but well worth a visit if you can penetrate the infuriating defences of its traffic system. Its central Corso Vannucci really comes to life during the evening 'passeggiata' (walkabout); the Brufani (page 137) lies at one end of it, and just along it is another hotel worth knowing about – La Rosetta (Tel 075 20841); it is much bigger, but not worryingly impersonal, and indisputably better value.

In the north-eastern extremity of Umbria is Gubbio – an unusual little town with plenty to interest the visitor for a day or two, but a scarcity of outstanding small hotels. The Bosone (page 135) is an acceptable overnight stop, but we should much prefer to wholeheartedly recommend a hotel for a longer stay. Our wish may eventually be fulfilled when the restoration of the Grand Hotel ai Cappuccini – housed in a 16thC monastery about one km out of town – is completed. (When we visited in 1989, that event seemed remote.) Its pre-restoration prices were appreciably higher than those of the Bosone; its pre-restoration phone number was 075 927 3441. Meanwhile, other small hotels to bear in mind are at the opposite end of the market: the neat little Gattapone (Tel 075 927 2489), right in the midst of the mainly pedestrianised old town, but watched over by a fierce little man who would not show us the rooms; and the cheap, simple, unpronounceable but quite friendly Oderisi-Balestrieri (Tel 075 927 3747), next to the main road skirting the town and close to the main entrance on the south-west side.

This *Charming Small Hotel Guide* contains summaries like the one above at the start of several sections – in general, those covering parts of Italy where we are conscious that our main recommendations form less than a complete picture. We aim to fill gaps in our coverage by suggesting other hotels in the area – some inspected but rejected as full entries, others on our agenda for future inspection, others again too big to merit a full entry in a guide to small hotels. We are particularly keen to have reports from readers on hotels in these areas. See page 206.

Umbria

Country House

An unassuming guest-house standing amid fields and orchards, yet within walking distance of the main westerly gates of Assisi. Silvana Ciammarughi has had the brilliant idea of running two complementary businesses in one small and beautifully restored little country house – really little more than a cottage. From the ground-floor rooms she sells antiques, and in the upper rooms (furnished with pieces borrowed from below) she accommodates guests. Extra rooms on a lower level have recently been added, with doors opening on to the garden. Ms Ciammarughi is a charming hostess and speaks excellent English.
Nearby the sights of Assisi.

San Pietro Campagna 178, Assisi 06081 Perugia
Tel (075) 816363
Location in countryside, about 10 minutes' walk from Assisi; free private car park
Food & drink breakfast
Prices rooms L35,000-L70,000
Rooms 10 double, all with bath; 2 single; 5 family rooms, all with bath; all rooms have central heating
Facilities sitting-room with bar, sitting-room, large terrace
Credit cards AE, V
Children accepted
Disabled 2 rooms accessible
Pets accepted
Closed never
Proprietor Silvana Ciammarughi

Fontebella

There is certainly no reason to prefer the Fontebella to the Umbra (page 131), but it is worth knowing about in case the Umbra is full. The hotel occupies an old *palazzo* lying on one of the well-worn routes from the central piazza to the basilica of St Francis, and its chief merit is the immaculate condition in which everything is kept – elegant dining-chairs stand on dangerously shiny marble floors in the sitting-room. There are good reports of the proprietors, but we (and others) have encountered a dour receptionist. Some bedrooms are 'incredibly small', and street noise can be a problem.
Nearby basilica of San Francesco, cathedral, church of San Pietro.

Via Fontebella 25, Assisi 06081 Perugia
Tel (075) 812883
Location within city walls, with private garden; car parking in front of hotel
Food & drink breakfast, lunch, dinner
Prices rooms L69,000-L164,000; 30% reduction for children under 6
Rooms 23 double, 7 single, 8 family rooms, all with bath or shower; all rooms have central heating, phone, TV
Facilities dining-room, TV room, bar, reading-room
Credit cards AE, DC, MC, V
Children accepted
Disabled no special facilities
Pets accepted
Closed never
Proprietor Giovanni Angeletti

Umbria

Town hotel, Assisi

Umbra

Assisi, a place of pilgrimage for hundreds of years, is surprisingly not well endowed with places to stay. The largest and least charming are concentrated close to the Basilica which is the town's main attraction. But tucked away down a little alley off the main square is this delightful little family-run hotel, with a restaurant worth a visit in its own right.

The Umbra consists of several small houses – parts date back to the 13thC – with a small gravelled courtyard garden shaded by a pergola. The interior is comfortable and in parts more like a private home than a hotel; there is a bright little sitting-room with Mediterranean-style tiles and brocaded wing armchairs, and a series of bedrooms, mostly quite simply furnished but each with its own character and some with lovely views over the Umbrian plain. We like the elegant dining-room, where imaginative regional dishes triumph over the bland cooking you so often find in hotel restaurants. But a reader complains of a sombre atmosphere and poor food. In fine weather, meals are served outside. The Umbra offers all the peace and tranquillity which you might hope to find in Assisi, and nothing is too much trouble for Alberto Laudenzi, whose family has run the hotel for more than 50 years.

Nearby basilica of St Francis, church of Santa Chiara, medieval castle, cathedral.

Via degli Archi 6, Assisi
06081 Perugia
Tel (075) 812240
Location in middle, off Piazza del Comune, with small garden; nearest car park at Piazza Santa Chiara, 300 m away
Food & drink breakfast, lunch, dinner
Prices rooms L48,000-L138,000
Rooms 23 double, 16 with bath, 5 with shower; 4 single, 2 with bath, 2 with shower; all rooms have phone, central heating
Facilities 3 sitting-rooms, bar, dining-room
Credit cards AE, DC
Children tolerated
Disabled access difficult
Pets not accepted
Closed mid-Nov to mid-Dec, mid-Jan to mid-Mar
Proprietor Alberto Laudenzi

Umbria

Restaurant with rooms, Campello sul Clitunno

Le Casaline

Here is one of those restaurants out in the country which attract families from miles around on holidays; no further testimony to the quality of the food is necessary. The bedrooms are very much a sideline – so much so that the *padrone* has been known to throw a room in with the price of a good meal (not as extravagant as it sounds, when you know how little he charges for them normally). The rooms are in converted outbuildings a little way from the delightfully rustic restaurant, and they really are as simple as you would expect for such low prices.

Nearby Spoleto (14 km), Assisi (35 km).

Località Poreta, Campello sul Clitunno 06042 Perugia
Tel (0743) 520811
Location 3 km E of Campello, isolated in countryside; in gardens, with ample car parking
Food & drink breakfast, lunch, dinner
Prices rooms L65,000; meals L30,000

Rooms 7 rooms, 2 with bath, 5 with shower
Facilities dining-room, terrace, TV room
Credit cards AE, DC, V
Children welcome **Disabled** access to 2 bedrooms possible
Pets accepted
Closed restaurant only, Mon
Proprietor Benedetto Zeppadoro

Umbria

Restaurant with rooms, Castelleone

Nel Castello

Deruta is a valley town famous for its long-established ceramics industry; high above it is the walled village of Castelleone, and higher still stands this little castle. It could be a modern folly, so neat are its warm-stone crenellations, but it is apparently of 11thC origin.

The food here is dependable although unexciting, the rooms quite pretty, with colourful tiled floors. There is only a small sitting area off the stone-walled dining-room, but there are also a number of chairs outside in the shady garden, which is a lovely place to sit and watch the sun go down across the broad valley below.

Nearby Assisi (38 km), Perugia (25 km).

Castelleone, Deruta 06053 Perugia
Tel (075) 971 1302
Location 5 km SE of Deruta, on hilltop; surrounded by gardens, with car parking
Food & drink breakfast, lunch, dinner
Prices DB&B L95,000
Rooms 9 double, one family room; all with bath and shower; all rooms have phone; some rooms have TV, minibar
Facilities dining-room, sitting-room; swimming-pool
Credit cards AE, DC, V
Children accepted
Disabled no special facilities
Pets not accepted
Closed Nov to Mar
Proprietor Sg Carlo Mari

Restaurant with rooms, Foligno

Villa Roncalli

Few drivers on the main road south from Assisi to Terni deviate into Foligno, which worthy guide-books describe as 'commercially important'. But this smart little restaurant with rooms is one good reason to pause. It is a neat, little villa in a woody garden, its light, vaulted dining-room (with huge paintings on the walls) occupying much of the ground floor. Above this, a grand central hall provides some sitting space as well as access to the high-ceilinged, sparely furnished first-floor bed-rooms; those on the top floor are more compact, but still comfortable.

Nearby Assisi (18 km), Perugia (35 km), Terni (59 km).

Via Roma 25, Foligno 06034 Perugia
Tel (0742) 670291
Location 1 km S of middle of Foligno; with private car parking
Food & drink breakfast, lunch, dinner
Prices rooms L62,000-L94,000; meals L35,400
Rooms 10 rooms, all with bath or shower; all rooms have TV, phone
Facilities dining-room, hall, TV room
Credit cards AE, DC, V
Children accepted
Disabled no special facilities
Pets not accepted
Closed 2 weeks Aug; restaurant only, Mon
Proprietors Angelo and Sandro Scolastra

Umbria

Converted castle, Monte vibiano

Castello di Monte Vibiano

This handsome hilltop castle, rebuilt in the 17thC and renovated earlier this century, has been a hotel only since 1988. Despite its size, it accommodates only 12 guests, so there is no danger of tripping over one another in the vaulted public rooms of the house or on the beautifully kept lawns of the grounds (which enjoy grand views of the Umbrian hills). You share the elegantly furnished house with the proprietors, who have novel ideas about hotel-keeping: all drinks are included in the quoted prices.
Nearby Perugia, Lago Trasimeno (25 km).

Monte Vibiano, Mercatello 06050 Perugia
Tel (075) 878 3371; Florence booking office (055) 218122
Location in hills SW of village, 25 km SW of Perugia – take road through Pila and turn off after Spina; ample car parking space
Food & drink breakfast, lunch, dinner
Prices DB & B L200,000-L230,000; FB L240,000-L270,000; includes all wine
Rooms 6 double, all with bath; all rooms have central heating
Facilities dining-room, 3 sitting-rooms; swimming-pool, tennis court
Credit cards not accepted
Children accepted, but children under 8 must eat separately **Disabled** no special facilities **Pets** not accepted **Closed** Nov to first week of Easter **Proprietor** Dr Andrea Fasola Bologna

Country hotel, Assisi

Le Silve

Here is a rustic gem, close enough to Assisi for sightseeing expeditions but remote enough for complete seclusion – and with good sports facilities immediately on hand.

It is an old farmhouse (parts of it very old indeed – 10thC) converted to its new purpose with great sympathy and charm – all tiled floors, stone or white walls and beamed ceilings, and furnished with country antiques. The hotel is virtually self-sufficient, the farm producing its own oil, cheese and meat.
Nearby sights of Assisi.

Località Armenzano, Assisi 06081 Perugia
Tel (075) 812659
Location in countryside 12 km E of Assisi, on road between S444 and S3; ample car parking space
Food & drink breakfast, lunch, dinner
Prices rooms L100,000-L200,000; DB & B L140,000; FB L180,000; reductions for children
Rooms 11 double, 3 single, all with bath; all rooms have central heating, phone, TV
Facilities dining-room, 2 sitting-rooms, bar; swimming-pool, tennis, sauna, riding, archery
Credit cards AE, DC, V
Children welcome
Disabled no special facilities
Pets not accepted
Closed mid-Jan to mid-Feb
Manager Daniela Taddia

Umbria

Town hotel, Gubbio

Bosone

While the Cappuccini is out of action (see page 129) the Bosone rates as best in town. It occupies a *palazzo* which is as old as some of the sights you visit Gubbio to see, but its antiquity is not much in evidence. Most of the bedrooms are furnished in anonymous modern style, and the public areas mainly look worn rather than antique. But there are two remarkably grand bedrooms decorated in a highly flamboyant Renaissance style: staying in them could be entertaining. There is no restaurant, but meals may be taken at the nearby Taverna del Lupo, which is quite jolly.

Nearby historic sights of Gubbio.

Via XX Settembre 22,
Gubbio 06024 Perugia
Tel (075) 9272008
Location in heart of historic city; access and parking difficult, but private garage available
Food & drink breakfast, lunch, dinner; meals taken in nearby Taverna del Lupo
Prices B&B L31,000-L43,000; DB&B L44,000-L56,000

Rooms 16 double, 2 single, 16 family rooms; all with bath; all rooms have phone
Facilities bar, sitting-room with TV
Credit cards AE, DC, MC, V
Children accepted **Disabled** access possible; lift/elevator to bedrooms **Pets** accepted
Closed Jan or Feb
Manager Alfonso Meletti

Restaurant with rooms, Orvieto

Villa Ciconia

While the Cappuccini is out of action (see page 129) the Bosone rates as best in town. It occupies a *palazzo* which is as old as some of the sights you visit Gubbio to see, but its antiquity is not much in evidence. Most of the bedrooms are furnished in anonymous modern style, and the public areas mainly look worn rather than antique. But there are two remarkably grand bedrooms decorated in a highly flamboyant Renaissance style: staying in them could be entertaining. In common with many small establishments, there is no restaurant but meals may be taken at the nearby Taverna del Lupo, which is quite jolly.

Nearby historic sights of Gubbio.

Via XX Settembre 22,
Gubbio 06024 Perugia
Tel (075) 9272008
Location in heart of historic city; access and parking difficult, but private garage available
Food & drink breakfast, lunch, dinner; meals taken in nearby Taverna del Lupo
Prices rooms L54,000-L81,000

Rooms 16 double, 2 single, 16 family rooms, all with bath; all rooms have phone
Facilities bar, sitting-room with TV
Credit cards AE, DC, MC, V
Children accepted
Disabled access possible; lift/elevator to bedrooms
Pets accepted
Closed Jan or Feb
Manager Mario Cannevali

Umbria

Converted monastery, Orvieto

La Badia

This marvellously preserved former Benedictine abbey ('badia') dating from the 12thC is probably the best place from which to visit the Etruscan town of Orvieto, with its splendid cathedral. It is a sight worth seeing in its own right, with its 12-sided tower and beautifully harmonious Romanesque arches. The mellow stone buildings, the view across to the dramatically sited town and the swimming-pool are powerful attractions, regardless of the qualities of the place as a hotel. In the first edition of the guide we were critical of some aspects.

Recent reports have been entirely favourable – 'I particularly enjoyed its quiet, modest luxury, and regional cooking,' says a discerning American reader. But the outraged management will not co-operate with us unless allowed to vet their new entry. This we will not permit, so the details below may be inaccurate.

Nearby cathedral and other sights of Orvieto; lake of Bolsena, Todi (40 km).

La Badia, Orvieto Scalo 05019 Terni
Tel (0763) 90359
Location 1 km S of Orvieto, off Viale 1 Maggio towards Viterbo; in large park with parking for 200 cars
Food & drink breakfast, lunch, dinner
Prices rooms L115,000-L210,000; FB L210,000-L270,000
Rooms 15 double, 14 with bath, one with shower; 3 single, 2 with bath, one with shower; 4 suites, 2 with bath, 2 with shower; all rooms have phone, air-conditioning, central heating
Facilities dining-room, bar, sitting-room with TV, conference hall; swimming-pool, 2 tennis courts
Credit cards AE, MC, V
Children welcome
Disabled access difficult
Pets no dogs
Closed Jan and Feb; restaurant only, Wed
Proprietor Luisa Fiumi

Umbria

Town hotel, Orvieto

Virgilio

Orvieto is probably best known outside Italy for the crisp white wines of the surrounding region, but the city itself also has much to offer. Without doubt, the centrepiece is the astonishing, glistening façade of the *duomo*, more of a work of art than of architecture. Look left as you confront it and you will see the engag- ingly shabby-looking Virgilio. As you do so you will already have appreciated this hotel's prime virtue: its position right at the heart of things. Inside, sadly, it has been left shiny but soulless by modernization, but it is comfortable, and prices are moderate.

Nearby cathedral, Etruscan and medieval museums; Arezzo, Rome, Perugia, Siena all within reach.

Piazza del Duomo 5/6, Orvieto 05018 Terni
Tel (0763) 41882
Location in heart of city – follow signs to Piazza Duomo; 2 public car parks 100 m away
Food & drink breakfast
Prices rooms L57,000-L87,000; 35% reduction for children sharing parents' room
Rooms 14 double, 2 with bath, 12 with shower; 2 single, both with shower; all rooms have phone
Facilities bar, breakfast room, TV room
Credit cards not accepted
Children accepted **Disabled** one ground-floor room; lift/elevator **Pets** cats and dogs accepted **Closed** never
Proprietor Virgilio Pedetti

Town hotel, Perugia

Brufani Palace

This is included especially for disciples of Conrad Hilton, who, according to legend, asserted that "only three things matter about a hotel: location, location and location". The Brufani stands at the south-west extremity of the *corso*, on top of one of the cliffs which circumscribe central Perugia – so you get great views south to Assisi and west to the setting sun. It is a polished little hotel, with a refined lobby (reception is at the back, beyond it), a smart restaurant, a glossy and fashionable 'American' bar, and bedrooms which are comfortable enought, but of no great charm.

Nearby old town of Perugia.

Piazza Italia 12, Perugia 06100
Tel (075) 62541
Location at southern end of central *corso*; garage (L20,000 a night)
Food & drink breakfast, lunch, dinner
Prices rooms L196,000-L369,000; meals from L40,000
Rooms 21 double, one single, one suite, all with bath; all rooms have central heating, phone, TV, hairdrier, minibar
Facilities bar, sitting-room, dining-room
Credit cards AE, DC, MC, V
Children accepted
Disabled access possible – lift/elevator to bedrooms
Pets small dogs only accepted
Closed never
Manager Sg M Ferrante

Umbria

Medieval manor, Ospedalicchio de Bastia

Lo Spedalicchio

Despite the attractions of Assisi and of a sound central hotel such as the Umbra (page 131), for the touring motorist there is much to be said for staying out of town in an hotel easily accessible by car. This one is the best around: a four-square manor house on the road to Perugia.

The ground-floor public rooms have high, vaulted brick ceilings and tiled floors with the occasional rug – whether you approach from the 'back' door as most drivers do or from the 'front' door opening directly on to the village square, the immediate impression is of centuries of calm living. The restaurant (which enjoys a high local reputation) is on one side – stylishly set out with bentwood chairs and pink napery; sadly, the sitting-room bar area which occupies much of the rest of the ground floor is not nearly so welcoming. Bedrooms vary widely – some high-ceilinged, some two-level affairs with sitting space (an attractive possibility, given the poor public sitting area) – but all those we have seen are spacious and inviting. The staff are courteous and helpful; their French is better than their English. A recent visitor confirms that the hotel is 'absolutely excellent'.

Nearby Assisi (10 km), Perugia (10 km); Gubbio, Orvieto, Todi and Spoleto all within reach.

Piazza Bruno Buozzi 3,
Ospedalicchio di Bastia
06080 Perugia
Tel (075) 8010323
Location between Assisi and Perugia on S147; in garden with ample car parking
Food & drink breakfast, lunch, dinner
Prices rooms L55,000-L83,000; meals approx L28,000
Rooms 20 double, 2 single, 3 family rooms; all with shower; all rooms have central heating, phone, colour TV
Facilities dining-room, American bar, TV room, conference rooms
Credit cards AE, DC, V
Children welcome; special meals, baby-sitter, small beds on request
Disabled no special facilities
Pets small ones only
Closed never
Manager Sg G Costarelli

Umbria

Town hotel, Spoleto

Gattapone

Although chiefly known for its summer Festival of Two Worlds, Spoleto has interesting year-round sights too – among them the 14thC Bridge of Towers, a tremendously high crossing of the steep-sided Tessino valley, of which the Gattapone has a grandstand view. The house was converted into a hotel in the 1960s, and much of it is evocative of Italian style of that era – notably the split-level bar/sitting-room; but there are also old-fashioned rooms in the older part of the house, and all the rooms we saw were admirably spacious.

Nearby Ponte delle Torri, duomo, basilica of San Salvatore.

Via del Ponte 6, Spoleto
06049 Perugia
Tel (0743) 36147
Location on W fringe of
town, with garden and
private car parking
Food & drink breakfast
Prices rooms L105,800-
L166,800
Rooms 13 double, 10 with
bath, 3 with shower; minibar

in 7 rooms; TV on request
Facilities American bar,
hall, meeting-room
Credit cards AE, DC, MC, V
Children accepted
Disabled no special facilities
Pets accepted
Closed never
Proprietor Filippo Hanke

Country hotel, Todi

Bramante

In a more competitive part of the country, the Bramante would frankly not rate an entry here: it is a little too big and impersonal for comfort. But applying our acid test – would we or would we not wish to know about it while touring in this area? – we get a positive result. The most important things in its favour are an amiable old stone house at the core of the hotel, restrained modern decoration and furnishings, and a splendid position on the hillside just along from Todi's most distinctive building – the church of Santa Maria, which looks like the work of the celebrated Bramante, but is not.

Nearby church of Santa Maria della Consolazione.

Via Orvietana, Todi 06059
Perugia
Tel (075) 884 8381
Location just outside town
on Orvieto road; in gardens,
with ample car parking
Food & drink breakfast,
lunch, dinner
Prices rooms L110,000-
L180,000
Rooms 43 double, 2 family
rooms, all with bath and
shower; all rooms have
phone, air-conditioning,
TV; some rooms have

minibar
Facilities sitting-rooms (one
with TV), dining-room,
conference room, terrace,
piano bar; fitness room,
tennis
Credit cards AE, DC
Children welcome
Disabled access possible
Pets accepted
Closed never
Proprietor Sg M Montori

Umbria

Le Tre Vaselle

On paper, the Tre Vaselle sounds disturbingly impersonal – it has 50 bedrooms (above our usual limit) and several conference rooms. But the hotel is entirely without ostentation, its modest entrance on a narrow street scarcely detectable. Friendly and courteous staff make you feel instantly at home, while the maze of ground-floor sitting-rooms – with massive arches, white walls, rustic beams, terracotta floors, shabby armchairs and sofas, card-table and stone fireplaces – is immediately captivating.

Bedrooms, some in a more modern building behind the main one, do not have such character, but are smart and civilized. The cavernous main dining-room is also a weak spot. Breakfast is served in a much more atmospheric room on the main ground floor. The food at the Tre Vaselle is excellent, and well complemented by the wines for which the owner, Dr Lungarotti, has made Torgiano well known (don't miss the fascinating wine museum a street away from the hotel).

This is the sort of place which the touring visitor hesitates to leave, knowing for sure that the next night's hotel will be inferior. Console yourself in this case with the thought that it is also pretty certain to be cheaper.

Nearby Perugia; Assisi (25 km).

Via Garibaldi 48, Torgiano 06089 Perugia
Tel (075) 982447
Location in side street of village, 12 km SE of Perugia; ample car parking nearby
Food & drink breakfast, lunch, dinner
Prices rooms L180,000-L260,000
Rooms 50 double, most with bath, rest with shower; all rooms have central heating, phone, minibar
Facilities sitting-rooms, dining-room, breakfast room, bar, conference rooms
Credit cards AE, DC, MC, V
Children accepted
Disabled access possible – lift/elevator to bedrooms
Pets not accepted
Closed never
Manager Romano Sartore

Marche

Taverna alla Selva

Cingoli is a hilltop town renowned for its views down towards the Adriatic, and we have tried but failed to find a recommendable hotel in the town itself. The Taverna is some miles away in the valley bottom, and is best thought of as a restaurant with rooms – though it has a pool, it does not have much in the way of indoor sitting areas. The restaurant is rather over-ornamented, and the entrance bar distinctly dreary, but the bedrooms are furnished with simple good taste and there is a small sitting area with a table and sofa on the upstairs landing.
Nearby Macerata (30 km), Ancona (52 km).

Via Cicerone 1, San Vittore, Cingoli 62011 Macerata
Tel (0733) 617119
Location 12 km NE of Cingoli; in open countryside with ample car parking
Food & drink breakfast, lunch, dinner
Prices rooms L40,000-L50,000; 30%-50% reduction for children; meals L18,000-L28,000
Rooms 8 double, all with bath all rooms have phone
Facilities dining-room, bar, sitting-room; swimming-pool, tennis, bowls
Credit cards AE, DC, V
Children welcome
Disabled not suitable
Pets small dogs accepted in public rooms
Closed Jan
Proprietors Giacomo Cesarini and Adolfo Vitale

Villa Pigna

This substantial pink villa must once have been surrounded by fields and vineyards; now it is enveloped by a prosperous dormitory of Ascoli Piceno (though once inside its tiny grounds the surroundings are not intrusive – the dawn chorus is more so). It is very much a business hotel – breakfast consists of pastries and coffee from the bar, taken standing up at peak times – and the comfortable bedrooms lack character. But the ground-floor sitting areas are exceptionally welcoming, and satisfactory food is served in the smooth modern dining-room.
Nearby old quarter of Ascoli Piceno (4 km).

Viale Assisi 33, Folignano 63040
Tel (0736) 491868
Location 4 km N of Folignano; in private grounds, with garage and car parking
Food & drink breakfast, lunch, dinner
Prices rooms L79,800-L140,000; meals about L25,000
Rooms 50 rooms, 4 suites; all with bath; all rooms have phone, TV, minibar, balcony
Facilities dining-room, bar, conference room, private chapel
Credit cards AE, DC, V
Children accepted
Disabled no special facilities
Pets accepted
Closed restaurant only, 3 weeks July-Aug
Proprietor Anna Maria Rozzi

Marche

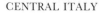

Country villa, Montecassiano

Villa Quiete

Macerata is a sizeable hilltop town a few miles inland from the Adriatic, and remarkable mainly for its huge 19thC arena, the Sferisterio, scene of a major opera festival in the summer. The Villa Quiete, across the valley at Montecassiano, is a substantial house of mixed merits: dreary sitting-rooms, smart cafe-style dining-room, bedrooms varying widely – some ordinary, some grand and furnished with antiques. Its key asset, perhaps, is the moderate-sized garden with its pines, palms and geraniums.

Nearby Porto Recanati – Adriatic coast (30 km); Ancona (40 km).

Vallecascia di Montecassiano, 62010 Macerata
Tel (0733) 599559
Location 3 km S of Montecassiano; in large shady park, with car parking
Food & drink breakfast, lunch, dinner
Prices rooms L57,000-L104,000
Rooms 40 double, 10 single; all with bath or shower; all rooms have central heating, phone, TV

Facilities 2 dining-rooms, 2 bars, sitting-rooms; conference facilities
Credit cards AE, DC, V
Children accepted
Disabled some rooms suitable
Pets dogs not accepted
Closed never
Proprietor Sg Bianchi

Seaside hotel, Portonovo

Fortino Napoleonico

And now for something completely different: a single-storey fortress (said to be 'ancient' but looking suspiciously recent), right on the sea next to the popular beach of Portonovo. Bedrooms, contained within the ramparts, are simple and somewhat gloomy, but spacious – many can accommodate three or four – and real value for the families who make up the bulk of the clientele. The restaurant and bar/sitting-room are also simple, clean and roomy.

Nearby Monte Conero; Ancona.

Portonovo 60020 Ancona
Tel (071) 801124
Location 12 km SE of Ancona, on promontory near beach; with ample car parking
Food & drink breakfast, lunch, dinner
Prices rooms L100,000
Rooms 26 double, 4 with bath, 22 with shower; all rooms have central heating, phone
Facilities dining-room, sitting-room, bar, terrace

Credit cards AE, DC, MC, V
Children welcome
Disabled access possible – single-storey building
Pets accepted
Closed never
Manager Sg Roscioni

Marche

Country villa, Pesaro

Villa Serena

The Adriatic coast south of Rimini is not short of hotels, but it is *very* short of our kind of hotel – which makes this one a find. It is a handsome 17thC mansion with some token castellations, standing in a wooded park high above the hubbub of the coast. In this oasis the Villa Serena lives up to its name.

The villa has always belonged to one family – the counts Pinto de Franca y Vergaes, who used it as a summer residence until, in 1950, they turned it into a small hotel to be run like a family home. Renato Pinto does the cooking and serves up some better-than-average dishes; Mario sees to guests and reception; while their mother, Signora Laura, busies herself in the house and garden. All three are reassuringly down-to-earth, and the emphasis in their house is on character, simplicity and tranquillity, rather than luxury. There are salons of baronial splendour, antiques and curiosities wherever you go, and corridors delightfully cluttered with ceramics and potted plants. A few faded corners reinforce the villa's appealing air of impoverished aristocracy. No two bedrooms are exactly alike but antiques and fireplaces feature in most of them. A couple could do with a lick of paint and some trees lopped to let in the light.

Sadly, we have a report from an unimpressed reader who was offered only biscuits for breakfast, and no other meals.

Nearby municipal museum, Ducal Palace at Pesaro; Gabicce Mare corniche road (NW 27 km) starting from Pesaro.

Via San Nicola 6/3,
61100 Pesaro
Tel (0721) 55211
Location 4 km from Pesaro and beach, in a large wooded park on hillside with private car parking
Food & drink breakfast, lunch, dinner
Prices rooms L80,000
Rooms 10 double, all with bath or shower; all rooms have central heating, phone
Facilities 4 sitting-rooms, dining-room, bar, terrace
Credit cards AE
Children accepted
Disabled access difficult
Pets accepted
Closed never
Proprietor Renato Pinto

Marche

Town hotel, Santa Vittoria in Matenano

Farfense

San Vittoria is an out-of-the-way little hilltop town midway between the Adriatic coast and the Sibillini mountains. The surrounding countryside is distinctive and pretty – a delightful patchwork of tiny fields covering the steep slopes of little valleys cut by streams in the soft soil. The Farfense is a very simple, old-fashioned, family-run hotel with spotless bedrooms and a charming little restaurant down in the brick vaults (as well as a bigger room upstairs, brought into action to feed the locals for weddings and feast days). Good views from a tiny terrace and some of the rooms.

Nearby Sibillini mountains.

Corso Matteoti 41, Santa Vittoria in Matenano 63028 Ascoli Piceno
Tel (0734) 780171
Location 35 km SW of Fermo, in middle of town; car parking on street
Food & drink breakfast, lunch, dinner
Prices rooms L31,000-L52,000
Rooms 8 double, 2 single, all with bath or shower; all rooms have central heating
Facilities sitting-room, bar, dining-room
Credit cards not accepted
Children accepted
Disabled no special facilities
Pets dogs not accepted
Closed 2 weeks end Sep/beginning Oct; restaurant only, Mon
Proprietor Eva Pepinelli

Converted monastery, Sirolo

Monteconero

Yet another example of a religious house in a prime position – on the very summit of Monte Conero, 500 metres above the nearby sea, with superb views south-east along the coast. The bedrooms give no sign of historic origins – they are simple, adequate, modern – but there is an atmospheric little stone-vaulted restaurant on the lower floor (as well as a bigger, more anonymous one), and some pleasantly polished sitting areas. The big bar is another asset, with a terrace overlooking the coast.

Nearby Sirolo; Ancona (21 km).

Monte Conero, Sirolo 60020 Ancona
Tel (071) 936122
Location 3 km N of Sirolo, in woods on shoulder of Monte Conero; with ample car parking
Food & drink breakfast, lunch, dinner
Prices rooms L50,000-L90,000
Rooms 34 double, 4 single; all with shower; all rooms have phone
Facilities sitting-room, bar, 2 dining-rooms; outdoor swimming-pool, tennis
Credit cards AE, DC, V
Children welcome
Disabled access difficult
Pets small dogs only accepted
Closed Nov to Easter
Proprietor Augusto Melappioni

Marche

Emilia

Although the Emilia is a seaside hotel, it stands aloof from the beaches south of Ancona, on the flanks of Monte Conero above the little resort of Portonovo (which is a car-journey away for all but the most energetic). It is a modern building of no great architectural merit. But its proprietors some years ago hit on a clever way of giving the hotel a distinctive appeal: they invited artists to come and stay, and to pay their way in kind. The results continue to accumulate on the walls: score upon score of paintings (none, we are assured, has ever been sold). Among the Italian signatures, our inspector spotted the artist Graham Sutherland's.

Even without the extraordinary wall-covering, the hotel would have an attractive air. A long, low sitting-room with clusters of chunky modern armchairs links reception to the large, light, simply furnished dining-room, which has big windows looking on to a passable imitation of a *prato inglese* (a lawn). Bedrooms are thoroughly modern and snazzy. Most are in the older part of the hotel, ranged at an angle so as to give each room a sea-view and a small balcony.

Food is taken seriously, although it no longer earns a Michelin star. Fish dominates, and is competently cooked, though expensive.

Nearby church of Santa Maria (at Portonovo), Monte Conero; Ancona (12 km).

Via Poggio, 149/A
Portonovo, Ancona 60020
Tel (071) 801145
Location 2 km W of
Portonovo on cliffs; ample
private car parking
Food & drink breakfast,
lunch, dinner
Prices rooms L70,000-
L106,000
Rooms 23 double, 2 with
bath, 21 with shower; 2
single, both with shower; 5
family rooms, one with bath,
4 with shower; all rooms
have central heating, phone,
colour TV, minibar
Facilities dining-room, TV
room, conference room, bar,
gazebo-bar; swimming-pool,
tennis
Credit cards AE, V
Children accepted **Disabled**
some ground-floor rooms
Pets accepted
Closed Dec and Jan
Proprietor Lamberto Fiorini

Lazio

Area introduction

Lazio hotels

Rome is a city of grand hotels rather than small and charming ones, which is why we have fewer listed here than we have for Florence or Venice. Suggestions from readers for additional entries would be gratefully received.

Among the hotels we have looked at but not given an entry to are a trio of simple but adequately comfortable places in the peaceful residential area of Aventino which are well known to travellers on a budget – the Domus Maximi (Tel 06 578 2565), the Sant'Anselmo (Tel 06 574 3547) and the San Pio (Tel 06 575 5231). At or close to the opposite extreme of the market is the luxurious 50-room Lord Byron (Tel 06 361 5404) – certainly less impersonal than most smart hotels, but still impressively ritzy rather than genuinely welcoming.

Location may not be as important in Rome as in some capital cities – the able-bodied can get around the whole of the central area on foot – but some locations are undoubtedly more equal than others. The position of the Sole (Tel 06 678 0441) can hardly be beaten – on the piazza in front of the Pantheon, which is not only the single most astonishing building in Rome but is also at the heart of tourist Rome as a whole. When last we saw it the hotel was only partly renovated; to judge by its new brochure, the process has been successfully completed – the place appears to have been transformed.

The modern Italian region of Lazio, like the old Latium, is dominated by Rome. The only tourist highlights outside the capital – the very different villas of Emperor Hadrian and the 16thC Cardinal d'Este – are 30 km NE at Tivoli. This is within day-trip range of Rome, but if you want to stay overnight, go for the Torre Sant'Angelo (Tel 0774 23292).

Town guest-house, Rome

Gregoriana

An unprepossessing building in a narrow street running away from the top of the Spanish Steps, the Gregoriana is distinguished by its friendly and personal atmosphere and its highly individual decor. There is something for everyone – leopard-skin wallpaper on one landing, raffia on another, Liberty prints on a third. Rooms are uniform in style, modern and slightly glamorous, but vary appreciably in size; some have a little terrace. There is no public room apart from the tiny reception area, and breakfast is served ('with commendable speed') in your bedroom.

Nearby Spanish Steps, Villa Borghese, Fontana di Trevi.

Via Gregoriana 18, Rome 00187
Tel (06) 6797988
Location 100 m from the top of the Spanish Steps, with car parking on the street or in garage 50 m away
Food & drink breakfast
Prices rooms L112,000-L180,000
Rooms 15 double, 12 with bath, 3 with shower; 4 single, all with shower; all rooms have central heating, air-conditioning, TV, phone
Facilities tiny lobby; bar service in rooms
Credit cards not accepted
Children welcome **Disabled** no special facilities **Pets** small ones only **Closed** never
Proprietor Ernesto Bagat

Lazio

Town hotel, Rome

La Residenza

The Via Vittorio Veneto is one of Rome's most fashionable addresses, and the location of some of its grandest hotels. The Residenza is not one of them, but its position only a block away from this sweeping tree-lined avenue gives it a head start. The Spanish Steps and the Villa Borghese are about equidistant, to the west and north respectively.

The Residenza is part of the small Giannetti chain of hotels, concentrated in dreary Lido di Jesolo – not a good sign. But Signor d'Arezzo does a sound job as manager and the front desk staff are friendly and helpful.

Another key aspect of the hotel's appeal is its bar and sitting areas on the elevated ground floor, which are comfortable and welcoming, with a mixture of modern and antique furniture. (An attractive area in which to relax over a drink is a rarity in modest Rome hotels.) A better-than-average help-yourself breakfast is served in a more ordinary, windowless room at the back of the hotel, with bright red cafe-style chairs.

Bedrooms are comfortable and well equipped, but uniformly furnished with no great flair or character. Those at the back are quieter than those at the front, which despite their double glazing suffer from noise from a nearby nightclub. Some have fair-sized terraces, and there is also a communal roof-top terrace with interesting views.

Nearby Spanish Steps, Villa Borghese.

Via Emilia 22, Rome 00187
Tel (06) 460789
Location in side-street off Via Veneto; limited car parking
Food & drink breakfast
Prices rooms L95,000-L170,000
Rooms 24 double, all with bath; 3 single, all with shower; all rooms have central heating, minibar, satellite TV, air-conditioning, hairdrier, phone
Facilities sitting-rooms, bar, breakfast room, patio, terrace
Credit cards not accepted
Children accepted
Disabled access difficult
Pets not accepted
Closed never
Manager Adriano d'Arezzo

Lazio

Town villa, Rome

Villa Florence

On the broad Via Nomentana to the north-east of the middle of Rome, this well-run hotel has particular attractions for motorists reluctant to tangle with the worst of Rome's traffic (in addition to a convenient location, it has private parking in the garden behind the house).

The villa's other chief merit is the welcoming ambience of its public areas. Great efforts have been made to give the little sitting area (off reception) and the adjacent café-style breakfast room some interest and warmth. Dotted around all the public areas are interesting archeological fragments which have been discovered on the site of the hotel.

There is a small secluded terrace behind the house, with sun-beds as well as tables and chairs. The bedrooms (some of them in outbuildings, with doors opening on to the garden) are comfortable, and we are told that the characterless melamine unit furniture has been replaced.

The cheerful proprietor makes an effort to see that breakfast is more than usually satisfying, with yoghurt, cheese and ham as well as the standard fare.

Nearby Villa Borghese.

Via Nomentana 28,
Rome 00161
Tel (06) 4403036
Location about one km NE
of Via Veneto, with private
car parking in garden
Food & drink breakfast
Prices rooms L110,000-
L180,000; 30% reduction
for children sharing parents'
room
Rooms 32 double, one
single, 4 family rooms; all
with bath or shower; all
rooms have colour TV,
minibar, air-conditioning,
phone
Facilities breakfast room,
TV room, bar
Credit cards AE, DC
Children accepted
Disabled no special facilities
Pets not accepted
Closed never
Proprietor Tullio Cappelli

Lazio

Portoghesi

This is a good example of the kind of sought-after small hotel that may be common in Florence or Venice but is all too rare in Rome: unpretentious, functional but attractively old-fashioned, and fairly priced – at least considering its very central position, which is ideal for the foot-slogging tourist (if not for the motorist).

The sights of Rome are distributed all around, with the delightful Piazza Navona and the stunning Pantheon only yards away. Furnishings are simple, service is polite and efficient rather than notably warm. There is a pleasantly sunny breakfast room (with a small terrace), and an overwhelming choice of places for dinner within a short stroll.

Nearby Piazza Navona, Pantheon.

Via dei Portoghesi 1, Rome 00186
Tel (05) 6864231
Location just N of Piazza Navona, with roof terrace
Food & drink breakfast
Prices rooms L61,000-L102,000
Rooms 27 rooms, 22 with bath or shower; all rooms have phone
Facilities breakfast room, sitting-room
Credit cards MC, V
Children accepted
Disabled access possible – large lift/elevator
Pets small ones only accepted
Closed never
Proprietor Mario Trivellone

Sitea

The Sitea is a well-maintained hotel with only a reception area on the ground floor and its other public areas up on the sixth. Great effort has clearly gone into the elaborate decoration of the bar and sitting-rooms up there, though it is not quite clear which era of Roman history their designers were aiming to evoke. The bedrooms we saw were comfortably furnished in traditional style and generally spacious, with somewhat old-fashioned bathrooms. Many have apparently been renewed.

Nearby Fontana di Trevi, Via Veneto.

Via Vittorio Emanuele Orlando 90, Rome 00185
Tel (06) 4754696
Location in middle of city, close to Piazza della Repubblica; public garage and car parking nearby
Food & drink breakfast; lunch and dinner available in coffee shop
Prices rooms L145,000-L225,000
Rooms 31 double, 27 with bath, 3 with shower; 6 single, one with bath, 4 with shower; all rooms have central heating, phone, air-conditioning; hairdrier and radio on request
Facilities sitting-room, roof-garden bar
Credit cards AE, DC, MC, V
Children welcome **Disabled** no special facilities **Pets** accepted by arrangement; not allowed in public rooms
Closed never
Proprietors Giovanni and Giuseppe de Luca

Lazio

Villa delle Rose (see opposite)

Scalinata di Spagna

The Spanish Steps are a favourite spot for visitors to Rome to sit around soaking up the atmosphere and the afternoon sun, and at the top of them are two hotels – the Hassler (100 rooms costing L500,000 a night each) and, facing it across the piazza, this highly individual little *pensione*.

The idiosyncratic character of the place is obvious as soon as you walk in the door, when you come face to face with Cacao, the resident parrot. Beyond the tiny reception area, a corridor dotted with antiques and paintings leads to old-fashioned bedrooms of varying size with bathrooms which by Italian standards are rather plain. For eight months of the year breakfast is served on the roof-top terrace, from which many of the famous sights of Rome can be spotted across the neighbouring roofs, whilst enjoying the early morning sunshine; at other times a tiny room off reception is brought into play.

Signor Bellia is charming and helpful, and clearly tickled by the wave of publicity his captivating little house has received in recent years, particularly in the United States. His prices are no longer low, yet demand for rooms continues to exceed supply. The rational response is to raise prices further; we hope the temptation can be resisted. Book early.

Nearby Spanish Steps, Villa Borghese, Via Veneto.

Piazza Trinita dei Monti 17,
Rome 00187
Tel (06) 6793006
Location at the top of the Spanish Steps; car parking 50 m away
Food & drink breakfast
Prices rooms L107,500-L165,000
Rooms 10 double, 2 with bath, 8 with shower; 4 single, one with bath, 3 with shower; all rooms have central heating, minibar, radio, phone
Facilities breakfast room, roof garden
Credit cards not accepted
Children accepted
Disabled no special facilities
Pets not accepted
Closed never
Proprietor Giuseppe Bellia

Lazio

Town villa, Rome

Villa delle Rose

Via Vicenza 5, Rome 00185
Tel (06) 4451788
Location close to main
railway station with small
garden; parking for 4 cars,
public car park 200 m away
Food & drink breakfast
Prices rooms L78,900-
L132,800
Rooms 29 double, 8 single,
nearly all with bath or
shower; all rooms have
central heating, phone
Facilities large sitting-room
with bar, breakfast room
Credit cards AE, DC, MC, V
Children very welcome
Disabled access difficult
Pets accepted if well behaved
Closed never
Proprietor Claude Frank

If an economical night or two
near Rome's railway station is
necessary, this calm old villa
certainly takes some beating.
The bedrooms are neat, and
gradually being improved by
the enthusiastic owner Claude
Frank (who is Swiss), and there
is a grand little bar/sitting-
room with marbled pillars and
a beautifully frescoed ceiling.
Breakfast is served in a cool
arched cellar with linen on
the tables and bentwood
chairs, and there is a shady
terrace surrounded by flowers
and greenery in the little
garden.
Nearby Piazza della Repub-
lica, church of Santa Maria
Maggiore.

Town hotel, Rome

Valadier

If you know the Valadier of old, you are in for a shock next time
you go back. When we visited it in 1987 a transformation was
under way: out were going its ornate antique furnishings, and in
were going beautifully crafted modern fittings, giving the compact bedrooms something of the flavour of an expensive yacht –
except that the weight of marble in the new bathrooms would be
sufficient to sink a liner. The end result, recent visitors say, is
rooms which are small to the point of claustrophobia, but 'exceptionally well appointed'.
Nearby Spanish Steps, Villa Borghese.

Via della Fontanella 15,
Rome 00187
Tel (06) 3610559
Location off Via del Corso,
close to Piazza del Popolo;
garage 100 m away
Food & drink breakfast
Prices rooms L165,000-
L270,000
Rooms 40 double, 6 suites;
all with bath and shower; all
rooms have central heating,
phone, minibar, TV, piped
music, air conditioning
electronic safe, hairdrier
Facilities piano/American
bar, dining-room, conference
rooms; solarium

Credit cards AE, DC, MC, V
Children accepted
Disabled access difficult
Pets small ones only
Closed never
Proprietor Simonetta
Battistini

Lazio

Country hotel, Grottaferrata

Villa Fiorio

The hill villages south of Rome known as the Castelli Romani are perhaps of more interest to Romans escaping the heat of the city than visitors from abroad. But if you too want to get out of town without leaving the orbit of Rome altogether – or if easy access to Ciampino airport is attractive – this comfortable villa fits the bill. The interior of the rambling 18thC villa is richly decorated, with impressively gracious bedrooms, but the great attraction is the garden, with its lawns, pines, olive groves and sizeable swimming-pool. Prices are very attractive by comparison with those of central Rome, too.

Nearby Rome (20 minutes), Castelli Romani.

Viale Susmet 25,
Grottaferrata, Rome 00046
Roma
Tel (06) 945 9276
Location 21 km SE of Rome; in large park with ample car parking
Food & drink breakfast, lunch, dinner
Prices rooms L113,000-L156,000; meals L35,000
Rooms 20 rooms, all with bath or shower; all rooms have phone, TV, minibar

Facilities sitting-room, dining-room, bar; swimming-pool
Credit cards AE, DC, MC, V
Children accepted
Disabled no special facilities
Pets not accepted
Closed never
Proprietor Pierino Maccari

Converted castle, Formia

Castello Miramare

High on the hillside above Formia, with tremendous views of the huge, sweeping bay of Gaeta, stands this modest little folly or 'castle', built in the late 19thC and converted in the 1970s. It is emphatically a restaurant with rooms rather than a hotel – the only sitting area is a claustrophobic hall with a barrel ceiling. The main dining-room runs all along the front of the building, but in summer a glamorous marquee affair is erected on a rear terrace, and there are other little terraces in the gardens for breakfast and drinks.

Nearby Gaeta (8 km); Sperlonga, Terracina, San Felice Circeo all within reach.

Balze di Pagnano,
Formia 04023 Latina
Tel (0771) 700138
Location on hill above town, in gardens, with private car parking
Food & drink breakfast, lunch, dinner
Prices rooms L61,000-L77,000; meals from L35,000
Rooms 10 rooms, one with bath, 9 with shower; all rooms have minibar, colour TV, hairdrier, air-conditioning
Facilities 3 sitting areas, bar, dining-room
Credit cards AE, DC, MC, V
Children accepted
Disabled no special facilities
Pets accepted
Closed Nov
Proprietor Carla Celletti

Lazio

Seaside hotel, San Felice Circeo

Punta Rossa

San Felice is an amiable village at the foot of the 550-metre Monte Circeo, which is an isolated lump of rock at the seaward point of a flat area, once marshland but now drained except for zones which have been declared a national park to preserve the flora and fauna. The Punta Rossa lies around the mountain in a secluded setting above an exposed and rocky shore.

The hotel has the form of a miniature village. Reception is in a lodge just inside an arched gateway, and beyond that is a little piazza enclosed by white-walled buildings in rough Mediterranean style. Bedrooms are spread around in low buildings at or near the top of a garden beyond the piazza which descends steeply to the sea. They are pleasant, varying in size, many with colour schemes which look a bit dated; all have balconies with sea views. The main attraction of the suites is their admirable size. The restaurant is part-way down the garden (already bursting with colour when we visited in spring) towards the sea and pool, with views from its terraces.

Nearby Terracina (20 km); Circeo national park.

San Felice Circeo 04017
Latina
Tel (0773) 528085
Location 4 km W of San Felice, isolated on rocky shore; in gardens, with ample car parking
Food & drink breakfast, lunch, dinner
Prices rooms L170,000-L240,000; DB&B L170,000-L220,000
Rooms 27 double, 6 single, 7 suites; all with bath or shower; all rooms have phone, minibar, colour TV; all double rooms have sea-view balcony or terrace, air-conditioning
Facilities bar, dining-room, terrace, courtyard; outdoor swimming-pool, small beach
Credit cards AE, DC, V
Children welcome
Disabled access difficult
Pets small dogs accepted by arrangement
Closed never
Manager Maria Fiorella Battaglia

Abruzzo

Converted castle, Balsorano

Castello di Balsorano

High on a wooded, rocky hill, the Castello di Balsorano is a fine-looking 13thC fortress – one of the few to have survived the Barbarian attacks and earthquakes of the Abruzzo region. Inside, it still has the atmosphere of a medieval castle, unchanged by the modern amenities which have been installed. Downstairs there are grand rooms with coats of armour and shields, swords and daggers and ancient shotguns. Bedrooms are in similar medieval style, some with ornately carved baronial beds and silk wall hangings. In this quite a remote part of Abruzzo it is normally essential to speak Italian. But the Castello is an exception: Mary Ricci is English.

Nearby Abruzzo National Park within reach.

Castello di Balsorano,
Balsorano, Sora 67025
L'Aquila
Tel (0863) 95236
Location on rocky hilltop in
village; with private car
parking
Food & drink breakfast,
lunch, dinner
Prices rooms L74,000; suite
L104,000; meals about
L35,000-L40,000

Rooms 5 double, one suite,
all with bath; all rooms have
central heating
Facilities dining-room, bar
Credit cards not accepted
Children accepted
Disabled access difficult
Pets not accepted, in dining-room
Closed Nov
Proprietors Nino and Mary
Ricci

Country hotel, Scanno

Mille Pini

Scanno lies surrounded by the massive 2,000-metre peaks of Abruzzo, the highest of the Appennine range of mountains. The Lago di Scanno is the local beauty spot, and there are hotels beside it; but those with an eye on the hills should make for this modern hotel (as its name suggests, surrounded by pines) at the foot of the chair-lift up to Monte Rotondo. It is simple and neat, in Alpine chalet style, and quiet at most times of the year. Few foreign visitors penetrate this far into the mountains, so don't expect to speak English.

Nearby Sulmona (31 km).

Via Pescara 2, Scanno 67038
L'Aquila
Tel (0864) 74387
Location slightly out of
village, at foot of chair-lift; in
small garden, with car
parking on quiet road
Food & drink breakfast,
lunch, dinner
Prices rooms L68,000-
L96,000; meals L35,000-
L40,000
Rooms 15 double; 5 single;

one family room; all with
bath; all rooms have central
heating, phone
Facilities dining-room,
sitting-room, games room,
TV room
Credit cards not accepted
Children accepted
Disabled no special facilities
Pets dogs not accepted
Closed restaurant only, Tue
Proprietor Silla Carmelo

Campania

Area introduction

Campania hotels

Campania has three components: the frantic city of Naples (where, somewhat to our surprise, we have succeeded in finding one attractive small hotel – the Miramare, page 156); the extremely popular seaside resorts to the south of Naples on the Sorrento peninsula and the islands of Capri and Ischia (where there is a super-abundance of such hotels); and the coast and countryside away from Naples, where we have drawn almost a complete blank.

Ischia is hard work for the seeker for small hotels. Tourism there was originally nad is still closely linked with the island's thermal springs, and large hotels with spa facilities are the norm – accounting partly for the island's domination by German visitors, who are much keener on mud baths than most other nationalities.

One of the most popular excursions is to Sant'Angelo on the south coast – a tiny fishing village on a narrow isthmus leading to a rocky point. Sant'Angelo would be a pleasant place to stay for longer than an hour or two – indeed, it is at its best before the daily coaches arrive or after they depart – and apart from the San Michele (page 165) it has a couple of other hotels which do not quite merit full entries in this guide but which make acceptable bases. The Miramare (Tel 081 999219) is almost at sea level on the east side of the village, with a big terrace on the waterside which gets the morning sun. Just behind it up the steep hillside, with views over the rooftops from its little terraces, is La Palma (Tel 081 999526).

Seaside villa, Baia Domizia

Della Baia

This low-lying white building stands well away from the main part of Baia Domizia. Inside the three Sello sisters have successfully reproduced the peaceful atmosphere of a stylish private villa: spotless white stucco walls, cool quarry-tiled floors and white sofas are offset by bowls of fresh flowers and potted plants and the antique and modern furnishings blend well together. Bedrooms are no less attractive; some have balconies.
Nearby Gaeta (29 km); Naples within reach.

Via dell'Erica, Baia Domizia
81030 Caserta
Tel (0823) 721344
Location in S part of resort, with gardens leading down to long sandy beach; ample car parking
Food & drink breakfast, lunch, dinner
Prices FB L85,000- L105,000; reductions for children
Rooms 54 double, 18 with bath, 36 with shower; 2 single, one with bath, one with shower; all rooms have central heating, balcony, phone
Facilities two sitting-rooms, TV room, bar, terrace, dining-room; tennis, bowls, private beach
Credit cards AE, DC, V
Children welcome
Disabled no special facilities
Pets small, well-behaved ones accepted
Closed Oct to mid-May
Proprietors Elsa, Velia and Imelde Sello

Campania

Town hotel, Naples

Miramare

This waterfront hotel, a couple of blocks from the very grand Excelsior in Santa Lucia (as in the song) is handy for ferries to the islands, and for several of the major sights. Rooms are cleverly designed to make the most of their compact dimensions, and are reached by the most elegant, creaky old lift we have encountered. Good breakfasts are served in a smart, light penthouse with views of the famous bay, surrounded by a roof terrace. Staff are friendly and helpful. Prices cannot be called low, but are reasonable by local standards.

Nearby Palazzo Reale and Castel dell'Ovo.

Via Nazario Sauro 24, Naples 80132
Tel (081) 427388
Location in Santa Lucia
Food & drink breakfast
Prices rooms L150,000-L207,500
Rooms 27 double, 4 single; all with bath or shower; all rooms have air-conditioning, phone, colour TV, minibar

Facilities sitting-rooms, breakfast room, bar, TV room, meeting room
Credit cards AE, DC, MC, V
Children welcome if well behaved
Disabled ground-floor bedrooms
Pets welcome if well behaved
Closed never **Proprietors** Enzo and Bibi Rosolino

Seaside hotel, Vico Equense

Capo la Gala

The Sorrento coast road is squeezed between mountain and sea, but space has been found on the steep hillside below to create this neat modern hotel, arranged in a series of terraces. On the first level down from the shady car park and reception are double-bedded rooms, reached from an interior corridor; below that are twin-bedded rooms reached via an outdoor terrace; all are uniformly done out with tiled floors, plain walls and pretty cane furniture. Just above sea level is the fair-sized pool and restaurant – a pleasant spot for serious sunbathing.

Nearby Pompeii (10 km), Sorrento (10 km), Naples (34 km); Capri (30 min by boat), Ischia (one hr by boat).

Via Luigi Serio 7, Capo la Gala, Vico Equense 80069, Naples
Tel (081) 8798278
Location 3 km N of Vico Equense, below coast road, in steep gardens with undercover car parking
Food & drink breakfast, lunch, dinner
Prices rooms L180,000; DB&B L145,000
Rooms 18 double, all with bath and shower; all rooms have phone, minibar,

balcony with sea-view
Facilities 3 bars, dining-room, TV and video room, games room; swimming-pool (thermal sulphur spring fed), sauna, solarium, private beach
Credit cards AE, V
Children flexible attitude
Disabled lift/elevator available **Pets** at proprietors' discretion
Closed Nov to Mar
Proprietors Antonio and Maria Savarese

Campania

Converted monastery, Amalfi

Cappuccini Convento

A rickety-seeming elevator from the roadside is your unimpressive introduction to this extraordinary hotel, perched in an apparently impossible position on the cliff face above Amalfi; not surprisingly, one of its great attractions is the superb views of the rugged Amalfi coast shared by the flowery, creeper-covered terraces and many of the rooms.

But the other merits of this 12thC monastery soon become clear, too. The public areas are light and airy, with a striking sense of space, many original features retained, and antiques lining the wide hallways. The salon/bar has Oriental rugs on tile floors, with comfortable pink-covered armchairs and sofas, a newly built brick fireplace and a piano adding to the clubby atmosphere. The large dining-room is a delight, with superb vaulting and columns, crisp white tablecloths and bentwood and cane chairs on a tiled floor. The bedrooms are mostly large and charmingly furnished with antiques; most have tile floors with rugs, and quite a few have both a sea view and a balcony.

The recently restored cloisters are the cool, dignified venue for occasional piano and other recitals.

Nearby Grotta dello Smeraldo (4 km); Ravello (7 km), Sorrento (33 km).

Amalfi 84011 Salerno
Tel (089) 871008
Location 300 m from middle of Amalfi, high up on cliffs, reached by lift/elevator up from main road; garden and private car parking at road level
Food & drink breakfast, lunch, dinner
Prices rooms L70,000-L150,000
Rooms 44 rooms, all with bath or shower; all rooms have phone
Facilities dining-room, sitting-rooms, bar, solarium, conference facilities; beach
Credit cards AE, DC, V
Children accepted
Disabled no special facilities
Pets accepted
Closed never
Proprietor Alfredo Aielli

Campania

Converted monastery, Amalfi

Luna

The middle of Amalfi is crowded and bustling, and the most desirable hotels lie just outside it or well above it up on the rock-face. The Luna Convento is one of the former – about five minutes' walk uphill from the cathedral. It occupies two separate buildings, separated by the winding coast road – one of them an old Saracen tower perched right on the sea.

The hotel opened in 1825 (it is one of the oldest in Amalfi), and has been in the same family for five generations. But you only have to step inside to see that the building's history goes back much further than the 19thC. The unique feature is the Byzantine cloister, enclosing a garden and ancient well. The arcade serves as a quiet and civilized sitting area and breakfasts are served within the actual cloister – a delightful spot to start the day. You have the choice of modern or traditional bedrooms, and for a premium you can have your own private sitting-room. Lunch and dinner (specialities are cannelloni, *crêpes* and fish risotto) are taken either in the vaulted restaurant in the main building, where large arched windows give beautiful views of the bay, or better still across the road where the terrace and parasols of the tower restaurant extend to the water's edge. The swimming-pool forms part of the same complex – as does the somewhat incongruous disco.

Nearby cathedral of Sant'Andrea and cloisters of Paradise (in Amalfi); Valle dei Mulini (one hr walk); Ravello (6 km).

Via P Comite 19, Amalfi
84011 Salerno
Tel (089) 871002
Location short walk from middle of resort, overlooking sea, with private garage
Food & drink breakfast, lunch, dinner
Prices rooms L75,000-L155,000; FB L120,000-L150,000; 20% reduction for children under 6, sharing parents' room

Rooms 45 double, 5 single, 5 family rooms; all with bath; all rooms have minibar, phone
Facilities 2 dining-rooms, 2 bars, Byzantine cloister; swimming-pool, disco
Credit cards AE, DC, MC, V
Children welcome
Disabled 2 lifts/elevators
Pets accepted, but not in restaurant or by pool
Closed never
Manager A Milone

Campania

Seaside hotel, Capri

Flora

On the edge of the fashionable little town of Capri, the Flora looks out to the sea and the ancient cliff-top Certosa di San Giacomo. It is a modest but well cared-for little hotel (recently refurbished to gain an extra star), immersed in greenery and flowers, with calm and spacious bedrooms (many with balconies sharing the view) and an attractive sun-terrace. Breakfasts are excellent, and the lack of a dining-room is no problem – there is a wide choice of restaurants within easy strolling distance.

Nearby Carthusian monastery of San Giacomo, Augustus gardens, beach at Marina Piccola.

Via Federico Serena 26, Capri 80073 Napoli
Tel (081) 837 0211
Location about 200 m from middle of Capri town; with flowery terrace and fine sea views; no private car parking
Food & drink breakfast
Prices rooms L280,000
Rooms 16 double, one single, 7 family rooms, all with bath; all rooms have air-conditioning, TV, minibar; most rooms with terrace, phone
Facilities breakfast room, sitting-room, bar, terrace
Credit cards AE, DC, MC, V
Children accepted
Disabled access difficult
Pets accepted
Closed Nov to Feb
Proprietor Virginia Vuotto

Seaside hotel, Capri

Luna

In comparison with some of the ritzy alternatives on Capri, the Luna strikes you as somewhat old fashioned – in the nicest sense. A delightful path shaded by vines forms the entrance to the hotel; inside, public rooms are spacious, quiet and civilized, with beautiful views of the sea from the dining-room terrace, and bedrooms have the sort of space and comfort you expect from a top-class hotel. The setting is one of the most desirable on the island – perched on cliffs plunging down to the dark blue water and facing the strange islets of the Faraglioni.

Nearby old town of Capri; Certosa di San Giacomo.

Viale Matteotti 3, Capri 80073 Napoli
Tel (081) 837 0433
Location about 250 m from middle of Capri town, on cliffs; in large garden
Food & drink breakfast, lunch, dinner
Prices rooms L150,000-L276,000; meals L45,000
Rooms 46 double, 2 single, all with bath; all rooms have air-conditioning, phone, minibar
Facilities dining-room, 4 sitting-rooms, TV room, bar, terrace, conference facilities; swimming-pool
Credit cards AE, DC, V
Children accepted
Disabled no special facilities
Pets accepted, but not allowed in dining-room
Closed Nov to Mar
Proprietor Raffaele Vuotto

Campania

Seaside hotel, Capri

La Pineta

Despite its increase in size (and gloss) over the years, the Pineta retains what was always its greatest asset – the location. 'Pineta' means pine-wood and the modern, low-lying buildings lie right among the trees, on a hillside overlooking the sea and the rocky south coast of the island. Flowery terraces shaded by pines and the spacious balconies of the apartments focus on this spectacular panorama. Breakfasts are buffet-style, and the pool-side restaurant serves tempting meals from noon to 5pm.

Nearby town of Capri (three minutes' walk); Marina Piccola (2 km).

Via Tragara 6, Capri 80073 Napoli
Tel (081) 8370644
Location among pines close to the middle of town; no private car parking
Food & drink breakfast, lunch; dinner at Ristorante Campanile in Capri town
Prices rooms L60,000-L210,000; lunch about L30,000; special weekly rates
Rooms 40 double, 8 single, 6 family rooms, all with bath; all rooms have central heating, air-conditioning, TV, phone, minibar
Facilities breakfast room, bar, piano bar, 3 terraces; gym, sauna, heated outdoor swimming-pool
Credit cards AE, DC, MC, V
Children accepted if well-behaved **Disabled** no special facilities **Pets** small ones accepted **Closed** never
Proprietor Costanzo Vuotto

Seaside villa, Capri

Villa Sarah

A steep walk up from the middle of Capri will bring you to the Villa Sarah – a whitewashed building among the vines, well away from the bustle of the town. (Carry on along the path and you come to the remains of the Villa Iovis, one of 12 palaces on the island belonging to Tiberius – local guides will tell you he kept a different mistress in each one of them.) Originally the Villa Sarah was built by an English aristocrat and though much modernized, it still has the friendly air of a private home. Rooms are cool, whitewashed and simple and the only public area is the breakfast room – though most guests prefer to take breakfast on the terrace, soaking up the morning sun.

Nearby Capri town (500 m); Villa Iovis (30 minutes' walk).

Via Tiberio 3/a, Capri 80073 Napoli
Tel (081) 8377817
Location on road leading from middle of Capri town to Villa Iovis; with shady garden
Food & drink breakfast
Prices rooms L60,000-L140,000
Rooms 25 rooms, all with bath or shower; all rooms have phone
Facilities breakfast room, terrace
Credit cards AE
Children accepted
Disabled no special facilities
Pets dogs not accepted
Closed Nov to Mar
Proprietor Sga C Vuotto

Campania

Seaside hotel, Capri

Scalinatella

No expense has been spared in the creation of this small, exclusive hotel. A spotless white building with a profusion of arches and oriental ornamentation, it feels distinctly Moorish. Inside a world of cool luxury awaits you. Every corner is air-conditioned and the rooms have all the trimmings that you might expect for the very high price you will be paying – telephones in the bathroom, private terraces and beds that disappear into alcoves, converting your rooms into a sitting-room by day. Furnishings vary from the simple and refined to the extravagant and perhaps over-rich. But there are few other flaws in this luxury hotel. Its location, with beautiful views to the Carthusian monastery of San Giacomo, leaves little to be desired; the garden and pool (where buffet lunches are served) are immaculate. The hotel is being refurbished in 1989.

Nearby Monastery of San Giacomo (overlooked by hotel); Capri town (about five minutes' walk).

Via Tragara 8, Capri 80073 Napoli
Tel (081) 8370633
Location on Punta Tragara road; with garden and ample car parking
Food & drink breakfast, buffet lunch by pool
Prices rooms L350,000-L420,000
Rooms 28 rooms, all with bath and jacuzzi; all rooms have air-conditioning, phone, TV, minibar
Facilities sitting-rooms, breakfast room, bar; swimming-pool
Credit cards not accepted
Children not accepted
Disabled no special facilities
Pets accepted
Closed Nov to mid-Mar
Proprietors Morgana family

Campania

Villa Krupp

After the bustle of Capri town, the Augustus gardens are a welcome retreat, terraced on a gentle hillside above the sheer cliffs and little beaches of Marina Piccola. Quite high up is the Villa Krupp, a serene white villa whose main claim to fame is that both Lenin and Gorky lived here for a while – you can still see the desk where they wrote. There are no public rooms, but bedrooms are bright, clean and mainly spacious, with floral tiled floors and the occasional rug. Walls are whitewashed and there are some pretty antique pieces and wicker chairs with cushions. Each of the rooms has a balcony, and breakfasts are taken on a terrace overlooking the gardens.

Nearby middle of Capri a few minutes' walk; Marina Piccola.

Via Matteotti 12, Capri
80073 Napoli
Tel (081) 837 0362
Location in the Augustus gardens, up from the middle of Capri town
Food & drink breakfast
Prices rooms L52,000-L106,000
Rooms 12 rooms, all with bath or shower; all rooms have balcony
Facilities small terrace
Credit cards V
Children accepted
Disabled not suitable
Pets not accepted
Closed Nov to May (but open for Easter)
Proprietor Sga Settanni

Villa Brunella

The Brunella was built in 1970 and its modern façade has no great distinction. What really makes the place is its setting, perched on terraced slopes in the south-east of the island, with superb views of the rugged cliffs and azure waters that characterize Capri. You can admire the views from the balcony of your room, from the terrace where a buffet lunch is served, or from the pool which lies below the hotel. The atmosphere is relaxed and the bedrooms are spacious, light and modern. The busy town of Capri, with its chic shops, is not far away; alternatively, a scramble down the slopes will bring you to the sea.

Nearby beach of Faraglioni, Carthusian monastery of San Giacomo, Capri town.

Via Tragara 24, Capri 80073
Tel (081) 8370122
Location on terraced slopes, overlooking sea and cliffs, a few minutes' walk from Capri town; no proper road or car parking
Food & drink breakfast, lunch, dinner
Prices rooms L70,000; meals about L35,000
Rooms 18 double, all with bath; all rooms have central heating, air-conditioning, phone; 5 rooms have sitting area
Facilities 2 sitting-rooms, 2 bars, swimming-pool, panoramic terrace
Credit cards AE, V
Children accepted
Disabled no special facilities
Pets not accepted
Closed Nov to mid-Mar
Proprietor Vincenzo and Brunella Ruggiero

Campania

Converted monastery, Ischia

Il Monastero

Ischia Ponte gets its name from the low bridge giving access from the 'mainland' of Ischia to the precipitous islet on top of which stands the original settlement of Ischia, known collectively as the Castello although it consists of several buildings. One of these is an old monastery which is now run as a simple but entirely captivating *pensione*.

A lift reached by a tunnel into the rock of the island takes you up to the Castello (though there are steps as an alternative). Discreet signs bring you to the locked door of the *pensione*, and a ring on the bell summons the amiable *padrone*. Up a final flight of stairs and at last you are there. Many paintings hang on the plain walls of the hallway and the neat little sitting-room. The dining-room has satisfyingly solid wooden furniture. Bedrooms are monastically simple; some are reached from inside, some from the outside terrace, which gives a breathtaking view of the town and island of Ischia.

We have no first-hand experience of the food, and half-board is inescapable; but we know that the cooking is good enough to keep the Monastero full in spring and autumn when other hotels are half-empty.

Nearby Castello d'Ischia.

Castello Aragonese 3, Ischia Ponte 80070 Napoli
Tel (081) 992435
Location on island E of Ischia town, linked by causeway
Food & drink breakfast, dinner
Prices DB & B L40,000
Rooms 15 rooms, 13 with bath or shower
Facilities dining-room, TV room, large terrace
Credit cards not accepted
Children accepted
Disabled not suitable
Pets not accepted
Closed mid-Oct to mid-Mar
Proprietor Ciro Eletto

Campania

Town villa, Porto d'Ischia

La Villarosa

This is a sharp contrast to the Monastero in every way: it is immersed in a jungle of a garden right in the heart of the little town of Ischia, and its great attraction (apart from the garden and pleasant little pool) is its series of delectable sitting-rooms, beautifully furnished with comfortable armchairs and ornate antiques. The bedrooms are, by comparison, rather plainly furnished, but perfectly acceptable.

The light, welcoming restaurant upstairs leads out on to a terrace overlooking the garden and the roof-tops of Ischia, and meals are served there in summer. Only full-board terms are offered, and regretably we have no evidence about the standard of cooking – so anyone who books in for more than a night or two is clearly taking a risk.

Like many hotels on the island, the Villarosa offers thermal treatments of various sorts – though the atmosphere is far removed from that of the traditional spa hotel. (The 'Scottish shower' mentioned in the brochure is presumably a localized drizzle.)

Nearby port of Ischia (500 m), Castello d'Ischia (2 km).

Via Giacinto Gigante 5,
Porto d'Ischia 80077 Napoli
Tel (081) 991316
Location 200 m from lido;
with limited car parking
Food & drink breakfast,
lunch, dinner
Prices HB L80,000-
L100,000; FB L90,000-
L110,000
Rooms 34 double, 20 with
bath, 14 with shower; 6
single, all with shower; all

rooms have central heating
Facilities sitting-room, bar,
dining-room, TV room,
terrace; thermal outdoor
swimming-pool, sauna
Credit cards MC, V
Children not suitable
Disabled access possible –
lift/elevator to bedrooms
Pets not accepted in public
rooms or dining-room
Closed Nov to Mar
Proprietor Paolo Amalfitano

Campania

Seaside hotel, Forio d'Ischia

La Baggatella

In a quiet and slightly shabby beach resort area, this extra-ordinary modern hotel offers a sort of simulation of the ornate decoration and furnishings apparently once favoured by the Neapolitan aristocracy. It is crammed with elaborately carved antiques or convincing reproductions, and richly coloured fabrics. It is all beautifully kept, to suit the German clientele at whom it is aimed. In a luxuriant garden behind the house is an attractive pool, and the separate, more restrained restaurant.
Nearby Sant'Angelo (6 km).

Via Commaso Cigliano, Spiaggia di San Francesco, Forio d'Ischia 80075 Napoli
Tel (081) 986072
Location between Lacco Ameno and Forio, 100 m from beach; with garden and some car parking
Food & drink breakfast, lunch, dinner
Prices rooms L60,000-L100,000
Rooms 35 rooms, all with shower; all rooms have phone
Facilities dining-room, 2 sitting-rooms, 2 bars (one by pool); beauty centre and partial mud baths, swimming-pool, thermal pool, (covered)
Credit cards not accepted
Children not very suitable
Disabled not suitable
Pets dogs not accepted
Closed Nov to 3rd week Mar
Manager Sergio Masucci

Seaside hotel, Sant'Angelo

San Michele

This villa-style building is not a remarkable hotel in itself. The bar/sitting-room has a tile floor and a dark, comfortable atmo-sphere, with deep modern armchairs; the dining-room is more traditional, with a terrazzo floor, raffia-seated chairs and a shady terrace; bedrooms too have tile floors small rugs and modern (though not ugly) furniture – and each has a small balcony. The real attraction is the exceptionally peaceful loca-tion and lush gardens; there are thermal facilities neatly tucked away, lovely terraces with plenty of tables and chairs and a delightful swimming-pool set among pine trees.
Nearby boats to Ischia town.

Sant'Angelo, Isola d'Ischia 80070 Napoli
Tel (081) 999276
Location on rocky headland with garden; access by foot only: public car parks (one paying, one free) 5 minutes' walk away
Food & drink breakfast; lunch and dinner in season
Prices rooms L70,000-L100,000
Rooms 52 rooms, all with bath or shower; all rooms have phone
Facilities hall, bar, conference facilities, 2 terraces; sea-water pool
Credit cards not accepted
Children accepted
Disabled not suitable
Pets accepted
Closed Nov to Mar
Proprietor Claudio Iacono

Campania

L'Ancora

This modern and unpretentious hotel shares the views of the famous and over-priced Syrenuse, next door – and its close proximity to the heart of the resort. The public areas are large, light and simply furnished, with rather loud tiled floors. The spacious dining-room opens out on to the terrace, which overlooks the sea and gets the sun for most of the day; it is partly shaded by a creeper-covered awning. The bedrooms, all of which have balconies overlooking the sea, are traditionally decorated. They are sparsely furnished and seem quite large, but what furniture they have is well chosen and there are rugs on the tiled floors. Bathrooms are clean, tiled and in good order.

Nearby Amalfi (17 km), Sorrento (17 km), Ravello (23 km).

Via C Colombo 36, Positano 84017 Salerno
Tel (089) 875318
Location a short walk from middle of resort, with private car parking
Food & drink breakfast, dinner
Prices DB&B L80,000-L95,000
Rooms 18 double, all with bath; all rooms have phone, TV, minibar; some rooms have balcony, air-conditioning
Facilities sitting-room, dining-room, terrace
Credit cards AE, DC, MC, V
Children accepted **Disabled** no special facilities **Pets** accepted, but not in dining-room **Closed** mid-Oct to Mar
Proprietors Savino brothers

Marincanto

Like most hotels in Positano, the Marincanto is no bargain. But for a hotel of its category, the rooms in the main building are surprisingly spacious and well furnished (those in the annexe are less impressive). The views from the flowery terraces of dazzling blue seas and the colourful houses of Positano jostling on the hillside are hard to forget. There is no restaurant, which is probably an advantage in a resort where half-board terms may be a rip-off and good food is abundant. The public rooms are confined to an open-plan reception and sitting area – breakfast is taken on a pretty sea-view terrace. Several flights of steps lead down to a pebble beach. In a resort where parking is a problem the hotel car park is a bonus – but watch the charges.

Nearby Amalfi (17 km), Ravello (23 km), Sorrento (17 km).

Positano 84017 Salerno
Tel (089) 875130
Location built into hillside directly above sea and beach; with terrace and private (paying) car park
Food & drink breakfast
Prices rooms L90,000-L110,000
Rooms 23 rooms, all with bath or shower; all rooms have phone, minibar
Facilities sitting-room, bar
Credit cards AE, DC, MC, V
Children accepted
Disabled no special facilities
Pets dogs not accepted
Closed mid-Oct to week before Easter
Proprietor Sga Celesti Manna

Campania

Miramare

On the steep hill to the west of the beach and the fishing boats, the Miramare is a series of old fishermen's houses joined to make a charming and thoroughly comfortable hotel. The sitting-room has a vaulted ceiling, Oriental rugs, antique furniture and lots of plants and flowers. The dining room is a delight – a glassed-in terrace with bougainvillaea hanging from the ceiling trellis, smart modern chairs and a memorable view shared by all tables. Each bedroom has a balcony overlooking the sea – and in some cases even the bath gives a view.

Nearby Amalfi (17 km), Ravello (23 km).

Via Trara Genoino 25-27, Positano 84017 Salerno
Tel (089) 875002
Location 3 minutes W of main beach; with private parking for 10 cars
Food & drink breakfast, lunch, dinner
Prices rooms L70,000-L240,000; dinner L50,000
Rooms 10 double, 3 single, 5 suites; all with bath and shower; all rooms have central heating
Facilities dining-room, bar, 3 sitting-rooms
Credit cards AE, V
Children not encouraged
Disabled not suitable
Pets not allowed in dining-room
Closed never; restaurant Nov to mid-Mar
Proprietor Sg Attanasio

Casa Albertina

This family-run hotel excites great enthusiasm in some visitors. Our most recent inspector was less impressed than most, finding his room ordinary, his bathroom drab and quite badly maintained, and his dinner poor value. But there is no denying that the house is attractive – arches, white walls, tiled floors, plenty of plants and ornaments – and the welcome warm. There is a small terrace off the dining-room, and the better bedrooms have their own (the *casa* faces east across the bay, so gets the morning sun). It is rather inaccessible, reached by seemingly endless stairs up from the chaotic one-way street through the resort.

Nearby Emerald Grotto (9 km), Sorrento (17 km), Amalfi (17 km), Ravello (23 km).

Via della Tavolozza 4, Positano 84017 Salerno
Tel (089) 875143
Location 200 m uphill from the middle of resort, reached up alleys from street; paying car park 300 m away
Food & drink breakfast, lunch, dinner
Prices DB&B L80,000-L135,000
Rooms 16 double, one single, 2 suites; all with bath; all rooms have central heating, hairdrier; half the rooms have air conditioning
Facilities 2 sitting-rooms, dining-room, bar, TV room, 3 terraces
Credit cards AE, DC, MC, V
Children welcome in low season; special meals available **Disabled** access very difficult **Pets** quiet, small ones accepted
Closed never
Proprietor Lorenzo Cinque

Campania

Palazzo Murat

Most hotels in this picturesque and fashionable little resort are ranged up the steep hills either side of the ravine leading down to the sea. Such positions are fine for views, but imply strenuous climbs back from the beach or the middle of the resort. The Palazzo Murat is by no means viewless, but it is much more in the heart of things – just inland of the *duomo*, and reached by one of the pedestrian alleys lined with trendy boutiques.

The main building is a grand L-shaped 18thC palazzo, easily identified from most parts of the resort by its pitched, tiled roof. Within the L is a charming courtyard – a well in the middle, bougainvillea trained up the surrounding walls, palms and other exotic vegetation dotted around – where you can take breakfast (though in spring early risers will find it sunless). Along one side of this courtyard run the interconnecting sitting-rooms, which are beautifully furnished with antiques.

Bedrooms in the palazzo itself are attractively traditional in style – some painted furniture, some polished hardwood – and have doors opening on to token balconies (standing room only). We have not seen rooms in the more modern extension on the seaward side of the palazzo, but most of them do have the attraction of bigger balconies.

A breakfast-only hotel could scarcely be better placed: Positano's many restaurants are mainly congregated behind the beach, a short stroll away.

Nearby tour of Amalfi coast and Sorrento peninsula.

Via dei Mulini 23, Positano
84017 Salerno
Tel (089) 875177
Location in heart of resort, in pedestrian street; paying car park nearby
Food & drink breakfast
Prices rooms L155,000-L175,000
Rooms 28 double, all with bath and shower; all rooms have phone, balcony
Facilities sitting-room, TV room, terrace, bar
Credit cards AE, DC, V
Children accepted **Disabled** access difficult **Pets** small ones only accepted
Closed Nov to Easter week
Proprietor Carmela Cinque

Campania

Seaside hotel, Positano

Villa Franca

Provided you are not worried by heights, or by remoteness from the centre of things, this smartly traditional hotel – all arches, white walls and tiled floors – has much to commend it. The position high on the western side of the Positano ravine gives an excellent view of the resort and the coast beyond from the windows and terraces, the bedrooms and public rooms are spacious and comfortable. A reporter found the proprietors and staff welcoming, and the food satisfying and freshly prepared. There is a private bus to and from the beach at certain times.
Nearby Amalfi (17 km), Sorrento (17 km), Ravello (23 km); boat trips to Capri.

Via Pasitea 318, Positano
84017 Salerno
Tel (089) 875735
Location on main road above middle, with fine sea views
Food & drink breakfast, dinner
Prices rooms L100,000-L160,000; DB&B L140,000; meals L40,000-L50,000
Rooms 28 double, 1 single, all with bath; all rooms have central heating, radio, satellite TV, phone
Facilities dining-room, bar terrace; swimming-pool
Credit cards AE, MC, V
Children welcome
Disabled not suitable
Pets accepted, but not allowed in dining-room
Closed never
Proprietor Mario Russo

Town villa, Ravello

Giordano Villa Maria

With its views down to the sea, the shady garden restaurant of this charming old villa is not surprisingly popular for lunch and dinner, and there is a traditionally furnished dining-room for cooler days; bedrooms are simple but comfortable. Guests have the use of a large modern pool at the nearby Hotel Giordano, which is under the same ownership. Carla Palumbo will patiently talk you through the menu in excellent English.
Nearby Amalfi (6 km); Vesuvius, Pompeii, Sorrento within reach.

Via Santa Chiara 2, Ravello
84010 Salerno
Tel (089) 857170
Location on path to Villa Cimbrone, in garden; private car parking available
Food & drink breakfast, lunch, dinner
Prices rooms L84,000-L94,000; DB&B L60,000-L75,000 (min 3 days)
Rooms 10 double, 5 with bath, 5 with shower; 2 single, with shower; 2 family rooms, both with bath; all rooms have central heating, phone; TV and minibar on request
Facilities dining-room, TV room, lounge bar, sitting-room; heated swimming-pool, hydromassage
Credit cards AE, MC, V
Children accepted at proprietor's discretion
Disabled no special facilities
Pets not accepted
Closed never
Proprietor Vincenzo Palumbo

Campania

Seaside hotel, below Ravello

Marmorata

Despite the address, the Marmorata is not up in the hill-top town of Ravello, but set on the rugged shoreline. Originally a paper mill, the building has been smartly converted into a four-star hotel with a nautical design theme. It is stylishly modern, cool and comfortable. Large windows make the most of the sea views, and the main terrace is perched directly above the water.
Nearby Ravello (6 km); Positano, Sorrento within reach.

Strada Statale 163, Localita Marmorata, Ravello 84010 Salerno
Tel (089) 877777
Location 3 km E of Amalfi; on hillside below coast road, with private car parking
Food & drink breakfast, lunch, dinner
Prices rooms L75,000-L210,000; DB&B L70,000-L150,000
Rooms 38 double, one with bath, 37 with shower; 3 single, 2 with bath, 1 with shower; all rooms have central heating, colour and satellite TV, radio, minibar, air-conditioning, phone
Facilities hall, dining-room, bar, conference room; terraces, solarium, sea-water pool
Credit cards AE, DC, MC, V
Children accepted
Disabled access difficult
Pets accepted if well behaved
Closed never
Proprietors Camera d'Afflitto family

Converted monastery, Ravello

Parsifal

Wagner was one of the many illustrious visitors who stayed at Ravello's Villa Rufolo, and the gardens there are said to have been the inspiration for the second act of the opera from which this little hotel takes its name. No doubt Wagner would have been equally inspired by the stunning sea-views from this simple but charming little hotel. It was converted from a monastery, and part of the cloister, along with Corinthian columns and vaulted ceilings, have been preserved. Home-made pastas, cannelloni and *crêpes* are the specialities of the house, and you can enjoy them on a creeper-clad terrace.
Nearby Villa Rufolo and Villa Cimbrone at Ravello; Amalfi (7 km), Positano (18 km); Pompeii within reach.

Via G d'Anna 5, Ravello 84010 Salerno
Tel (089) 857144
Location in quiet street on fringe of town, well signposted from approach road; car parking on street
Food & drink breakfast, lunch, dinner
Prices rooms L55,000-L80,000; meals L20,000-L40,000
Rooms 15 double, 8 with bath, 4 with shower; 2 single, one with shower; 2 family rooms with bath; all rooms have central heating
Facilities sitting-room, dining-room, veranda and terraces, cloister
Credit cards AE, DC, MC, V
Children accepted **Disabled** no special facilities **Pets** accepted, but not in dining-room **Closed** 7 Oct to end Mar
Proprietor Nicola Camera

Campania

Town hotel, Ravello

Caruso Belvedere

The Caruso Belvedere is one of several hotels in this justly popular beauty spot which have been converted from old *palazzi*. Ever since it opened in 1903 it has been in the capable hands of the Caruso family. The grandeur may have faded somewhat and the rooms cannot be called luxurious, but unaffected, informal charm is the key to its success.

Many of the original features, such as the Corinthian columns and marble pillars, still survive; the antiques, faded sofas and open fireplaces are entirely in keeping with the setting. Bedrooms are perhaps simpler than you might expect, though you can always opt for a 'de luxe' room and enjoy the views from a huge balcony. The restaurant is simple, light and spacious, but the best feature is the summer terrace commanding sensational views of the rugged coast and the Gulf of Salerno. There are mixed reports about the food, though most people seem to enjoy the wines that come from the Caruso's own vineyards.

Perhaps the most romantic feature of all is the terraced garden, with its timeless views of the sea far below.
Nearby Villa Rufolo, Villa Cimbrone; Amalfi (7 km).

Via San Giovanni del Toro 52, Ravello 84010 Salerno
Tel (089) 857111
Location 500 m from the main piazza, with garden; public car parking in front of hotel
Food & drink breakfast, lunch, dinner
Prices DB & B L95,000; FB L112,000
Rooms 22 double, 2 single, all with shower; 2 family rooms, both with bath; all rooms have central heating, phone
Facilities dining-room, bar, TV room, solarium
Credit cards AE, DC, MC, V
Children welcome
Disabled no special facilities
Pets small ones only accepted, and not allowed in public areas
Closed never
Proprietor Paolo Caruso

Campania

Town hotel, Ravello

Palumbo

A Moorish-inspired *palazzo*, built for a nobleman in the 12thC, the Palumbo was bought by a Swiss hotelier in the mid-19thC and is still run by his family. No expense has been spared in its conversion to a five-star hotel, but what distinguishes it from most other hotels of its category is its understated luxury and elegance.

Public rooms focus on a 13thC inner courtyard where Corinthian-topped columns, oriental arches and a profusion of flowing plants provide a cool, civilized sitting-area. The restaurant is equally elegant, though more French than Moorish, with its peach tablecloths, gilt mirrors, mouldings and bentwood chairs. But on fine days the choice location for breakfast, lunch or candlelit dinners is the restaurant balcony, where you look down over terraced vineyards to dazzling blue seas below. Various other balconies and terraces (hung with vines and roses) share this same stunning panorama. Throughout the hotel there are beautiful antiques, water-colours and paintings – including what is purported to be a Caravaggio. Bedrooms are light and airy and tastefully furnished with antiques, tiled floors and rugs. Those in the annexe are more modern in style, but, for anyone on a tighter budget, are much cheaper.

Nearby Villa Cimbrone, Villa Rufolo; Amalfi (7 km).

Via San Giovanni del Toro 28, Ravello 84010 Salerno
Tel (089) 857244
Location perched on cliffs; with garden, sun terrace and private car parking
Food & drink breakfast, lunch, dinner
Prices DB&B L260,000
Rooms 21 rooms, 3 apartments; all with bath; 7 rooms are in annexe close to main building; all rooms have phone
Facilities sitting-rooms, bar, dining-room
Credit cards AE, DC, MC, V
Children accepted
Disabled not suitable
Pets dogs not allowed in dining-room
Closed never
Proprietors Vuilleumier family

Campania

Town villa, Ravello

Villa Cimbrone

Along with the Villa Rufolo (the beauty of which was the inspiration of the Garden of the Flower Maidens in Wagner's 'Parsifal') the Villa Cimbrone is the greatest attraction of Ravello. What the visitors go to see is not the villa itself but its gardens, suspended high above the sea and the wonderful views from the cliff-top belvedere, stretching over the Gulf of Solerno as far as Paestum. Few realize that the villa at the entrance, with its fine Gothic cloisters and crypt, is a guest-house.

The building was restored by an eccentric English lord earlier this century, but being forbidden from owning property in Italy once the Fascists were in power, he handed it over to Marco Vuilleumier, who is still the owner. The bedrooms may not be the ultimate in modern luxury (there are several without private bathrooms) but they all have immense charm and individuality, furnished with some fine antiques and many preserving the mosaics and frescos from the original villa. Getting there involves a 10-minute stroll from the middle of Ravello along a delightful path, past villas and overhanging gardens – not quite so delightful though, if you are laden with suitcases. As the guide went to press, we learned that the guest house was closing for six months in the winter of 1989-90 for total refurbishment. We trust that the character of the house will not be lost.

Nearby Villa Rufolo, about ten minutes' walk.

Ravello 84010 Salerno
Tel (089) 857138
Location about 10 minutes' walk from central square; with famous gardens and view; cars must be left in public parks
Food & drink breakfast
Prices rooms approximately L150,000
Rooms 20 rooms, 5 with bath or shower

Facilities reading-room, TV room, breakfast room, cloister
Credit cards not accepted
Children all but tiny ones accepted
Disabled not suitable
Pets dogs not accepted
Closed never
Proprietor Marco Vuilleumier

Campania

Converted monastery, Sant'Agnello

Cocumella

Sant'Agnello is just to the west of Sorrento, and almost a part of it; the Cocumella lies in a quiet residential street close to the sea, in a large, luxuriant garden which ends at cliffs above a beach and a little harbour (reached by a lift). It may not be the most personal of hotels, but the building – originally a 16thC Jesuit monastery – is as attractive as the setting. Bedrooms are delectably restrained, public areas a bit more showy, with reproduction antiques.

Nearby Sorrento (2 km).

Via Cocumella 7,
Sant'Agnello 80067 Napoli
Tel (081) 878 2933
Location in residential area between town and sea, on cliffs; in extensive grounds with ample car parking
Food & drink breakfast, lunch, dinner
Prices rooms L110,000-L230,000; reductions for children under 16
Rooms 45 double, 5 single; all with bath and shower; all rooms have central heating, air-conditioning, phone, minibar, TV, radio, hairdrier
Facilities sitting-rooms, dining-room, bar, disco; sauna, tennis, sea-water swimming-pool; beach and jetty reached by lift/elevator
Credit cards AE, DC, MC, V
Children accepted; cots available **Disabled** access possible – lift/elevator to bedrooms **Pets** accepted, but not in dining-room
Closed never
Proprietor Giovanni del Papa

Seaside hotel, Sorrento

Belair

Since it opened in 1967, the Belair has been a favourite among British travellers. Public rooms are prettily furnished with antique-style furniture in pink velours, bedrooms have dark-wood reproduction furniture on tiled floors. But the most striking feature is the setting, at one end of the bay of Sorrento on plunging cliffs. From the restaurant terrace, and from many of the bedrooms, there are superb views. The pool is perched even more dramatically over the sea. The walk up from the middle of Sorrento can seem a hike on a hot day.

Nearby sights of Sorrento; Vesuvius, Pompeii within reach.

Via Capo 29, Sorrento 80067 Napoli
Tel (081) 8071622
Location 1 km W of middle of resort, on cliffs overlooking sea, with parking for 40 cars
Food & drink breakfast, lunch, dinner
Prices rooms L150,000-L218,000; meals L45,000
Rooms 36 double, 2 family rooms; all with bath and shower; all rooms have central heating, TV, radio
Facilities dining-room, sitting-room, bar, TV room; swimming-pool
Credit cards AE, DC, MC, V
Children accepted **Disabled** access difficult **Pets** small animals accepted
Closed Nov to Mar
Proprietors Russo family

Campania

Seaside hotel, Sorrento

Bellevue Syrène

This is one of the older and nobler establishments of Sorrento – a far cry from the usual package-style seaside hotel. The grandeur has faded somewhat, but there are still some fine antique furnishings and paintings, and the rooms preserve the atmosphere of a rambling mansion. The simple, spacious main dining-room has large windows overlooking the sea and creating a bright, sunny atmosphere – compensating in part for mediocre meals. A second (à la carte) restaurant gives you the chance to eat in the garden – a delightful spot to admire the sunset and beautiful views. Bedrooms range from fair-sized doubles with sea-view balconies and old-fashioned furniture to the smaller, simpler annexe rooms at the back.

The fact that the hotel does not have a pool is perhaps the main disadvantage – particularly if you go in high season. But there is ample compensation in the location of the hotel and the old-fashioned charm of its rooms – and for views it is hard to beat. The building is perched dramatically on cliffs; a private lift takes you down to the hotel beach and to deck-chairs stretched out along a wooden jetty.

Nearby Sorrento Peninsula (Amalfi, Positano); excursions to Vesuvius, Pompeii and Herculaneum.

Piazza della Vittoria 5, Sorrento 80067 Napoli
Tel (081) 878 1024
Location on clifftops, close to central square; with private garden/terrace and some car parking
Food & drink breakfast, lunch, dinner
Prices rooms L100,000-L150,000
Rooms 51 rooms, all with bath or shower; all rooms have phone
Facilities sitting-rooms, bar, 2 dining-rooms; lift down to beach
Credit cards AE, DC, MC, V
Children accepted **Disabled** no special facilities **Pets** dogs not allowed in dining-room
Closed for a period of renovation and expansion in early 1990
Proprietors Mario Fluss and family

Campania

Regina

A mid-sixties hotel furnished with leather-effect chairs does not sound very promising. But the Regina is set in a pretty garden, with chairs among orange trees and sweet-smelling flowers; it is on a quiet dead-end street; and being close to the cliffs of Sorrento it enjoys superb views of the bay of Naples from its glass-walled roof-top restaurant and terrace. The ground-floor sitting-room and bar are comfortable, with modern furniture and rugs on terrazzo floors, and plenty of plants and pictures. Bedrooms are large and plain with tiled floors and each has its own reasonably sized balcony.

Nearby excursions to Vesuvius, Pompeii and Herculaneum.

Via Marina Grande 10, Sorrento 80067 Napoli
Tel (081) 878 2722
Location on cliffs, on W edge of resort, with garden and private car parking
Food & drink breakfast, dinner
Prices rooms L50,000-L90,000
Rooms 36 rooms, all with bath or shower; all rooms have phone
Facilities dining-room, sitting-room, bar, TV room
Credit cards AE
Children accepted
Disabled no special facilities
Pets dogs not allowed in dining-room
Closed Nov to Mar
Proprietor Sg Amitrano

La Tonnarella

Perched high on cliffs at the western extremity of Sorrento's sweeping bay, La Tonnarella enjoys superb sea views from its restaurant and flowery terraces. The restaurant is at the heart of the operation, and the sitting-room, although charmingly furnished with antiques, is on the small side; but the bedrooms are more numerous and more attractive than is usual in most Italian restaurants-with-rooms. A lift takes you to a small private beach. Signor Gargiulo is unfailingly courteous.

Nearby Naples, Vesuvius, Ponpeii, Capri and Ischia all within reach.

Via Capo 31, Sorrento 80067 Napoli
Tel (081) 8781153
Location about one km from middle of resort, on cliffs overlooking the sea, with lift/elevator to beach; private car parking
Food & drink breasfast, lunch, dinner
Prices rooms L55,000; meals L18,000
Rooms 16 double, 2 family rooms, all with bath; all rooms have central heating
Facilities dining-room, bar, TV room
Credit cards AE, DC, V
Children welcome
Disabled no special facilities
Pets small ones accepted in bedrooms and in dining-room
Closed Dec to late Mar
Proprietor Carlo Gargiulo

The 'heel' of Italy

Hotels in the 'heel'

To say that good small hotels in the heel of Italy are difficult to find is a wild understatement. It would be nearer the truth to say that they don't exist. The half-dozen hotels which have full entries in the following pages are the best you will find, but none of them is particularly captivating in the way that many hotels in Tuscany or Venice or the lakes can be. These hotels are spread over an area about 300 km by 50 km, which means that some alternative recommendations may be helpful, even if they are further still from our idea of an attractive hotel.

Lecce is a city of Baroque architecture which is well worth exploring; the Risorgimento (Tel 0832 42125) is in a splendid central building, but way overdue for refurbishment. If your ambition is to make it right to the southern tip of the heel, you could aim for L'Approdo (Tel 0833 753016) a well-run seaside holiday hotel at Marina di Leuca.

None of the major cities of the area is particularly alluring; each has a handful of routine big hotels. But if circumstances dictate a night in Foggia the place to head for is the Cicolella (Tel 0881 3890), which has an attractive restaurant, star-rated by Michelin. To the north at Peschici, on the other side of the Gargano peninsula from our Mattinata recommendation, is the Gusmay (Tel 0884 94032), a civilized and peaceful beach hotel.

Alba del Gargano

Mattinata is a lively little resort a short bus-ride from the beach; both the town and this part of the coast have escaped major development. The hotel itself is low-rise and unobtrusive; inside it is simply, but not starkly, decorated and furnished. The high-points of a stay here are al fresco dining in the courtyard (the emphasis is on fresh fish) and going out in one of the sons' motorboats for a tour of the spectacular coast.

Nearby coast of Gargano peninsula; Monte Sant'Angelo (19km).

Corso Matino 102,
Mattinata 71030 Foggia
Tel (0884) 4771
Location at end of main
street; garage and car
parking in courtyard
Food & drink breakfast,
lunch, dinner
Prices rooms L38,400-
L120,000; air-conditioning
L15,000; reductions for
children under 6
Rooms 20 double, all with
shower; 3 single, all with
shower; 16 family rooms; all
rooms have phone; 9 rooms
have air-conditioning
Facilities dining-room,

outdoor dining area, TV
room, games room, bar
Credit cards V
Children welcome
Disabled some bedrooms on
ground floor
Pets small ones accepted, but
not in certain rooms
Closed Oct to May;
restaurant only, Tue
Proprietor Francesco
Piemontese

The 'heel' of Italy

Trulli hotel, Alberobello

Dei Trulli

The 'heel' of Italy has only one major tourist attraction: _trulli_ – tiny stone buildings with conical, pointed roofs, usually joined in jolly little groups to make up multi-roomed houses. In Alberobello, a whole sector of the town consists of _trulli_, making it the natural goal of most visitors to the heel – though there are plenty of _trulli_ dotted around the countryside, too.

The Dei Trulli offers _trulli_ enthusiasts the irresistible opportunity to go the whole hog – not just to peer at these quaint dwellings but to actually stay in one. The hotel is a sort of refined holiday camp – it consists of little bungalows, each partly contained in a _trullo_, set among pines and neat flower beds. You get a small living-room as well as a spacious bedroom and compact bathroom, plus seats outside your front door.

There is a rather plain restaurant staffed by waiters whose charming demeanour quickly evaporates when problems arise. The cooking is competent, but the price for half-board is unreasonably high; the hotel does not publicize a bed-and-breakfast rate, but will quote one on request – and there are restaurants in the town (within walking distance, through the main _trulli_ zone).

Nearby coast (15-20 minutes by car).

Via Cadore 28, Alberobello
70011 Bari
Tel (080) 721130
Location 5 minutes' walk from middle of Alberobello; with private car parking
Food & drink breakfast, lunch, dinner
Prices rooms L82,000-L179,000
Rooms 28 double apartments, 11 with bath, 17 with shower; 11 family apartments all with bath and shower; all rooms have phone, sitting-room, TV, minibar
Facilities dining-room, bar; swimming-pool, playground
Credit cards AE, V
Children welcome
Disabled no special facilities
Pets small ones only accepted **Closed** Never
Manager Luigi Farace

The 'heel' of Italy

La Silvana

This friendly, family-run hotel (not to be confused with the much larger Sierra Silvana, in the same hill-top resort community) makes a useful and economical base from which to explore the *trulli* district – Alberobello, where you will see the best examples of these distinctive buildings, is only a short drive away. It is a modern though not brand-new place with clean, spacious but plainly furnished rooms – some with large balconies and attractive views. The big restaurant attracts many non-residents, and there is a wide tiled terrace with sun-shades. Most important of all, the proprietors are welcoming and helpful.

Nearby Alberobello (15 km).

Viale dei Pini 87, Selva di Fasano, Fasano 72010 Brindisi
Tel (080) 9331161
Location 2 km W of Fasano, in wooded residential area; with ample car parking and garage
Food & drink breakfast, lunch, dinner
Prices rooms L77,000-L79,000; DB&B L60,000-L70,000, minimum stay 3 days

Rooms 13 double, most with bath or shower; 2 singles; 3 suites with bath; all rooms have central heating
Facilities dining-room, TV room, terrace
Credit cards V
Children welcome
Disabled not suitable
Pets accepted, but not allowed in dining-room
Closed restaurant only, Fri in winter
Proprietor Anna Palmisano

Orsa Maggiore

Castro Marina is a small resort and fishing port midway along the dramatic and beautiful rocky strip of coast which forms the bottom of Italy's heel. The Orsa Maggiore is situated a little way out along the coast road heading north: a modern building high above the sea, its modest grounds dotted with many olive trees. The hotel is run amiably and competently by five brothers, who inherited it from their mother. You will find that it is a straightforward place – well kept, with the occasional antique alongside the everyday furniture, and a high reputation locally for its food (wedding feasts are a regular weekend hazard).

Nearby Lecce (48 km); fine drives along coast to N and S.

Litoranea per Santa Cesarea 303, Castro Marina 73030 Lecce
Tel (0836) 97029
Location 2 km N of Castro Marina, with ample private car parking
Food & drink breakfast, lunch, dinner
Prices rooms L63,000-L90,100; DB&B L55,000-L75,000
Rooms 30 double, 28 with bath, 2 with shower; all rooms have central heating, phone, small terrace
Facilities dining-room, hall, bar, 2 sitting-rooms, veranda
Credit cards AE, MC, V
Children accepted if well behaved **Disabled** no special facilities **Pets** well behaved ones accepted **Closed** never
Proprietors Ciccarese family

Restaurant with rooms, Castel del Monte

Castel del Monte

Ostello di Federico

The extraordinary and conspicuous 13thC Castel del Monte is a favourite spot for local day-trippers as well as tourists, and the Ostello di Federico – only a little way down from the hilltop castle – is set up to feed them in large numbers, with its rustic pizzeria (wood-burning oven, of course), polished restaurant and expanses of terrace. But it also has a handful of simple rooms. As this edition goes to press, major alterations are under way, and the management are unable to predict the results. The information given below is probably out of date.

Nearby 13thC castle giving panoramic views.

Castel del Monte, Andria
70031 Bari
Tel (0883) 83043
Location 18 km S of Andria,
next to castle in countryside;
with ample car parking
Food & drink breakfast,
lunch, dinner
Prices B&B L27,500-
L40,000; meals L20,000-
L40,000
Rooms 4 double, all with
bath
Facilities bar/sitting-room,
TV room, dining-room,
pizzeria, terrace
Credit cards not accepted
Children accepted
Disabled access difficult
Pets accepted, but not
allowed in bedrooms
Closed 2nd week Jan for one
month, and every Mon
Manager Avvocato Sperone

The 'heel' of Italy

Seaside hotel, Polignano a Mare

Covo dei Saraceni

This is a modern hotel close to the heart of the attractive little resort of Polignano, but on a secluded promontory. It overlooks a rugged little cove where once, presumably, the Saracens invaded Apulia; now it is a popular shingly sand beach. The building, on several split levels, copies the traditional flat-roofed style of these parts and is painted white; inside it has a nautical atmosphere owing to a predominance of blue and white. Bedrooms are bright and modern, some with terraces. A competitively priced alternative to the Grotta Palazzese, although of limited appeal for the longer stay.

Nearby Alberobello (30 km).

Via Conversano 1, Polignano a Mare 70044 Bari
Tel (080) 740696
Location on cliffs, close to middle of town; with large car park
Food & drink breakfast, lunch, dinner
Prices rooms L38,500-L91,000
Rooms 26 rooms, all with shower; all rooms have air-conditioning, phone, TV, minibar, radio, sea view
Facilities dining-room, bar, sitting-room, TV room, terrace; solarium
Credit cards AE, DC, MC, V
Children accepted
Disabled no special facilities
Pets accepted
Closed never
Manager Vito Consoli

Seaside hotel, Polignano a Mare

Grotta Palazzese

The little town of Polignano stands right on the edge of abrupt, low cliffs which are in places eroded to form caverns. The great attraction of this otherwise unremarkable hotel is its position directly over such a cavern, with a terrace restaurant on a rock bridge at its mouth. Dining here on a warm summer's evening is a memorable experience, and the 250 available seats are easily filled; naturally, fish is the speciality. A reader tells us that hotel guests receive a 20% discount. There is a much more ordinary dining-room for use in bad weather, and a couple of small, pleasant sitting-rooms with sea views. The bedrooms we have seen are very small, with dreary pine panelling.

Nearby Alberobello (30 km).

Via Narciso 59, Polignano a Mare 70044 Bari
Tel (080) 740261
Location in middle of resort, on cliffs; car parking difficult, but garage available
Food & drink breakfast, lunch, dinner
Prices rooms L52,000-L105,000
Rooms 15 double, 2 single, all with bath or shower; all rooms have air-conditioning, phone, minibar, TV
Facilities sitting-room, dining-room, terrace
Credit cards AE, DC, MC, V
Children welcome
Disabled access difficult
Pets dogs not accepted
Closed never
Proprietor Pietro Mongardi

The 'toe' of Italy

Hotels in the 'toe'

For most foreign tourists, the toe of Italy is a region simply to be traversed on the motorway to Sicily (or to be ignored altogether). For travellers with time to spare, the SS18 makes a slow-paced alternative to the A3, sticking to the eastern coast south of Lagonegro where the motorway takes a long detour inland. Two of our three recommended hotels in the area are at the northern end of this stretch of coast, and there are a couple of places further south that are worth bearing in mind. At Diamante is the Mediterranean-style Ferretti (Tel 0985 81428), with terraces overlooking the sea and a highly reputed restaurant. The 65-room Grand Hotel San Michele (Tel 0982 91012) at Cetraro is rather more swish – a well-restored old house in an attractive informal garden on cliffs above the beach.

The main tourist attraction of the toe, however, is on the other side of the A3 – the magnificently wild landscape of the Sila mountains east of Cosenza and north of Catanzaro. Each of these towns has a handful of acceptable hotels. There are also several modest hotels in the ski resort of Camigliatello Silano, none of which can compete for value with the simple Dino's (Tel 0984 992090) in the more easterly town of San Giovanni in Fiore.

If your plans require a night on the mainland before or after crossing the Straits of Messina, a good compromise between comfort and cost is the Primavera (Tel 0965 47081) on the northern side of Reggio di Calabria.

Villa Cheta Elite

This gracious art nouveau building stands out from the modern blocks that characterize so much of the Italian coastline. It stands among flowery terraces, enjoying beautiful views of the coast. Inside, lace table cloths, chintz sofas and carefully chosen period pieces create the air of a private villa. In the restaurant, fish and typical southern dishes are the specialities to be enjoyed along with sea views from the terrace.

Nearby Maratea (8 km); corniche road between Sapri and Praia a Mare.

Via Nazionale, Acquafredda di Maratea 85046 Potenza
Tel (0973) 878134
Location 1.5 km S of Acquafredda, in gardens overlooking sea; private car parking
Food & drink breakfast, lunch, dinner
Prices rooms L78,000-L96,000; DB&B L70,000-L105,000
Rooms 16 double, 1 with bath, 15 with shower; 2 family rooms, both with shower; all rooms have central heating, phone
Facilities dining-room with sea-view terrace, TV and reading-room, bar
Credit cards AE, DC, MC, V
Children welcome if well behaved
Disabled access difficult
Pets small ones only accepted; allowed in dining-room in low season only
Closed mid-Oct to Mar
Proprietors Marisa and Lamberto Aquadro

The 'toe' of Italy

Santavenere

The Santavenere lies just outside the charming old town of Maratea, close to the sea, and is undoubtedly one of the most refined hotels of the deep south, furnished throughout in impeccable taste. The building is low-lying and arcaded, set on a promontory with lawns stretching to cliffs which plunge down sheer to the sea. The beach is not far away, but it is pebbly and the hotel's garden, pool and terrace are all so inviting there is not much temptation to stray far. Inside, the public rooms boast a fine collection of antiques, and prettily upholstered sofas – the sort you might find in an elegant country home. Bedrooms are equally inviting, with many of them enjoying sea views from a terrace or balcony.

Nearby old town; dramatic coastal scenery.

Fiumicello di Santa Venere, Maratea 85040 Potenza
Tel (0973) 876910
Location close to beach in Maratea; with garden and private car parking
Food & drink breakfast, lunch, dinner
Prices rooms L203,000-L476,000
Rooms 44 rooms, all with bath; all rooms have phone, TV, minibar; half the rooms have terrace or balcony
Facilities sitting-rooms, dining-room, bar, terrace; swimming-pool, tennis, beach
Credit cards AE, DC, MC, V
Children accepted **Disabled** no special facilities **Pets** not allowed in dining-room
Closed Oct to Apr
Manager Davide Naestripierei

Baia Paraelios

Few hotels in the deep south of Italy can boast a setting as fine as that of the Baia Parelios, on a promontory overlooking a bay of fabulous white sands washed by crystal clear waters. It consists of bungalows, staggered on the hillside above the bay, each one with a terrace and sitting-room. The communal areas are the prettily furnished reception area at the top of the hill, an inviting pool and open-air bar in the middle of the complex, and a dining-room and sitting-room down by the beach.

Nearby fishing port of Tropea.

Parghelia, Tropea 88035 Catanzaro
Tel (0963) 600004
Location W of Parghelia; in gardens; private car parking
Food & drink breakfast, lunch, dinner
Prices FB L110,000-L175,000; reductions for children
Rooms 72 bungalows, all with bathroom; all rooms have sitting-room, terrace, phone, ceiling fan
Facilities dining-room, sitting-room, open-air bar; swimming-pool, tennis, boutique, massage room, chapel
Credit cards AE, DC, V
Children welcome
Disabled no special facilities
Pets accepted if well behaved
Closed 4th week Sep to 4th week May
Proprietor Adolfo Salabe

West coast

Area introduction

Sicily Hotels

Although a popular destination for seaside package holidays, Sicily has enormous attractions for the sightseer, with its heritage of Greek, Roman, Saracen and Norman remains – plus Europe's largest volcano, Mount Etna.

The package holiday trade concentrates on Taormina, on the east coast close to Etna and to the airport of Cetania. It is an attractive although overcrowded little town in a remarkable setting, and has the island's greatest concentration of desirable hotels both large and small; our recommendations include several here. The San Domenico Palace (Tel 0942 23701) is far too big to be given a full entry (as well as extremely expensive), but cannot be ignored: it is partly contained in the remains of an ancient monastery and has superb colourful gardens with glorious views of the coast and Etna.

Palermo, the capital and main port of Sicily, towards the north-west corner of the island, can be an intimidating place but for the dedicated sightseer is one of Italy's most compelling cities. Most of its hotels are either big and grand or small and simple; the best bet in the latter category is the Villa Archirafi (Tel: 091 285827), in a relaxed area near the botanical gardens and the sea.

In Syracuse, choose between the engagingly shabby Grand Hotel Villa Politi (Tel 0931 32100), with a large pool, and the cheap, simple Panorama (Tel 0931 32122) – handy for the splendid archaeological zone.

Town hotel, Erice

Moderno

Erice is in every sense remote from the tourist haunts of eastern Sicily – a medieval town with paved streets perched on a rocky outcrop at the north-western extremity of the island. The place to stay is the Moderno – in the heart of the town, and run with flair and warmth by the Catalano family. Some parts of the hotel are, as its name suggests, smartly modern – notably the split-level sitting-room – but some bedrooms are elegantly traditional, and there are pictures, ornaments and plants everywhere. The sunny terrace gives fine views.

Nearby Trapani (14 km) (with daily car ferry service and hydrofoil to the Egadi islands); Segesta temple (35 km).

Via Vittorio Emanuele 63, Erice 91016 Trapani
Tel (0923) 869300
Location in middle of town
Food & drink breakfast, lunch, dinner
Prices rooms L50,000-L90,000; DB&B L70,000-L80,000
Rooms 33 double, 10 with bath, 23 with shower; 7 single, all with shower; all rooms have central heating, phone

Facilities dining-room, sitting-room, bar, terrace
Credit cards AE, DC, V
Children accepted
Disabled lift/elevator
Pets small ones only accepted, but not in public areas
Closed never
Proprietor Giuseppe Catalano

East coast

Seaside hotel, Taormina

Villa Paradiso

Next to the public gardens and close to the heart of historic Taormina, the Villa Paradiso also has the advantage of a glorious panorama along the coast and across to the hazy cone of Etna. The only drawback to the location is that it is on a main road, which means some noise for back rooms and major problems with parking in high season. The hotel is a well-maintained white building, and the public rooms have all the style and atmosphere of a private villa: white arches, patterned carpets on tiled floors, stylish sofas and an imaginative collection of prints, paintings and water-colours. The restaurant on the fourth floor makes the most of the views, and the food is distinctly above average. Every bedroom has a balcony, and inevitably the most sought-after are those at the front with sea views. The majority are larger than you would expect from a 'pensione'; some have attractive painted furniture. You can reach the beaches by cable-car or – more convenient – the hotel minibus, which takes you to the Villa Paradiso Lido.

Nearby Greek theatre, Corso Umberto and public gardens; excursions to Etna.

Via Roma 2, Taormina 98039 Messina
Tel (0942) 23922
Location on SE edge of town; small public car park next door, paying garage nearby
Food & drink breakfast, lunch, dinner
Prices rooms L65,000- L200,000; DB&B (preferred) L75,000- L130,000
Rooms 30 double, 28 with bath, 2 with shower; 3 single, all with shower; 9 suites, all with bath; all rooms have central heating, air-conditioning, phone, radio,
Facilities 2 sitting-rooms, bar, dining-room, terrace
Credit cards AE, DC, MC, V
Children welcome; special meals and baby-sitting on request **Disabled** access possible – some ground-floor rooms **Pets** small cats and dogs only accepted
Closed early Nov to mid-Dec
Proprietor Salvatore Martorana

East coast

Arathena Rocks

For peace-lovers the gardens and pool of the Arathena Rocks provide an attractive alternative to the busy sands of Giardini-Naxos; and there is swimming in the sea from the rugged black lava rocks or a man-made private beach. Rooms throughout the hotel are light and cheerful, with whitewashed walls and painted furniture. The dining-room overlooks the garden and sea, as do some bedrooms. The friendly Arcidiacono family speak English, and will do their best to make sure that your stay here is an enjoyable one.

Nearby Taormina; excursions to Etna.

Via Calcide Eubea 55, Giardini Naxos 98035 Messina
Tel (0942) 51349
Location 5 km SW of Taormina on private road, overlooking own gardens and sea; with private car parking
Food & drink breakfast, lunch, dinner
Prices DB&B L79,000-L84,000
Rooms 42 double, 10 single, all with bath or shower; all rooms have phone
Facilities 2 sitting-rooms, dining-room, bar, snack-bar by pool; sea-water swimming-pool, tennis
Credit cards MC, V
Children welcome; special meals on request **Disabled** no special facilities **Pets** dogs not accepted in dining-room
Closed Nov to Mar
Proprietors Arcidiacono family

Villa Fiorita

Built into the rock high on a mountain terrace, the Fiorita is a small hotel with a grand panorama of the bay below Taormina. Bedrooms are spotlessly clean and surprisingly well equipped for a hotel of its category. Downstairs there are various sitting-rooms, though the main attractions in summer are the outdoor terraces, garden and pool. And for those who prefer the beach the funicular down to sea-level is only a couple of minutes' walk away. The Fiorita is principally a bed-and-breakfast place, but evening snacks are served on request.

Nearby Greek theatre, beach (via funicular).

Via L Pirandello 39, Taormina 98039 Messina
Tel (0942) 24122
Location about 5 minutes from middle of resort, on NE side; with garden and (paying) garage
Food & drink breakfast
Prices rooms L90,000
Rooms 24 double, 23 with bath, one with shower; all rooms have air-conditioning, phone, TV, radio, minibar
Facilities sitting-room, breakfast room, games room, sauna, heated swimming-pool
Credit cards AE, MC, V
Children not encouraged
Disabled no special facilities
Pets not accepted
Closed never
Proprietor Antonietta Colombo Papa

East coast

Seaside villa, Taormina

Villa Belvedere

The Belvedere is a simple but stylish hotel which has been in the same family since 1902, with each generation making its changes without altering the inherent charm of the place. Currently in charge is Frenchman Claude Pécaut and his Italian wife, both of them friendly and helpful.

One of the villa's great assets is its location. It is close to the middle of Taormina, commanding a spectacular panorama of the bay and the slopes of Etna to the south. Ask for a room at the front, and preferably one with a terrace. Not only do the few rooms at the back of the hotel lack these superb views – they are also noisy and gloomy by comparison.

Flowery gardens lead down to a small pool where the setting and poolside bar (snacks and light lunches) tempt guests to linger all day and postpone the more serious business of sightseeing. There is no proper restaurant, but this can scarcely be considered a drawback given the choice down the road in central Taormina. And the hotel does have two prettily furnished drawing-rooms, an indoor bar and a spacious breakfast room. All in all, a sound choice for a reasonably priced family hotel when you don't want to be tied down by meals.

Nearby Greek theatre, Corso Umberto, public gardens; excursions to Etna, half or whole day.

Via Bagnoli Croce 79, Taormina 98039 Messina **Tel** (0942) 23791 **Location** close to public gardens and old town, with garden and car parking space for 15 cars **Food & drink** breakfast **Prices** rooms L60,000-L120,000 **Rooms** 39 double, 3 single, all with bath or shower; all rooms have central heating **Facilities** 2 sitting areas, 2 bars, breakfast room; swimming-pool **Credit cards** MC, V **Children** accepted if well behaved **Disabled** no special facilities **Pets** welcome **Closed** Nov to Feb **Proprietor** Claude Pécaut

East coast

Villa Sant'Andrea

The Villa Sant'Andrea was originally built and furnished by an aristocratic English family. It was converted to a hotel in 1950, but even after modernization it still has the stamp of a rather elegant turn-of-the-century English home. Flowery fabrics (largely Sanderson), cool colours and a few carefully chosen antiques combine to create a light and inviting interior – helped by the big windows that overlook the bay. Some of the guest rooms are a little old-fashioned in comparison with the rest of the hotel, but the front rooms with terraces are hard to beat for views.

The hotel stands among dense sub-tropical terraces just above the pebbly beach of the bay of Mazzaro. One of the restaurants is right on the beach, and you can lunch or dine here in the shade of palm trees overlooking the bay – an inviting spot both by day and night, when you can watch the fishing boats glide silently out to sea. The main restaurant is crisp and fresh with sea breezes wafting through white arches which frame the bay.

Nearby Greek theatre, Corso Umberto and public gardens of Taormina, all reached by cable car; excursions to Etna.

Via Nazionale 137, Mazzaro, Taormina-mare 98030 Messina
Tel (0942) 23125
Location on NE side of town, in gardens overlooking private beach; parking for 30 cars
Food & drink breakfast, lunch, dinner
Prices rooms L100,000-L110,000; DB&B L145,000-L175,000; reductions for children under 12
Rooms 45 double, 30 with bath, 15 with shower; 3 single, one with bath, 2 with shower; all rooms have central heating, air-conditioning, phone
Facilities 2 dining-rooms, 2 bars, sitting-room; windsurfing, rowing-boats
Credit cards AE, DC, MC, V
Children accepted
Disabled no special facilities
Pets not accepted
Closed Nov to late Mar
Manager Francesco Moschella

South coast/Aeolian islands

Villa Athena

Agrigento was one of the richest cities of the ancient world, and the unique feature of the Villa Athena is its amazing setting in the Valley of Temples, where the ruins rise in isolated splendour.

From an 18thC villa it has been converted into a smart four-star hotel. The façade is classical and handsome. Sadly, the interior is somehow much more modern than you might expect and the atmosphere does tend towards the impersonal. But this is well outweighed by the beauty of the site – the grounds, the pool, the palms and the terraces where you can eat looking across to the timeless temples.

Nearby Valley of Temples.

Via dei Templi 33, Agrigento 92100
Tel (0922) 23833
Location 3 km south of Agrigento, in the valley of the Temples with own garden and ample car parking (supervised)
Food & drink breakfast, lunch, dinner
Prices rooms L85,000-L120,000
Rooms 35 double, 6 single; all with shower; all rooms have central heating, air-conditioning, radio, TV, phone
Facilities dining-room, bars, terrace, swimming-pool
Credit cards AE, MC, V
Children accepted; baby-sitting **Disabled** no special facilities **Pets** accepted
Closed never
Proprietor Francesco d'Alessandro

Villa Diana

Lipari is the largest of the volcanic Aeolian islands, and among its attractions are picturesque fishing villages, deep clear blue seas and the charming town of Lipari. The Pensione Diana is a skilfully restored villa whose ample terraces and quiet gardens overlook Lipari and the bays that frame it. It is a family home, furnished and looked after with care; there are antiques, paintings and ceramics in the dining-room, and some of the bedrooms have antiques too. Dinners include a variety of local dishes, served with wines made on the island.

Nearby Norman cathedral, Bishop's Palace (Eolian Archaelogical Museum), and other old buildings of Lipari.

Via Tufo, Lipari, Isole Eolie 98055 Messina
Tel (090) 9811403
Location about 15 minutes from middle of Lipari; in garden, with private parking
Food & drink breakfast, dinner
Prices B&B L30,000; DB&B L60,000
Rooms 11 double, 8 with bath, 3 with shower; 2 single, both with shower
Facilities dining-room, terraces, bowls
Credit cards V
Children welcome
Disabled no special facilities
Pets welcome
Closed Nov to Mar
Proprietor Anna Calabrese Hunziker

Inland

Country hotel, Oliena

Su Gologone

The Barbagia, in the heart of mountainous Sardinia, is a region which the locals say has never been tamed. The landscape is wild, the villages remote and bandits still thrive – though tourists are unlikely to encounter them.

The hotel is a low-lying white villa, covered in creepers, surrounded by flowing shrubs and set in a landscape of rural splendour: wooded ravines, fields of olives, pinewoods and the craggy peaks of the Supramonte mountains. It feels isolated, and it is; but the Su Gologone is far from undiscovered. Once, only a few adventurous foreign travellers found their way here; now, they come for the peace, or indeed for the food alone, which is typically Sard: cuts of local meats, roast lamb and the speciality of roast suckling pig – you can watch it being cooked on a spit in front of a huge fireplace. The wines are produced in the local vineyards. The dining-room spreads in all directions – into the vine-clad courtyard, the terrace and other rooms, all in suitably rustic style. The bedrooms are light and simple, again in rustic style, inkeeping with the surroundings. Walls are whitewashed, floors are tiled and there are lovely views.

Despite its size and range of facilities, the Su Gologone still feels small and friendly, and in most respects still typically Sard.
Nearby Gennargentu mountain range; Monte Ortobene – a 21-km drive.

Oliena 08025 Nuoro
Tel (0784) 287512
Location 8 km NE of Oliena, in remote mountain setting with private parking
Food & drink breakfast, lunch, dinner
Prices B&B L32,000-L46,000 DB&B L66,500; FB L80,000
Rooms 61 double, 4 family rooms, all with bath; all rooms have central heating, air-conditioning, phone; 15 rooms have colour TV, minibar
Facilities 5 dining-rooms, 2 bars, conference room; disco, swimming-pool, tennis, bowls, riding
Credit cards AE, MC, V
Children accepted **Disabled** no special facilities **Pets** accepted **Closed** Nov to Feb
Proprietor Giuseppe Palimodde

Sporting Hotel (see opposite)

Costa Smeralda

Cappricioli

The Capriccioli is a small, simple, family-run hotel, and its prices are a fraction of what you pay at the five-star luxury places on the Costa Smeralda. The Azara family have been here for a quarter of a century, starting with just a restaurant. The rustic villa-style building lies among the windswept *macchia*, close to a pretty beach of white sands. The style is predominantly rustic, but in the restaurant nets, boats and anchors provide the setting for *Risotto Pirata* and other local dishes. The key attraction is the restaurant terrace, with beautiful views of the coast.

Nearby sandy beaches of the Costa Smeralda.

Cappricioli, Porto Cervo 07020 Sassari
Tel (0789) 96004
Location in Cala di Volpe area, overlooking beach; with ample car parking
Food & drink breakfast, lunch, dinner
Prices DB&B L128,000-L145,000
Rooms 24 double, 3 with bath, 21 with shower; 4 single, all with shower; all rooms have central heating
Facilities dining-room with terrace, 2 bars, 2 TV rooms; tennis, beach with windsurfing
Credit cards AE, MC, V
Children welcome
Disabled no special facilities
Pets not accepted
Closed Oct to Apr
Proprietor Martino Azara

Sporting Hotel

The Sporting is another little Costa Smeralda oasis of luxury. Its series of neo-rustic houses lie on a peninsula, with sea views all around. The style is one of simple elegance, with beams, tiled floors and white stucco walls providing the setting for spotless white sofas and benches scattered with cushions. The atmosphere is quite clubby – it is popular with the wealthy yachting fraternity who moor their boats in the marina next door. Bedrooms with white walls and cushioned wicker seats are cool and restrained, and all have a terrace overlooking the sea.

Nearby beaches of Costa Smeralda.

Porto Rotondo, Olbia 07026 Sassari
Tel (0789) 34005
Location 15.5 km N of Olbia on a peninsula between sea and marina; with garden and ample car parking
Food & drink breakfast, lunch, dinner
Prices DB&B L392,700
Rooms 27 double, all with bath; all rooms have minibar, phone, balcony
Facilities dining-room, barbecue, piano bar; sea-water swimming-pool, beach, boat hire, water-skiing, windsurfing, tennis
Credit cards AE, DC, MC, V
Children accepted
Disabled no special facilities
Pets not accepted
Closed end Sep to mid-Apr
Manager Hans Teurer

Costa Smeralda

Pitrizza

The smart playground of the Costa Smeralda is liberally endowed with luxury hotels, but there is one that stands out from the rest: the Pitrizza. What distinguishes it (apart from its small size) is its exclusive, intimate, club-like atmosphere. No shops, disco or ritzy touches here. Small private villas are scattered discreetly among the rocks and flowering gardens, overlooking a private beach. Rooms are furnished throughout with immaculate taste, some of them amazingly simple. The style is predominantly rustic, with white stucco walls, beams and locally crafted furniture and fabrics. Each villa has four to six rooms, and most have a private terrace, garden or patio. The core of the hotel is the club-house, with a small sitting-room, bar, restaurant and spacious terrace where you can sit, enjoying the company of other guests or simply watching the sunset. A path leads down to the golden sands of a small beach and a private jetty where you can moor your yacht. Equally desirable is the seawater pool, which has been carved out of the rocky shoreline.

There is of course a hitch to the Pitrizza. The rooms here are among the most expensive on the entire Italian coastline.

Nearby beaches of the Costa Smeralda; Maddalena archipelago.

Porto Cervo 07020 Sassari
Tel (0789) 91500
Location 4 km from Porto Cervo, at Liscia di Vacca; ample car parking
Food & drink breakfast, lunch, dinner
Prices DB&B L293,000-L418,000; reductions for children sharing parents' room
Rooms 21 double, 6 single, one suite; all with bath; all rooms have air-conditioning, minibar, phone, TV, radio; most rooms have terrace or patio
Facilities bar, dining-room, terrace; sea-water swimming-pool; beach, water skiing, boat hire, windsurfing, private mooring
Credit cards AE, DC, MC
Children accepted
Disabled no special facilities
Pets not accepted
Closed Oct to mid-May
Manager Sg P Tondina

Costa Smeralda/East coast

Balocco

For those who cannot afford the five-star luxury that typifies the Costa Smeralda, the Balocco is a more than satisfactory four-star substitute. It is a small, well-equipped hotel and unlike most along this stretch of coastline, it is conveniently situated only a short walk from the shops and chic harbour of Porto Cervo. Subtropical gardens lead down to the swimming-pool, and from the bedrooms and terraces there are fine views of the sea and the yachts which frequent the port. The building is typically Mediterranean – white, tiled and built on various levels. Walls are whitewashed, and furnishings are a mix of modern and rustic. Every room has a terrace or balcony.

Nearby Porto Cervo; Maddalena archipelago.

Via Liscia di Vacca, Porto Cervo 07020 Sassari
Tel (0789) 91555
Location overlooking sea and port of Porto Cervo, in gardens with ample car parking
Food & drink breakfast
Prices rooms L110,000-L240,000
Rooms 34 double, 12 with bath, 22 with shower; all rooms have phone, TV, air-conditioning, balcony or terrace
Facilities hall, TV room, bar; swimming-pool, terrace, solarium
Credit cards AE, DC, MC, V
Children welcome
Disabled access difficult
Pets not accepted
Closed mid-Oct to Apr
Proprietor Antonio Verona

Don Diego

On an unspoilt stretch of coastline, the Don Diego faces the islands of Tavolara and Molara, with a well-equipped beach and jetty on the shore below. The hotel consists of individual Mediterranean-style cottages scattered amongst the 'macchia' and flowering gardens, each with its own terrace; the rooms are comfortably furnished and blissfully quiet. The main building houses the public rooms, attractively furnished in rustic style, including a restaurant where fish is the main speciality.

Nearby Olbia (15 km), Costa Smeralda.

Località Costa Dorata, Porto San Paolo, Vaccileddi 07020 Sassari
Tel (0789) 40007
Location 1.5 km SE of Porto San Paolo on the coast; in gardens, with private car parking
Food & drink breakfast, lunch, dinner
Prices DB&B L130,000-L150,000
Rooms 49 rooms, all in independent villas, all with bath or shower; all rooms have phone
Facilities dining-room, sitting-room; swimming-pool, tennis, beach
Credit cards not accepted
Children accepted
Disabled no special facilities
Pets dogs accepted, but not allowed in dining-room
Closed never
Manager Sg di Geronimo

West coast/North coast

Villa las Tronas

Lying on its own little rocky peninsula, the Villa las Tronas looks more like a castle than a hotel – which is not so surprising when you discover its background. Not so long ago it was a holiday home of the former royal family of Italy. Inside, as one might expect, the furnishings are suitably palatial. Ornate chandeliers, moulded ceilings, gilt mirrors create a grand, if rather formal setting and bedrooms are soberly elegant. Gardens surround the hotel and you can swim off the rocks below. But the main beach of Alghero lies well to the north.

Nearby Porte Conte and Neptune's Grotto (24 km).

Via Lungomare Valencia 1, Alghero 07041 Sassari
Tel (079) 975390
Location standing in gardens on rocky coastline close to old town, with private car park
Food & drink breakfast, lunch, dinner
Prices rooms L80,000-L204,000; lunch and dinner L36,000-L44,000; 20% reduction for children under 7 sharing parents' room
Rooms 25 double, 12 with bath, 13 with shower; 5 single, 3 with bath, 2 with shower; all rooms have central heating, minibar, colour TV, phone
Facilities 2 sitting-rooms, dining-room, bar, writing-room; bowls
Credit cards AE, DC, MC, V
Children accepted
Disabled access difficult
Pets not accepted
Closed restaurant only, winter
Proprietors Masia brothers

Shardana

Santa Teresa di Gallura is a small, busy town on the rugged northern tip of Sardinia, looking across to the cliffs of Corsica. The stylish Shardana lies well out of the town, on a quiet hillside close to a sandy beach. Accommodation is mainly in separate bungalows, laid out among the myrtle and juniper, with rooms furnished in an attractive rustic style. A restaurant specializing in fresh fish, a piano bar and a comfortable sitting area are located in the central clubhouse, along with a handful of bedrooms. The pool is small but prettily set on the sea side of the hotel, and there are watersports on the beach.

Nearby Maddalena archipelago.

Capo Testa, Santa Teresa Gallura 07028 Sassari
Tel (0789) 754031
Location 2.5 km from Santa Teresa Gallura
Food & drink breakfast, lunch, dinner
Prices rooms L72,000-L120,000
Rooms 51 rooms (45 in bungalows), all with bath or shower; all rooms have phone and minibar
Facilities dining-room, bar (piano bar in Jul and Aug); swimming-pool
Credit cards AE
Children accepted **Disabled** not suitable **Pets** small ones accepted in bedrooms
Closed Oct to May
Manager Nicola Lupo

Reporting to the guide

Please write and tell us about your experiences of small hotels, *pensioni* and inns, whether good or bad, whether listed in this edition or not. As well as hotels in Italy, we are interested in hotels in Britain, France, Spain, Portugal, Austria, Switzerland, Germany and other European countries, and those in the eastern United States.

The address to write to is:
Chris Gill,
Editor,
Charming Small Hotel Guides,
The Old Forge,
Norton St Philip,
Bath, BA3 6LW,
England.

Checklist
Please use a separate sheet of paper for each report; include your name, address and telephone number on each report.

Your reports will be received with particular pleasure if they are typed; and if they are organized under the following headings:
Name of establishment
Town or village it is in, or nearest
Full address, including post code
Telephone number
Time and duration of visit
The building and setting
The public rooms
The bedrooms and bathrooms
Physical comfort
   (chairs, beds, heat, light, hot water)
Standards of maintenance and housekeeping
Atmosphere, welcome and service
Food
Value for money

We assume that in writing you have no objections to your views being published unpaid, either verbatim, or in an edited version. Names of outside contributors are acknowledged, at the editor's discretion, on the final page of each guide.

If you would be interested in looking at hotels on a professional basis on behalf of the guides, please include on a separate sheet a summary of your travel experience and hotel-going.

Index of hotel names

An index of cities, towns and villages at which, or near which, hotels in the guide are located.

Index of hotel names

Index of hotel names

Index of hotel names

Index of hotel names

Index of place names

Index of place names

Index of place names

Index of place names

Index of place names

Acknowledgements

The editor is particularly grateful to:

Susie Bolton, Frances Roxburgh, Georgie Howarth, Jan North, Martin Hitchcock and Fiona Duncan

for assistance with hotel inspection and writing reports. Also to the many people – too numerous to mention by name – who sent in reports about their hotels, *pensioni* and other places to stay.